CHILDREN
OF
FACUNDO

DUKE UNIVERSITY PRESS   DURHAM AND LONDON 2000

Caudillo and

Gaucho

Insurgency

during

the Argentine

State-Formation

Process

(La Rioja,

1853–1870)

ARIEL DE LA FUENTE

Frontispiece illustrations

Left: Chacho Penàloza. Courtesy of Archivo General de la Nación.

Right: Facundo Quiroga. Daguerrotype courtesy of Archivo
General de la Nación.

© 2000 Duke University Press

Printed in the United States of America on acid-free paper ∞

Typeset in Galliard by Tseng Information Systems, Inc.

Library of Congress Cataloging-in-Publication Data appear
on the last printed page of this book.

To the memory of my father,
Jorge H. de la Fuente (1923–1998)

To my mother,
Matilde Saravia de de la Fuente

To Marcela Duprat

To Cecilia Tenorio,
Malena, and Agustina

El *Martín Fierro* y la *Vuelta* han adquirido una popularidad que nunca consiguieron las mejores producciones de [Hilario] Ascasubi. . . . [Ascasubi] creyó poder convertir sus cantos en arma de combate; e ignorante probablemente de nuestra historia, predicó el unitarismo en las campañas, donde la idea federal ha sido el credo que se pronunciaba en el martirio y el programa de lucha franca durante largos años. Las tradiciones no se borran de un día para otro, y menos cuando vienen empapadas en sangre. Ascasubi fracasó. José Hernández tiene campo abierto. — Review of the first edition of *La Vuelta de Martín Fierro*

El favor alcanzado por Martín Fierro había indicado la oportunidad de otros gauchos no menos acosados y cuchilleros. [Eduardo] Gutiérrez se encargó de suministrarlos. . . . Cuando se publicaron [sus novelas], sin embargo, nadie imaginó que esos temas fueran privativos de Hernández; todos conocían la pública realidad que los abastecía a los dos. — Jorge Luis Borges, "Eduardo Gutiérrez, Escritor Realista"

CONTENTS

List of Illustrations   x

Acknowledgments   xi

Introduction   1

1   Caudillos, Provincial Elites, and the Formation
     of the National State   17

2   Unitarians and Federalists in Famatina: The Agrarian Component
     of Political Conflict in a Valley of the Andean Interior   33

3   The Society of the Llanos   61

4   Gauchos, Montoneros, and Montoneras: Social Profile
     and Internal Workings of the Rebellions   75

5   Caudillos and Followers: The Forms of a Relationship   94

6   Facundo and Chacho in Songs and Stories: Oral Culture
     and Representations of Leadership   113

7   Whites and Blacks, Masons and Christians: Ethnicity and
     Religion in the Political Identity of the Federalist Rebels   143

8   State Formation and Party Identity: The New Meanings
     of Federalism in the 1860s   164

9   The Vanishing of Federalism   181

Conclusions   188

Notes   195

Bibliography   237

ILLUSTRATIONS

TABLES

1 Population of the Department of Famatina, Nineteenth Century 36
2 Families of Large Landowners in Famatina, 1855 40
3 Unitarians in the Department of Famatina, 1862 46
4 Federalist Montonera Leaders in the Department of Famatina, 1860s 48
5 Victims of the Montonera, 1867 53
6 Federalist Montonera Leaders from All Departments, Except Famatina, 1860s 80
7 Montoneros, Province of Origin, 1860s 81
8 Montoneros, Department of Origin, 1860s 81
9 Montoneros, Occupation, 1860s 81
10 Montoneros, Marital Status, 1860s 82
11 Montoneros, Age Range in Years, 1860s 82
12 Montoneros, Education, 1860s 82
13 Ethnic Composition of La Rioja's Population, 1778–1814 144

FIGURES

1 Proprietors of the Department of Famatina, 1855 38
2 Proprietors of the Department of Costa Alta de los Llanos, 1855 69

ACKNOWLEDGMENTS

THE RESEARCH FOR THIS BOOK was supported by a grant from the Joint Committee on Latin American and Caribbean Studies of the Social Science Research Council and the American Council of Learned Societies, as well as funds provided by the Andrew Mellon Foundation and Ford Foundation (1991–1992). In the doctoral stage of the project, the writing was subsidized by an International Doctoral Fellowship from the Fundación Antorchas in Argentina (1992–1993) and aided in many ways by the Department of History at the State University of New York at Stony Brook. Later, a research assignment at Purdue University gave me the time to work on the manuscript, and a fellowship from the Program in Agrarian Studies at Yale University (1998) made possible its completion. To all of them, my deep gratitude.

The intellectual, moral, and personal debts of this project are enormous. I wish to recognize the staffs of the archives in La Rioja for their tolerance and assistance. I owe special thanks to Doctor Ligia Da Costa de Matta, Aurelio "Alilo" Ortiz, and Professor Miguel Bravo Tedín, whose kindness and cooperation facilitated my work. "Chichi" Zamora opened her family archive to me and shared her enthusiasm for the history of La Rioja, and Eduardo Salinas, Patricia Orquera, and their children offered me their hospitality and warm friendship. I am deeply beholden to all of them.

In Córdoba, I would like to thank María del Carmen Ferreyra de Sánchez Bretón, whose historical sensibility, knowledge, and personal kindness gave me the opportunity to work in a rich collection of documents.

In Buenos Aires, I am grateful for the assistance I received from the staffs of the Museo Mitre, Museo Histórico Sarmiento, Archivo General de la

Nación, and Instituto Nacional de Antropología y Pensamiento Latino-americano. The help and cooperation of the Biblioteca Central de la Universidad de la Plata staff afforded me access to a valuable collection of newspapers.

I also thank José Carlos Chiaramonte, Sandra Gayol, Alejandra Irigoin, Gustavo Paz, Beatriz Ruibal, Beatriz Bragoni, and Roberto Schmit; their intellectual support and friendship was fundamental. In presentations at the Universidad de Buenos Aires and Universidad Torcuato Di Tella, several colleagues also offered their insightful comments and suggestions, particularly Noemí Goldman, Hilda Sábato, Ricardo Salvatore, and Sonia Tedeschi. I would like to recognize specially the assistance, encouragement, and opportunities Enrique Tandeter gave me in very uncertain moments of my education and career. I am particularly grateful to Alberto Britos and Edgardo Larreategui, whose generosity and support were crucial in the difficult times I went through in Buenos Aires. In addition, I am fortunate to have Fernando Boro as a colleague and friend. Since the early days of our studies at the Universidad de Buenos Aires, I have always benefited from his brilliant insights on Argentine history, his sensibility for things rural, and more important, his common sense.

My debts are numerous in the United States as well. The moral and intellectual support I received from the staff and faculty of the Department of History at the State University of New York at Stony Brook has had a tremendous impact on my life and career. I want to especially thank Paul Gootenberg, Brooke Larson, Barbara Weinstein, and Fred Weinstein, all of whom taught me a lot while also offering me their affection and friendship. I hope they know how appreciative I am. I owe a special debt to Julie Franks and Nadanja Skrabitz; they gave me their friendship and helped me through the first, crucial moments of my English literacy.

Other colleagues generously assisted my project in several crucial ways and provided the comments that helped improve this book. I would like to thank Jeremy Adelman, John C. Chasteen, Charles Cutter, Elliot Gorn, Tulio Halperín Donghi, Joel Horowitz, Nils Jacobsen, Gil Joseph, John Lynch, Enrique Mayer, Ricardo Piglia, Mariano Plotkin, David Rock, James C. Scott, and Eric Van Young. I am also grateful to all those who offered their thoughts on my presentations related to this book at Princeton University, the Colloquium Series of the Program in Agrarian Studies at Yale University, the University of Illinois at Champaign-Urbana, the

American Historical Association's annual meetings, and the Latin American Studies Association's international congresses.

Friends aided me in many ways and made life enjoyable throughout these years. I thank Guillermo Orti and Marcelo Carignano for their help with the graphics. For their warm friendship and inspiration, I owe gratitude to Héctor López, Silvia Echegoyen, Daniel Martínez, Maggie Parkins, Sandra Halpern, Marta and John Reichartz, Claudio González Chiaramonte, Liria Evangelista, Sergio Serulnikov, Silvana Palermo, Andrés Reggiani, Anahí Walton, Andrea Turcatti, Claudia Guerin, Pablo Serra, and Patricia Villata.

I would not have been able to write this book without my family. To my brothers, Hugo and Alvaro: we are one. I love and respect them, and owe them a great deal of the good things life has given me.

Finally, I dedicate this book to my father and mother, who both, without intending it, in the telling and retelling of family anecdotes and stories, brought me to this *metier,* or profession; to Marcela Duprat, who taught me a language, and showed me the beauty of words and colors; and to Cecilia Tenorio, Malena, and Agustina, who I love the most and give sense to my life.

INTRODUCTION

Shit on the savages [Unitarians], *I am a son of Peñaloza and I die for him, and if anybody wants to contradict me, come to the street* [to fight]; *because of the savages I am fucked up, for they do not give me even a dime and I will never take back what I say, not even if they put four bullets in me.*

THE INSULTS AND brags in the *pulpería* (tavern) of Caucete, in San Juan, went on the whole night of June 4, 1862.[1] The next morning, the Unitarian authorities arrested the gaucho who uttered them, and following the instructions of Governor Domingo F. Sarmiento, who had indicated before the necessity of severely punishing acts of insubordination, sentenced him to "400 clubs," or lashes. The gaucho had been willingly serving in the Unitarian militia, but against all expectations, had not been paid for his service. Angry and disappointed, he decided to openly manifest his political inclinations, leaving no doubt that he was a "son," or follower, of Federalist caudillo Chacho Peñaloza. Thus, a mix of money, perceptions of political parties, and personal loyalty fueled his emotions, and it seems, influenced some of his decisions as well.

In a way, the episode suggests the variety of forces and experiences that shaped caudillismo and the political participation of gauchos in nineteenth-century Argentina.[2] But how did the gauchos actually understand their relationship to the caudillos and politics in general? What did Unitarianism and Federalism mean for them? Why did they rebel? What was so special about Peñaloza and other caudillos that they could generate such loyalty and emotions? This book will attempt to answer these and other related questions, and in the process, establish a dialogue with the recent and growing body of Latin American historiography that is concerned with rural collective action and campesino consciousness, mentality, and motivations, and the way they shaped larger political processes, particularly those of nation and state formation. To do so, *Children of Facundo* will study caudillismo and popular politics in the northwestern province of La Rioja during the state-formation process.

Following the fall of the Federalist government of the Argentine Confederation in November 1861, the new national government led by the Unitarians from Buenos Aires began to impose its military and political control over the interior provinces, most of them still under the rule of the Federalist Party. This phase of state formation involved a great deal of contention and violence, especially in La Rioja. Between 1862 and 1868, Riojan Federalist caudillos and their gaucho followers revolted six times against the national and provincial governments. The resistance was initiated by one of the most legendary caudillos of nineteenth-century Argentina, General Angel Vicente Peñaloza (1798–1863), nicknamed El Chacho, and sustained throughout the 1860s by other Federalist leaders, like Felipe Varela.

This was not the first time, however, that Riojans had mobilized in the nineteenth century. La Rioja was the land of caudillos and *montoneras* (groups of gaucho rebels) par excellence. It was this province that gave rise to Facundo Quiroga (1788–1835), the archetypal Latin American caudillo immortalized by Domingo F. Sarmiento in *Facundo o Civilización y Barbarie* (1845). Facundo's rule from 1823 to 1835 (when he was murdered) was a foundational experience that began a decades-long tradition of caudillo and gaucho mobilizations, most of them on behalf of Federalism. Chacho Peñaloza, former follower of Facundo and his most notorious political offspring, became the strongman of the province from the late 1840s until his assassination in 1863. Like Quiroga, Chacho was also the object of Sarmiento's pen (and an obsession with Riojan caudillos) in *El Chacho: último caudillo de la montonera de los Llanos* (1866), the famous and controversial sequel to *Facundo*. Facundo and Chacho's own deeds and Sarmiento's writings put the Riojan caudillos at the heart of debates that involved other leading nineteenth-century intellectuals such as Juan Bautista Alberdi and Jose Hernández.[3] In the late nineteenth and twentieth centuries, Facundo and Chacho became the focus of works as diverse as Eduardo Gutiérrez's criollista literature and Jorge Luis Borges's poetry and prose.[4] The Riojan caudillos also occupied an important place in the political rhetoric of twentieth-century Argentina. Indeed, as late as the 1970s, the Peronist guerrillas called themselves montoneros, and in the late 1980s, Peronist Carlos Menem, former governor of La Rioja and president of Argentina (1989–1999), constructed his public image by associating himself with Facundo and Chacho's memories.

Yet, despite the centrality of Facundo, Chacho, and their followers to Argentina's history, culture, and politics since the mid–nineteenth century, no comprehensive study of caudillos, montoneras, and politics in La Rioja has been done, and we know little about them beyond the politically biased and fictionalized accounts left by Sarmiento, Hernández, and Gutiérrez. Nevertheless, I want to transcend La Rioja by using this case study to revise the received wisdom on caudillismo and question current explanations of the two-party type of strife that defined politics throughout the continent in the same period. And although the process of state formation is not the primary focus of this book, this research will help in understanding the conflicts and resistance that the process triggered in the rural areas of Latin America.

thesis

Caudillismo

Caudillismo was the most significant form of political leadership in nineteenth-century Latin America, and thanks to Sarmiento's reflections and intellectual legacy, Argentina provided the classic example for all Latin American history. For Sarmiento, caudillismo was the form that despotism, the typical government of Oriental societies, took in postindependence Latin America. Thus, caudillos were the embodiment, in Sarmiento's view, of barbarism.[5] Caudillismo has been more recently explained as a social system in which groups of patrons and clients used violence to compete for power and wealth.[6] Tulio Halperín Donghi has argued that the institutional vacuum created by the breakdown of the Spanish Empire and the militarization of politics in postindependence Argentina and Latin America gave rise to caudillos and ruralized political power.[7] In John Lynch's explanation, the caudillos emerged as protectors of the elite's interests and/or to represent backward regions in the conflicts that erupted after independence. In this thesis, the power of the caudillos depended on their ability to discipline the rootless and marginal lower classes, thereby transforming their peons into political followers.[8] Other historians have portrayed caudillos as folk leaders defending the traditional ways of life and Hispanic heritage of the majority of rural dwellers, who were under assault from modernizing, liberal elites.[9]

A common feature of these studies is that they have been concerned with the broad economic, social, or political factors that created the conditions for the development of caudillismo, and in this respect, they have critically contributed to a better grasp of the phenomenon. Yet certain fundamental questions have not received attention. With the exception of John Charles Chasteen's recent book,[10] which insists on the necessity of understanding the followers as well as the caudillos, studies on caudillismo have ignored the followers as political subjects, missing the fact that caudillista leadership was also their construction. It is not surprising, then, that most works have found it hard to explain why the urban and rural lower classes followed certain individuals who attained the status of caudillo. In this book, I contend that the gauchos' motivations for following a caudillo were many and varied: they ranged from their involvement in traditional and everyday forms of patron-client relations (which included the exchange of assistance and protection for political loyalty), to immediate material incentives, like the monetary rewards they expected to receive during a mobilization. But these motivations did not operate in a cultural or political vacuum. The material exchanges took place in a context of emotional attachment and cultural identification between leaders and followers, a tie constructed, in part, through the representations the followers had of their caudillos. Moreover, years of mobilization meant that the caudillo-follower relationships were established in light of political struggles in which party identities developed, and party allegiances were explicitly and publicly held. Caudillo-follower relationships thus created space for the political awareness of the followers, and eventually, the political identification between leaders and led. In short, it is my assertion that caudillismo should be seen through the followers' eyes as well as those of the leaders, and to accomplish this, historians must focus on the followers' social conditions and political culture.

Nineteenth-Century Politics

The nineteenth-century Latin American political landscape was dominated by two-party conflicts. The struggle between liberals and conservatives in Mexico, Colombia, Chile, and Brazil, and between liberals and protectionists in Peru, have attracted the attention of numerous scholars, who have devoted most of their efforts to analyzing the logic and nature of the disputes.[11]

The struggle between Unitarians and Federalists in Argentina has also been the subject of many interpretations. The earliest one, Sarmiento's, portrayed this as a conflict between urban, civilized Unitarians and rural, barbarian Federalists, or cities against the countryside.[12] In the twentieth century, historians have taken different approaches to the problem. The conflict, in some cases, has been portrayed as a fight between the nationalist values of the Federalists and the Europeanized ideas of the Unitarians.[13] Others have explained the political process through socioeconomic and institutional analyses.[14] More recently, scholars have turned to the discourse of intellectuals and political rhetoric, and some have studied electoral practices.[15] Few studies have focused on the formation of the Argentine state.[16] Yet lately, studies have looked at the ways in which laws, interests, and ideas interacted with the process of market formation, and how they impacted on the processes of nation and state formation.[17]

Halperín Donghi developed the most influential interpretation of nineteenth-century Argentine politics, which he later extended to the rest of Latin America.[18] In his explanation, the clash between Unitarians and Federalists becomes a factional one, an intraelite conflict that arose, in part, from competition for the spoils of government, fostered by the impoverishment that independence and civil wars inflicted on them. The parties did not represent different social groups with fundamental ideological disagreements, and therefore, the solidarity of their followers was based on cliental relationships that cemented their loyalty to a leader or group of men, rather than an identification with certain ideas. The nature of parties, in Halperín Donghi's analysis, allowed the protagonists to shift their political loyalties throughout the nineteenth century.

This body of literature has profoundly influenced our understanding of Argentina from the days of independence to the consolidation of the national state, and my own study has benefited enormously from its insights and findings. Yet some aspects of nineteenth-century politics still remain unaddressed, and consequently, unanswered. The majority of existing works focus on the city of Buenos Aires and/or its immediate hinterlands; few of them have ventured into the littoral provinces, and no comprehensive study has centered on any of the provinces of the interior, where more than half the population of Argentina lived in the 1850s. This concentration of research on Buenos Aires distorts our view as it tends to treat nineteenth-century politics in the capital city as equivalent to the national political process. In a similar fashion, it tempts historians to draw conclusions about the nature of nineteenth-century politics based on urban evidence, even though struggles were largely played out in rural areas.

More crucial, perhaps, is the tendency in many of these works to explain politics by privileging general economic or institutional processes over the historical actors' experiences and perspectives. And even when the subjectivity of the protagonists becomes a focus of research, historians have concentrated on prominent intellectuals and politicians who were close to the centers of power, and have left out the large majority of anonymous, usually illiterate people for whom politics also formed part of their lives and whose participation in the struggles was decisive.[19]

Thus, I believe that some of the methodological and theoretical assumptions that have dominated the political historiography of nineteenth-century Argentina need to be reconceptualized. The understanding of politics in a large country with a heterogeneous geography, diverse rural economies, strong regional identities, and few and weak federal institutions in place requires that studies account for these specificities, especially considering that daily political life was largely local and regional in character. This does not mean that the larger processes should be ignored. To the contrary, studies should focus on how the national or international contexts intersected with regional and local dynamics and traditions.

I also argue that politics cannot be explained solely through economic, social, or institutional analyses. Consequently, without neglecting the institutional or social contexts of political conflict, I focus on the actors, and the way their experiences and culture shaped their consciousness and informed their political actions. Following some of the recent developments in cultural history, then, my study pays attention to representations, language, symbolic actions, and everyday practices, which are not only windows into the protagonists' mentalities but also helped to constitute them.[20]

Recent studies of political history and peasant politics in Latin America and other regions have demonstrated the decisive participation of the peasantry in larger historical processes, such as party struggles, revolutions, and state or nation formation.[21] I contend that the historical process in nineteenth-century Argentina should be understood along these lines, and that the gauchos' political engagement fundamentally shaped political conflict and identities during the state- and nation-formation processes. That is, I regard gauchos as subjects aware of politics, and bring their experiences, culture, and behavior back into the study of political history, in a vein similar to recent studies on nineteenth-century Mexico, Brazil, and the Andes.

Politics in rural areas was not an activity monopolized by local elites, as the heterogeneous social backgrounds of the rebels in general and leaders in particular clearly demonstrates. In the La Rioja of the 1860s, party identities involved experiences that had developed over several time periods, and reflected processes at the local, national, and international levels. Several phenomena, from conflictive agrarian social relations along with ethnic and religious loyalties to the recruitment that gauchos experienced during the process of state formation, shaped Federalism in La Rioja. Some of them were local in nature, like the antagonistic agrarian relations and ethnic differentiation in the province, and had been at work since colonial times. Others, like the parties' relation to religion and the Federalists' resistance to military recruitment for the Paraguayan war, reflected specific aspects of the political struggle in different moments of the nineteenth century, involving both national and international levels of conflict.

As mentioned above, I also maintain that strong political identities were not incompatible with caudillista leadership. Caudillo leadership, moreover, could be one of the meanings that party identity took at the local level. On occasion, as shown by the folkloric narratives that featured Facundo as a protagonist, the figure of the caudillo served not only to represent but also to construct Federalist Party identity.

As seen from the Riojan countryside, Unitarianism and Federalism were highly differentiated party identities, with precise connotations and meanings, which occupied important places in the experience of rural dwellers. They were fundamental in orienting people politically, and it was the character of those identities that accounted for the consistency and commitment that rebels exhibited (throughout years of militancy and rebellion) in their political affiliations.

Argentina: From Colony to Nation

Since the sixteenth century, the Río de la Plata and city of Buenos Aires had occupied marginal positions in the Spanish colonies. It was not until 1776, when the Bourbon Reforms redrew the map of the colonies, that

Buenos Aires was named the capital of the newly formed viceroyalty of the Río de la Plata. The economic and administrative changes of the period transformed the city into a commercial and military center as well, propelling Buenos Aires into a position of leadership that it never relinquished.

It was in Buenos Aires that the process of independence began. On May 25, 1810, the revolutionaries formed the first patriotic government, and on July 9, 1816, independence was formally declared. Over the next two decades, the former viceroyalty would be fragmented into four incipient nations: Bolivia, Paraguay, Uruguay, and Argentina. Yet Argentina was far from being a nation.

In the first revolutionary decade of what would become Argentina, several attempts to form a national government failed, and in 1820, fourteen separate and autonomous provinces were left in the wake of this collapse. In 1826–1827, a new effort to form a central government under a Unitarian president, Bernardino Rivadavia, also failed. Federalist caudillo Juan Manuel de Rosas took control in Buenos Aires in 1829, and remained the most powerful figure in the provinces up until 1852. During that period, however, the only institutional link between the provinces was the Federal Pact of 1831, which delegated foreign relations to Buenos Aires. Still, Rosas exercised de facto political authority over the whole of the territory.

In 1852, General Justo J. de Urquiza, a Federalist caudillo from the littoral province of Entre Ríos, revolted, defeating Rosas in the battle of Caseros on February 2, 1852, and thus initiating the process of state formation, or the period of "National Organization." The provinces called a constitutional convention, which in 1853 passed a federal constitution establishing the Argentine Confederation. Buenos Aires had refused to participate in the convention, seceding from the other thirteen provinces in 1852, and for a decade remained a separate state in conflict with the confederation. This stalemate came to an end with the battle of Pavón, in September 1861, when General Bartolomé Mitre, the Unitarian governor of Buenos Aires, defeated Urquiza. The confederation collapsed, and in 1862, Buenos Aires Unitarians established the Argentine republic (maintaining the federal constitution). What followed was one of the most conflictive periods in the history of Argentina and a crucial phase in the process of state formation. The presidencies of Mitre (1862–1868), Domingo F. Sarmiento (1868–1874), and Nicolás Avellaneda (1874–1880) managed to establish the authority of the national government over the fourteen provinces, and thus, consolidate the national state. The process culminated in 1880, when the city of Buenos Aires was finally federalized and became the capital of Argentina.

The Province of La Rioja

La Rioja is located in northwestern Argentina and is 89,680 kilometers in size (roughly equivalent to the state of Maine). In the mid–nineteenth century, La Rioja shared borders, as it does today, with the provinces of Catamarca in the north, Córdoba in the east, San Luis and San Juan in the south, and the Republic of Chile in the west. In 1855, with 34,341 people, La Rioja was sparsely populated, a common phenomenon in a country that in 1859 only had 1.3 million inhabitants.[22] Riojan society was ethnically diverse: in the 1810s, one-fourth of the Riojan population qualified as Spaniard and another fourth as Indian, while the remaining half were people of African descent, most of them free.

During both the late colonial period and first revolutionary decade, La Rioja was a Tenencia de Gobernación dependent on the Gobernación Intendencia of Córdoba, but Riojans proclaimed their autonomy in March 1820, and the old Tenencia became a new province.[23] By the mid-1850s, the province was divided into seven departments (roughly equivalent to a U.S. county): the capital city of La Rioja and its immediate surroundings, Arauco, Famatina, Guandacol, Vinchina, Costa Alta, and Costa Baja (see map of La Rioja on page 10). These departments exhibited diverse geographies and economies. Famatina, Guandacol, and Vinchina occupied the valleys that, in the west, run parallel to the Andean Cordillera, from north to south. The haciendas and peasants of Indian background of those departments, like in Arauco in the north of the province, specialized in agriculture that depended on irrigation. They mainly produced wine and wheat, and cultivated alfalfa fields that were rented to cattle traders, who used them to fatten the cattle exported to Chile. The departments of Costa Alta and Costa Baja, in the Llanos, a large semidesert in eastern and southern La Rioja, specialized in cattle ranching. In 1855, the city of La Rioja, in the piedmont of the sierra of Velazco that separated the northern Llanos from the valley of Famatina, was populated by around 6,000 people, and was a small administrative and commercial center.

Situated west of the route traveled by the patriot armies sent from Buenos Aires to Upper Peru after 1810, La Rioja did not experience the

La Rioja, 1860s

wars of independence in its territory, although Riojans contributed to the war effort with troops and supplies. This relative tranquillity changed with the civil wars between Unitarians and Federalists that from the 1820s to 1870s engulfed the fourteen provinces and gave rise to Facundo Quiroga. Quiroga, a relatively large *criador* (cattle rancher) from the Llanos, began both his political and military careers in the late 1810s as a commander of militias, and by 1823, thanks to his capacity to mobilize, he was already the strongman of the province. After a hesitant and ambivalent participation in the conflicts of the new nation, Facundo embraced the Federalist cause in 1826, becoming the most important political and military leader in the interior until he was murdered in an ambush in 1835.

Political power in La Rioja remained in the hands of the Federalists. Yet, in 1840, some of Facundo's closest confidants, Chacho Peñaloza among them, joined the Unitarians in the Coalition of the North and rebelled against Rosas, while other Riojan leaders stayed loyal to Federalism. Two factors seemed to have influenced Chacho and other Riojan Federalists to align with the Unitarians: the certainty that Rosas's policies maintained Buenos Aires's privileges and the belief that the governor of Buenos Aires was responsible for Facundo's assassination. With the defeat of the coalition, Chacho went into exile in Chile, returning in 1842 and 1843 to lead two unsuccessful revolts against Rosas and his allies in La Rioja and other Andean provinces. In 1845, Peñaloza negotiated with General Benavídez, the Federalist governor of San Juan, Chacho's return to Argentina and the Federalist camp. Because of his anti-Rosista militancy, as late as 1848 Chacho would still be called "a savage (Unitarian)" by some of his local enemies, but he referred to Federalism as "my old and fixed cause."[24] Soon after his return, Chacho became the arbiter of politics in La Rioja, and thus, Federalists remained in control until his defeat in 1863.

1862–1863: The Two Rebellions of Peñaloza [Chacho]

After the defeat of Urquiza in the 1861 battle of Pavón, the new national government, controlled by the Unitarians of Buenos Aires, launched several military expeditions to impose its military and political authority over the Argentine interior, where the majority of the provinces were held by the Federalist Party.[25] The Federalists' responses were diverse. Peñaloza estimated that given their poverty and weakness, the provinces of the interior had to coordinate their resistance if they wanted to negotiate from a position of force, like the more powerful Entre Ríos province had done. Hence, Peñaloza invited Catamarqueño caudillo Octaviano Navarro to mobilize as many men as possible, place them in Córdoba, and then start negotiations with the new government. Navarro, however, declined Chacho's proposition. He did not believe in the military capacity of the interior to resist and was concerned about the devastating effects of a war in the provinces. Instead, Navarro chose the negotiation table to try to save as much as possible of what was left of the Federalist supremacy. Chacho went ahead with his plans nevertheless, and in March 1862, rebelled against the national government. The uprising encompassed La Rioja, western Córdoba, and northern San Juan and San Luis, ending three months later, in May 1862, when the national government signed a peace accord with the caudillo. In the treaty of "La Banderita," the new government acknowledged Peñaloza's rank as general, and for his part, Peñaloza was responsible for the obedience of the Federalists of La Rioja and other provinces of the interior to the new national government. The treaty reflected the ability of Peñaloza to resist, and the economic, military, and political limitations of Mitre's administration.

But the agreement did not work. On the one hand, the brand-new Unitarian governments of Córdoba, San Luis, and San Juan (the latter under the rule of Sarmiento) executed some Federalist gauchos that had participated in the rebellion. On the other, some lesser Federalist caudillos, stationed in the Llanos, launched retaliatory expeditions and executed the authorities of some rural departments in those provinces. The Unitarians accused Peñaloza of hidden complicity with the Federalists' reprisals, but the evidence suggests that although Peñaloza may have shown tolerance toward those caudillos, some of them acted with a certain degree of autonomy and, on occasion, even manipulated the name of Chacho to legitimate their actions.

By early 1863, Peñaloza was convinced that the Unitarian governments of the neighboring provinces had violated the treaty (especially the government of San Juan), and more important, began to realize the limitations that the new order was imposing on his ability to protect his followers and allies and how this was undermining his political base. So, in March 1863, Chacho again rebelled against the national government—a decision taken in complete political isolation. From the outset of his campaign, he was able to rely on the loyalty of subordinate chiefs, yet could count on neither the Federalists in the most crucial provinces, such as Córdoba, nor the leader of the Federalists, General Urquiza, whose support Chacho would continually and fruitlessly seek during the entire rebellion. Notwithstanding, Peñaloza showed himself to be a serious political obstacle for the Unitarians, and in June, was able to control Córdoba for several days. His military success was short-lived, however: national troops under the command of General Paunero defeated Chacho in Las Playas, on the outskirts of Córdoba. Peñaloza retreated to La Rioja with only a few men left. Persecuted by the Unitarians for nearly the next two months, Chacho managed to reassemble his people and form a new montonera of more than 2,000 gauchos. From that moment on, he tried to negotiate a new treaty with the national government, but this time, the government was convinced that the only way to ensure the political compliance of La Rioja was Chacho's military defeat, which Colonel Arredondo ultimately achieved in Caucete, San Juan. With his troops decimated, Peñaloza retreated to the Llanos, to be captured in the village of Olta and later assassinated, drawn and quartered by Commander Pablo Irrazábal on November 12, 1863. After eight months of war, the Federalist rebellion had finally been contained.

1865: The Montonera of Aurelio Zalazar

The peace imposed on La Rioja soon proved to be precarious. In May 1865, the national government declared war on Paraguay and ordered the provinces to recruit contingents of gauchos to be sent to the front. The recruitment met with strong resistance in La Rioja. In late June 1865, a few gauchos led by Aurelio Zalazar, a then obscure peon, attacked the contingent destined for the Paraguayan front, liberated the draftees, and gathered a montonera of around 500 gauchos that rebelled in the name of the Federalist Party and tried to topple the provincial government. Yet, in mid-July, the national troops defeated the montonera on the outskirts of the city of La Rioja, and Zalazar retreated to the Llanos, where he held out until his eventual capture in November.

1866: New Montoneras

In mid-1866, an old Federalist caudillo from the Llanos, Berna Carrizo, who had been one of Peñaloza's close confidants and during the rebellion of 1863 had managed to become governor of the province, rebelled against the provincial government. Carrizo mobilized a montonera of between 100 and 200 people, then marched against the city of La Rioja. He was defeated in the Llanos, however, and later executed in the capital. In November, political violence once more broke out in the Llanos. This time, a small Federalist montonera, made up of gauchos who a year before had participated in the rebellion headed by Zalazar, attacked and cut the throat of the principal commander of the department of Costa Baja in the Llanos, Andrés Galo Herrera. Galo Herrera had played a key role as an agent of both the provincial and national governments in fighting the montoneras, recruiting gauchos for the war against Paraguay, and no less significantly, collecting taxes for the provincial treasury.

1867: The Rebellion of Felipe Varela

A few weeks later, a large, new Federalist rebellion began that would shake the entire Andean interior. Its main leader was Felipe Varela (1819–1870). Varela was born and raised in a Federalist family in Catamarca. Like Chacho, he joined the Unitarians in 1840, went into exile in Chile after the defeat of the Coalition of the North, returned to Argentina in the late 1840s, and established himself as a grain and cattle trader in Guandacol, in western La Rioja. In the 1850s, Varela found paid positions in the army of the confederation in the provinces of Córdoba and Entre Ríos. He followed Urquiza to Pavón, and after Chacho's first revolt against Mitre's government, Varela became one of Peñaloza's closest allies and La Rioja's chief of police. In 1863, Varela rose with Peñaloza and later went into a new exile in Chile.

Together with Juan Saá and Juan de Dios Videla, caudillos from San Luis and San Juan respectively, and also in exile in Chile, Varela launched a rebellion in late 1866 that, during its organization, counted on the decisive tolerance of the Chilean government.[26] The expedition entered Argentina by way of Jachal, in the province of San Juan. According to the initial plans, Saá and Videla were to take the provinces of Mendoza, San Juan, and San Luis, whereas Varela had to secure La Rioja and Catamarca in order to control the rest of the north. If they were successful, they would then march toward the littoral provinces to overthrow the national government of President Mitre. As Chacho before, the leaders failed to gain the support of Urquiza.

In November, the Federalists of Mendoza had rebelled in what was called the "Revolution of the Colorados," and they already held that province. This facilitated Saá and Videla's campaign, and they were able to control Cuyo for about three months. On April 1, 1867, however, national troops defeated them in the battle of San Ignacio (San Luis) and forced them to make a chaotic retreat toward Chile. Meanwhile, by early March, Varela had been able to mobilize a force of more than 3,000 (one of the largest mobilizations ever seen in the interior) and was in control of the province of La Rioja. On April 10, in the battle of Pozo de Vargas outside the city of La Rioja, Manuel Taboada, a Unitarian from Santiago del Estero, decisively defeated Varela. Yet the Federalists resisted in the rural departments, and in May, subordinates of Varela returned to seize the city, only to be expelled at the beginning of July, marking also the beginning of the final phase of the rebellion. Without having been able to establish a firm base in the province of La Rioja, Varela began his retreat toward the north in an attempt to reach Bolivia, where the government offered him asylum. In the course of this three-month retreat, Varela captured the city of Salta, its only purpose being to supply his troops. Finally, defeated and after a year of campaign, Varela reached Bolivia in November 1867. The following year, while in Bolivia, he organized a new rebellion that also failed, never even reaching Argentine territory. Varela died in exile in Chile, in 1870.

1868: *The Montonera of Sebastián Elizondo*

Although Varela's failure was a turning point in the defeat of Federalism in the interior, it did not mean the end of Federalist resistance in La Rioja. In 1868, aware of the defeat of their party after years of struggle, some Federalist leaders sought an amnesty for themselves and their followers. Since the government rejected their request, the Federalist leaders decided to negotiate by force. Under the command of Sebastián Elizondo, a caudillo who had been a subaltern of Peñaloza and Varela, the Federalists mobilized more than 500 gauchos and, in August 1868, laid siege to the city of La Rioja for twelve days. The siege ended with the resignation of the Unitarian governor who had refused to honor a general amnesty. He was replaced by another Unitarian who granted the pardon, although the negotiation was later ignored by the national government. For some of the Federalist leaders, this meant prison; for others, it meant their execution.

1 / CAUDILLOS, PROVINCIAL ELITES, AND THE FORMATION OF THE NATIONAL STATE

F ROM INDEPENDENCE TO 1862, the provinces had lived under a system that allowed them to maintain most of their sovereignty, and in which the only means available to interior elites for governing and administering these areas were the provincial states.[1] The functioning of these provincial states affected members of the provincial elites in distinct ways, and this institutional experience became one of the factors that shaped their political affiliations and positions vis-à-vis the process of national state formation in the 1860s. Thus, in the 1860s, some members of the interior elite declared their support for a federal system of government, while others were convinced that a unitarian or centralized system was necessary.

The Provincial State

To understand the nature of the provincial state in La Rioja, it is essential to study public finances in the 1850s, using the budgets passed by the La Rioja legislature in various years of the decade.[2] The provincial treasury's dire poverty is immediately evident. For example, the annual budgets for 1856, 1857, and 1858 were, respectively, 18,986, 22,340, and 21,150 pesos.[3] Meager though the allocations were, the anticipated revenues were even more paltry: mainly property taxes and commercial licenses, they totaled 10,667 pesos in 1856 and 11,085 pesos in 1858.[4] These revenues were insufficient to cover even the most basic necessities; the deficit for 1858 was an estimated 10,65 pesos, almost half (48.5 percent) the budget. The deficit, it was hoped, would be covered by a subsidy from the government of the Argentine Confederation, itself on shaky financial ground.

The impoverished public finances of La Rioja would have surprised no one, since in the 1850s, even the most optimistic observers considered it to be the poorest of the fourteen provinces that became the Argentine republic in 1862. In contrast, the richest province, Buenos Aires, had allocated 3,961,260 pesos fuertes for 1859—that is, 187 times the budget of La Rioja.[5] While the state of La Rioja was the worst off, the budgets and allocations of the other interior provinces were far from the resources and revenues of Buenos Aires. The income of Córdoba, the richest of them after Buenos Aires, ranged from 198,061 pesos in 1853 to 83,015 pesos in 1855. These resources did not cover the expenditures of the provincial state, forcing the government to expand its public debt.[6]

The want of provincial monies throughout the nineteenth century in La Rioja and in other provinces has often been noted.[7] Yet it is necessary to go further, analyzing the consequences of the poverty of the "state" in the daily life and politics of the province. As a first step, we will examine the budgets in more detail so as to gain a better understanding of where the sparse resources were (or hoped to be) spent.

According to the information available for the 1850s, 1858 was a prosperous year for the state of La Rioja. Of the 21,150 pesos in the budget, more than two-thirds (69 percent, or 14,652 pesos) were destined to pay the salaries of officials and employees of the state, an amount that went well beyond the expected revenues of 11,085 pesos. Receiving these salaries were a mere sixty-four people, from the governor to the three individuals who sounded the drums at the garrison.[8] The remaining budget funds went to the maintenance and running of state offices.

The budget was divided into "portions" that corresponded roughly to the different powers and agencies of the state. The Department of Government received 21.5 percent of the total budget to cover its every expense, from the 3,000 pesos in salaries for the governor and Ministro General (2,000 and 1,000 pesos respectively) to 200 pesos in office expenses. The Department of Justice, with a total of fourteen employees (eight resided in the capital and six were judges in the rural departments), accounted for 22.7 percent of the budget. The legislature was assigned only 160 pesos, covering the salary of a clerk and maintenance expenses including the rental of a residence for the legislative body, whose members received no compensation for their work. Public Education received only 2,070 pesos, which was used to pay the salaries of the province's six teachers (one in each of the five rural departments and the other in the capital) and rent the houses used as schools, since the state did not have its own buildings for this purpose.

An important part of the budget (6,296 pesos, or 29.7 percent) went to the Department of Police and the Barracks of the Garrison, the agencies charged with maintaining public order. In the entire province, the Department of Police was represented by six agents: four in the capital and two in the town of Chilecito. The garrison, located in the city of La Rioja, was made up of twenty-two men, including the three drummers. Thus, the two provincial agencies of public order had at their disposal a force of twenty-eight. Their meager allotment allowed for the upkeep of three horses between the two agencies.

Finally, the Department of the *Hacienda,* which oversaw the public finances of the province, including tax collection, was allotted 865 pesos, which went almost entirely to the salaries of its two employees.

For the Federalists from the interior, the fiscal weakness of the provinces was intimately linked to the question of customs revenues collected in Buenos Aires. That city's monopolization of those revenues was responsible for the poverty of provincial states. As the Federalists argued, customs revenues were the product of the taxes paid by the inhabitants of all provinces.[9] But this assertion made sense only for the littoral provinces, whose growing integration into the Atlantic market gained them nothing under the control and intervention of Buenos Aires. In the case of the interior provinces (with the exception of Córdoba), given their commercial integration with the Chilean and Bolivian economies, their ports in the Pacific, and at the same time, the weakness and irrelevance, if not the nonexistence, of articulations between most of them and the Atlantic market, this argument lacked legitimacy.[10] The claim was a political appropriation of the littoral provinces' contention, through which the interior provinces sought to legitimate, and above all participate in, the benefits of an eventual nationalization of the revenues of the customhouse of Buenos Aires.

The Unitarians from the interior had a different rationale: they relied more on an analysis of the regional economies and tax bases of the provinces. Their diagnosis reproduced that of the Porteño Unitarians, as outlined by Régulo Martínez, who when visiting La Rioja in 1862, became convinced that "federation is not possible in [that] province," since most of its population paid "no sort of contribution."[11] In this explanation, the fundamental problem was the poverty of the regional economies and consequent impossibility of the provincial states to collect enough taxes to maintain themselves. This certainly was not unique to La Rioja. Other Unitarians from the interior were convinced that the provinces "would never be able to sustain their basic costs," and so declared themselves "enemies of provincial sovereignties," which they judged to be "damned and evil."[12] Others suggested that the scarce resources of the provinces be dedicated only to "municipal objectives" and "public instruction," while the administration of justice, police, military agencies, and elective positions be paid by the national government.[13] This type of proposal implied the dismantling of provincial sovereignty and acceptance of national sovereignty as exclusive, and derived from the belief that only the economic resources of the national government could form a state apparatus capable of administering and efficiently controlling the interior. For the Unitarians, then, the conflict over the system of government was also a problem of scale: the federal system demanded resources that were above the economic reach of the provinces. As a Tucumán Unitarian, disillusioned by the difficulties that he found in administering his province, vividly expressed, "The provinces are smaller at close range than from a distance, and are foundering in the [oversized] dress we have put on them."[14]

State, Clientalism, and Politics

The most important consequence of the lack of state funds in La Rioja was the state's inability to exercise a legitimate monopoly over violence. We have already seen that the budget approved for 1858 allocated funds for a combined "professional" public force of only twenty-eight. This small number was clearly not capable of maintaining order, especially in the countryside, and provincial authorities resorted to using citizens as more or less voluntary police.[15]

As a result, the state could not impose limits on political competition and conflicts nor could it impose and uphold its own authority. The exercise of private violence was the only alternative that actors had to guarantee their political rights and participation. Private violence arose from the skills that conflicting parties showed in cultivating their clientele, that is to say, the parties' capacity to mobilize people.

In La Rioja, this ability to mobilize had transformed the Federalists in general and El Chacho in particular into arbiters of politics in the province. When rumors of a second uprising by Chacho abounded in July 1862, Sarmiento wrote to Mitre that the hearsay was that "Peñaloza, who has rounded up people [in the Llanos], has gone to [the city of] La Rioja to change the government. . . . It would be strange if it were otherwise. *He has the people.*"[16]

The decisive factor in the political life of the province was, indeed, "the people." This clientele gave Chacho the possibility to install and depose governors almost at will. And it did not take Chacho a lot to succeed in these local enterprises. In 1848, Chacho entered the city of La Rioja at the head of a group of twenty-five gauchos and started a rebellion that ended with the appointment of Federalist Manuel V. Bustos as governor. In 1856, now leading eighty gauchos, the caudillo from the Llanos deposed another governor and appointed Bustos again. And in 1860, Chacho mobilized his gauchos once more, this time to depose Bustos and appoint Ramón Angel, another Federalist, as governor.[17]

The Unitarians of La Rioja tried to overcome their political limitations with a power whose base was outside the province, one that would not depend on their ability to mobilize the provincial population. The best alternative lay in the Buenos Aires political elites' ambition to take political control of the interior, following the fall of the confederation. According to General Paunero, the La Rioja Unitarians wished that "the army of Buenos Aires would make war [against Chacho] eternally, so that they, *who have no following among the masses,* might govern comfortably."[18]

In this context, a federal political system that guaranteed provincial sovereignty made sense only for those whom provincial politics offered a real possibility to exercise their political rights and ensure their representation. Not coincidentally, a Unitarian from the provinces considered that "provincial sovereignties were tyrannies" of local power groups.[19]

This provincial balance of power was significant in defining the position of both sectors of the La Rioja elite vis-à-vis the process of state formation led by the central government. In February 1862, when the Unitarian Porteño troops advanced on La Rioja, Lucas Llanos, an old rancher and Federalist caudillo from the Llanos, ordered a provincial representative to the city of La Rioja to support the governor, "so that he may freely proceed with all his administrative duties . . . [and] all the authorities established by our government, civil as well as military, might continue in their positions."[20]

In spite of these efforts, the Porteño troops occupied the province, and for some months, Unitarian officers exercised de facto control over the La Rioja government. The La Rioja Federalists clearly articulated their position in this respect. In May 1862, the Federalist caudillo Carlos Angel gave siege to the city where most of the Porteño troops and La Rioja Unitarians were located, informing them that he would lift the blockade only when Coronel Arredondo led his force "out of the city and out of the province." "With what right," the Federalist caudillo asked, "did Arredondo govern La Rioja, in the place of Señor Don Domingo Villafañe, legal governor of the province?"[21] A Federalist sympathizer was moved to remark, "One sees that the montoneros are not at all deficient in their understanding of public rights."[22] Thus the defense of the "Code of May," as the 1853 constitution was popularly known, and provincial sovereignty became the main themes of the resistance of La Rioja and other provinces after the battle of Pavón, to the extent that both the Unitarians and Federalists themselves would call Federalism "the Constitutional Party."[23]

The defense of the constitution and provincial sovereignty went along with a pronounced hostility to Buenos Aires. For instance, a Catamarca Federalist was outraged when he knew that a cabinet member in Buenos Aires had said, "The Argentine Republic is not formed, as people generally believed, by fourteen provinces; it is formed by thirteen provinces and one nation: that nation is Buenos Aires. 'Is this,' the Catamarqueño asked, 'the interprovincial equality sworn in the Constitution [of 1853] and in the [preexistent interprovincial] pacts?'"[24] By the late 1860s, these anti-Porteño feelings would achieve a particularly intense bitterness. In the proclamation that the Federalist caudillo Felipe Varela addressed to his followers in the rebellion of 1867, defending the constitution of 1853 meant fighting against "the odious centralism of the spurious children of the cultured Buenos Aires," a centralism that had divided Argentine citizens into two categories: "To be a Porteño is to be an exclusivist citizen and to be a provinciano is to be a beggar, without homeland, without freedom, without rights."[25]

But the La Rioja Unitarians had a different idea of the proper relation between the national government and their province. If the Porteño-controlled government had not yet decided to abolish the federal constitution, which largely preserved provincial sovereignty, it could at least do away with that institution in practice. Hence, a La Rioja Unitarian, who complained about the disturbing (but persuasive) presence of Chacho and his gauchos in the city of La Rioja when a new governor was about to be elected, and who declared himself to be "he who most belongs to the [Unitarian] cause in the province of La Rioja," indicated to General Paunero that "only the intervention of the national government, with whatever pretext or end, within the jurisdiction of the province could subordinate it to the triumph of Pavón."[26]

The provincial states' weakness and local elites' varying capacities to mobilize gauchos allows us to understand why a sector of the regional elites was disposed to negotiate political autonomy, whether partial or total, de facto or constitutional. This is an important factor in an explanation of the form that Unitarianism took in the provinces of the interior during the state-formation process. In this respect, some of the proposals that interior Unitarians made to the national government in the 1860s are illuminating. For example, a Unitarian from Salta reminded General Paunero in 1862 of the necessity to create an army, "forever doing away with the gauchos, who have cost this country so many tears and so much blood." Undoubtedly, he said, the province of Salta had "the best men . . . and could form an infantry of 500." Yet he hastened to add, "The resources of Salta would not be sufficient to finance this professional battalion"; this would require funds from the national government. While the proposal might have struck the government in Buenos Aires as onerous, the Unitarian pointed to the benefit it would bring: "Once formed, peace in the North would be an incontrovertible fact."[27] Salta's Unitarians were not the only ones with such proposals. Unitarians from Tucumán also tried to convince the national government of the value of installing professional battalions in their province, which would serve, among other things, "to contain Salta and Catamarca, where the majority is mashorquera."[28]

These projects, in practice, turned provincial political power over to the national government. Hence, such projects promoted, and actively participated in, the process of centralization. Interestingly, at least in the years immediately following the fall of the confederation, the Buenos Aires–controlled national government was itself unsure of how and at what speed centralization should proceed, given that government's own economic and political limitations. Writing to the governments of Mendoza and San Juan, General Paunero insisted that each of the provinces be responsible for maintaining order. He argued that "the national government cannot have barracks in each town, nor would such [a presence] be in any way in keeping with the federal system that governs us."[29]

In fact, with respect to the formation of a national state, certain differences existed within the Unitarian camp, which also help to clarify the use (though not exclusive) herein of the term Unitarian to refer to the party that the most recent historiography prefers to call liberal.[30] It is possible to distinguish two slightly different groups among the supporters of Buenos Aires in the provinces. First, there were the so-called Pure Unitarians (*Unitarios Puros*) who fought for the dissolution of provincial sovereignty and hegemony of Buenos Aires in the process of state formation. José Frías of Tucumán, defined by a friend as a Pure Unitarian, remarked that although he was "a provinciano" and loved his "country" (province), he also recognized that "these provinces needed the protection of Buenos Aires. . . . [they] owed Buenos Aires their well being, their organization and their progress." Moreover, he recommended that political power be concentrated in Buenos Aires, "the center where resources and intelligent men are; does any other province have them? Buenos Aires is the Argentine Republic; let's give her all and we will finally have patria."[31] The presence of this camp in provincial politics was acknowledged by Sarmiento, who only days after he had arrived with Porteño troops in his native San Juan, noticed, "A new revolution begins and that is the one of the old Unitarians who encouraged by the victory want to change the constitution and want to give to Buenos Aires a power that it cannot exercise."[32] For the "old Unitarians," the process of centralization should be achieved through the abolition of the federal constitution and formation of a centralized government controlled by Buenos Aires. This agenda, for Sarmiento, was beyond the economic and political capabilities of Buenos Aires, an assessment shared by Mitre. When his supporters from the interior asked Mitre to adopt the Unitarian system, the Porteño leader responded cautiously that "with respect to the form of government best-suited to us . . . time and experience will provide the solution."[33]

The second group was represented by a younger generation of Unitarians who frequently defined themselves as liberals. As a member of this group claimed, his position "had always been that there should be no influence [power] in the provinces other than the one of the national government."[34] This group also supported a strong, centralized power led by Buenos Aires, asked for the presence of national government agencies in the provinces, like the army, and advocated for the centralization of the application of justice. The liberal position, more in tune with Mitre and

Sarmiento's assessment of national politics, did not mean the complete abolition of provincial sovereignty.

It is important to note, however, that neither position was ever totally articulated or coherently presented by these supporters of Buenos Aires in the provinces. Moreover, although it is possible to notice these nuances within Unitarianism, it is also true that there was not a clear divide between the two camps. Even an individual could express support for one position or the other at different points in time.[35] These stances only differed in the mechanisms to be used in the process of centralization, and the extent and speed of the process; they both supported the process itself, with Buenos Aires in the leading role.

The common identity of these two centralist groups is clear in the continuity that the actors themselves saw in the nature of the partisan struggles between Unitarians and Federalists from the 1820s up to the 1860s. Federalist Ramón Gil Navarro Ocampo would say that in the process that began on September 11, 1852, and ended in the battle of Pavón, "the Unitarian flag finally triumphed with another name," while also noting the continuity in the use of symbols such as "the sky-blue ribbon of the Unitarian party or today's soi-disant liberal."[36] For some, it was even possible to personalize the continuity of these political identities and the nature of the conflict. Thus, when General Paunero defeated Chacho in Córdoba, in June 1863, he received the congratulations of a political friend who, in a flattering tone, said, "Our unforgettable General [José M.] Paz defeated the famous caudillo [Facundo] Quiroga on the outskirts of Córdoba; and you, disciple of the former, had the honor of defeating the most famous disciple of the latter, also on the outskirts of that city, thus giving the last blow to caudillaje and barbarism."[37] This perception was not limited to the elites; it was also assumed by the lower classes, most of them affiliated with Federalism and for whom the word *liberal* was unknown. The Federalist gauchos usually referred to Unitarians, as noted earlier, as "savages," a term used at least up until 1869.[38] Therefore, the predominant use of Unitarianism in this study reflects the language employed by the actors themselves, and has the benefit of emphasizing, like the protagonists of these struggles in the 1860s, the continuity of the partisan identities and nature of the conflict since the 1820s.

The problem of the provincial states' inability to exercise a monopoly on the legitimate use of violence, and the resulting significance of clientalism, according to Sarmiento, had always been a factor in provincial politics. As governor of San Juan, Sarmiento reflected that

> for a half a century these towns [of the interior] have spilled blood to resolve an impossible problem. *One party,* supported by the barbarity of *the masses,* tends to establish the autocratic government of the caudillo, with neither laws nor constitution nor form. *The other,* that draws from the cultured classes, tries to create a government but is *without power.*[39]

Sarmiento preceded this historical interpretation with the observation that the provincial governments were "very far from the action of the national government,"[40] recognizing that the former could not fulfill the basic functions of a state as long as they were confronted with the half-century "impossible problem"—that is, the gauchos' preference for one party identity, which restricted the other party's ability to effectively use private violence and govern. The only solution was the formation of a national state capable of expropriating civil society's exercise of violence.

Justice and Political Personnel

The indigence and weakness of these provincial states also had negative effects on the way in which justice was administered in the provinces, threatening the independence of judicial power and limiting the implementation of the principle of separation of powers.

Some of the limitations to the exercise of justice in the provinces are revealed in a legal dispute between Peñaloza and a prosperous criador in the Llanos, José María Vera. In December 1853, Chacho initiated an action against Vera and other criadores of the Llanos who, according to the caudillo, illegally occupied part of his lands in la Hediondita. Vera tried to find someone to represent him before the provincial court, but was unsuccessful. As Vera explained:

> [I was unable] to find anyone in this capital [La Rioja] who would represent me, since they are unwilling to put themselves on the wrong side of Señor Don Vicente Peñaloza, [and therefore I am going] to look for an individual in the Province of Córdoba who will answer [the charges].[41]

The judge refused to authorize this tactic, intended to minimize the caudillo's influence. The magistrate's decision was based on the opinion that "the fear that [Vera] showed toward the influence or power of the person of Don Vicente Peñaloza" was not justified.[42] Nevertheless, and despite the judge's declaration of his independence, the court decided in favor of Peñaloza, and Vera and the other criadores were expelled from the lands in question in April 1855.

The dispute did not end there. Ricardo and Gregorio Vera, sons of José María, would be among the few allies that the national government would have in the Llanos in the 1860s. Moreover, it was Ricardo who, in November 1863, captured Chacho and handed him over to Commander Pablo Irrazabal, who then assassinated Peñaloza. Following this, in 1864, Gregorio initiated proceedings to reclaim the lands that had been taken from his father, explaining that the delay in his claim was due to "the influence and power that the late Don Angel Vicente Peñaloza . . . [had exercised] in the entire province."[43] This time, the judgment favored the Veras.

The workings of patron-client relations also affected the application of justice. For instance, sometimes Chacho would use his influence on behalf of the gauchos. When a landless worker from the Llanos, the natural son of a well-established rancher, took legal actions against his richer stepbrothers in hopes of receiving some inheritance, Chacho supported his claims to such an extent that the worker himself declared, "General Peñaloza campaigned for his triumph in the complaint."[44] On other occasions, the clients themselves would manipulate their relation with the caudillo on their behalf and without Chacho's knowledge. When an illiterate labrador (peasant) was brought up on charges because of his supposed responsibility in the looting of a merchant's house in the city of La Rioja, he responded that both the merchant and chief of police "would pay for the damage their accusations had done to him when General Peñaloza arrived."[45] The threat worked; the complaint was dropped. But as with the Vera family's claim, the case was reopened in 1864, a few months after the assassination of the caudillo.

This interference of patron-client relations with the application of justice was one of the aspects of caudillismo that most disturbed the Unitarian elites. As late as the 1900s, an old Unitarian from La Rioja still remembered, not without a certain exaggeration, that not only for Chacho's followers but the lower classes of La Rioja in general, there were no judges, not even in civil justice, because he treated [interfered with] the justice, supporting always bad causes because only that type of people requested his support against the decisions of the judges, mocking the latter. . . . In short, this poor man [Peñaloza] was really damaging to morality and legal order.[46]

The weakness of the provincial states and resulting lack of an independent judicial power was common throughout the interior, and was frequently used by the Unitarians as proof of the impossibility of governing the country under a federal system. In 1865, a San Juan Unitarian enumerated the difficulties confronting the implementation of justice in his province, emphasizing that provincial officials "always work to organize [in their favor] the superior tribunals . . . [and therefore] cases are always decided by influence and not by law." This convinced him that at least "the administration of justice must be given Unitarian or national forms, removing it from local influence."[47] Justice, then, was another area in which the interior Unitarians hoped to further the process of centralization, thereby minimizing the power of some local groups.

Another problem for the adequate administration of justice was the scarcity of human resources, a consequence of both the poverty and small populations of provincial societies. Ideally, the functioning of the federal system required the availability of specialized personnel—in this case, lawyers—who could competently discharge their duties. The provinces simply did not have this personnel, even given their limited needs. The 1855 census of the La Rioja province showed no professional who could occupy any of the fourteen positions that were allocated for the judicial power in that region.[48] The situation seemed to have improved the following decade, since the 1869 national census registered eight lawyers in the province.[49]

The suggested solutions to this problem were diverse. In 1862, the governor of Mendoza proposed to his counterpart in San Juan that they form a single court for the three provinces of Cuyo. One of the advantages was that they could unite in one court the only two lawyers in these three provinces. Nevertheless, in order to secure the third magistrate that the court required, they would still have to recruit the lawyer from Argentine residents in Chile.[50]

The most common response to the scarcity of adequate personnel was to fill the positions with *legos*—that is, individuals who, while they did not have the specific training required, had a rudimentary understanding of the laws and functioning of justice. This solution brought its own problems, particularly the inefficient and slow administration of justice that derived from the legos' poor preparation.[51] Second, the fact that legos held their positions temporarily and not as a professional career certainly affected the differentiation of the judicial power from civil society. Furthermore, the pool of legos who could be called on in any provincial capital (which actually were small villages) was very small. It was not unusual for those individuals to take on multiple positions, in some cases being at once legislators, judges, and public prosecutors, which obviously disrupted the separation of powers.[52] In fact, the lack of personnel effectively paralyzed judicial power. Confronted with this situation, a Unitarian from Tucumán argued, "This proves that there is no reason for these provinces to claim their sovereignty as long as there is no administration of justice for lack of educated personnel."[53]

The legislative power also had difficulties functioning. In 1858, the state of La Rioja had only 160 pesos budgeted for the operations of this body, which paid for the rent of the building in which the chamber of representatives met and office expenses. The ten members of the chamber fulfilled their duties voluntarily, often turning the position into a burden. This was especially serious for representatives from rural departments, since they had to attend three-month-long sessions in the city of La Rioja. Their prolonged absences affected their own affairs negatively, and so it was not unusual for the legislative body, which according to the constitution of 1855 should have met for three months, to stay in session for barely one month. The representatives then delegated their power to the executive so that he could resolve the bulk of legislative concerns that the body could not attend to for lack of time.[54] On other occasions, the rural departments authorized the legislative body to elect a new legislator who, although residing in the city, could represent the interests of one or the other department. The new representative usually came from the small group of so-called decent people in the city, and owing to the nature of the problem, might for example represent the department of Vinchina one year and that of Arauco the next. Clearly, this arrangement limited a legislator's commitment to the district that was supposedly his responsibility.[55] On the other hand, it was not uncommon for these legislators to discharge the duties of provincial administration, again affecting the separation of powers in these small federalized states.

The Geography of Politics

In La Rioja, as seems to have been the case in other provinces of the interior, the majority of the Federalists were rural dwellers. Although Federalist loyalty was solid in all the departments, its stronghold was in the Llanos, home of Facundo Quiroga, General Tomás Brizuela, the governors Lucas Llanos and Hipólito Tello, and Chacho—the arbiters of provincial politics from 1823 to 1863.

The Unitarian Party, which was a minority, had supporters in the city of La Rioja, most of whom belonged to the decent people—that is, to the families of Spanish origin who had formed the local elite since colonial times and possessed modest fortunes derived from their commercial activities. The more affluent of this group also had rural properties, but they seemed to be of secondary importance, both in terms of the elites' economic activities and social life. In addition, members of these groups had a relatively high level of education, which together with their place of residence and social origin, facilitated their ascent to positions within the provincial administration. The fiscal poverty of La Rioja notwithstanding, these positions seemed to add to the incomes of some of these decent people.[56] A popular couplet characterized the Unitarians as follows:

> The savage Unitarians
> All want to be "doctors"
> Among them they make up the chamber
> of the would-be governors.[57]

The couplet associated Unitarianism with "doctors," educated individuals who resided in the small urban centers that were the provincial capitals of the time, and as such, Unitarians were seen as exercising a monopoly on political and administrative tasks. And, as the couplet infers, this group manipulated the conformation of the provincial legislatures whose members appointed the governors.

The urban and rural profiles of the parties gave conflicts a certain connotation. According to an inhabitant from the Llanos, when Chacho launched his first rebellion in 1862, his goal was "to have the [provincial] government and the city [of La Rioja] under his rule." At the end of almost four months of rebellion, the Llanisto said, a treaty was signed in which Peñaloza promised "not to raise arms against [the government of] the nation nor of the city of La Rioja."[58] Thus, the conflict between Unitarians and Federalists was also a struggle of the city of La Rioja against the rural departments.

But the most serious rivals of the caudillos of the Llanos were the Unitarians from the valley of Famatina.[59] The conflict between these two regions also shaped the perception that the actors had of the Unitarian-Federalist struggle in the La Rioja province. In 1866, in the middle of La Rioja's most troubled decade of the nineteenth century, the Unitarians would remember:

> The department of Famatina has been the asylum of order and liberties, persecuted from the woods of Los Llanos, whether under the bloody tyranny of Quiroga, or the brutish domination of [General Tomás] Brizuela, of [Lucas] Llanos, [Hipólito] Tello or Peñaloza. . . . [I]t is enough to say that the Ocampo, Dávila, San Román, Gordillo, García, Isaguirres, and Colina families and another thousand made Famatina into the bulwark of liberty against despotism.[60]

These families owned large haciendas dedicated to agriculture and were prosperous merchants. They were of Spanish origin, from families that had formed part of the economic and political elite of La Rioja since its colonization at the end of the sixteenth century, drawing a clear divide between them and the criadores of the Llanos. While the two groups did make up the provincial elite of the nineteenth century, the criadores of the Llanos had less economic power and education, and their regional status, like their prosperity, was of more recent origin, going back only to the eighteenth century.

But there were other phenomena at work that also marked a difference between the two groups, becoming relevant only after 1810. In the Llanos, agrarian conditions and the historical development of the region favored the construction of vertical relations of solidarity between criadores and gauchos, and consequently, facilitated (but did not automatically guarantee) the mobilization of larger followings. In contrast, in Famatina, some of those same factors had created a horizontal divide between landlords and gauchos that made the formation of vertical cleavages and mobilizations more difficult. Thus, in the Llanos well into the nineteenth century, land was still available for landless gauchos, while in Famatina by the early nineteenth century, access to land and water was a source of tension between landlords and gauchos. Similarly, the ethnic divide between elites and gauchos seemed to have been more clear and important in Famatina than in the Llanos. In Famatina, a large proportion of the gauchos were of Indian descent, and many of them were *comuneros* (Indian owners of communal lands) or lived in the old Indian villages of the department that exhibited a long history of accommodation or conflict with the landlords; at some point, this developed into an identity of opposition. In the Llanos, a good deal of the gaucho population was made up of people of African descent, but this relative ethnic homogeneity did not seem to fuel a seriously conflictive relationship with the landlords (as I will show, this homogeneity later worked the other way). In fact, this population was of more recent origin, made up of families that migrated to the Llanos in search of land from other areas of La Rioja or other provinces between the late eighteenth century and the first decades of the nineteenth, a situation that may have aided the acceptance of the criadores' leadership.

Finally, the relative poverty of the Llanos cattle-ranching economy and the consequent lower economic status of the Llanisto criadores translated into a narrower cultural gap between the larger criadores and the gauchos, facilitating their identification, while the richer, better-educated, and learned landlords of Famatina were culturally more distant from their potential clients.

These agrarian conditions and historical developments affected the form politics took in La Rioja in the nineteenth century. On the one hand, they gave the Llanisto criadores an edge in the competition for power in the province. On the other, while in Famatina and other departments party lines basically followed the horizontal social and ethnic divides, in the Llanos, affiliations tended to follow vertical lines, since both the most important Federalist leaders and few Unitarian dissidents (a rare specimen in the Llanos) belonged to the same social sector and ethnic background. In addition, the Llanisto Federalist resistance against the changes ushered in by the process of state formation was not limited to a single social sector but cut across classes.

As I said, these agrarian conditions and historical developments affected politics. Yet they were far from determining the political process in the province. Other factors, not necessarily related to or constrained by these agrarian conditions and social relations—such as how the national political process affected party struggles in La Rioja throughout the nineteenth century or the way oral culture was intertwined with politics, to name only a few—also counted in the workings of caudillismo as well as the forms that political conflicts and identities took, as we shall see.

URING THE 1860s, the valley of Famatina, to the west in La Rioja
province, would undergo the most conflict-ridden period of the
nineteenth century. In June 1862, a montonera of 400 or 500 men
attacked Chilecito, the capital of the department and residence of the legal
authorities, and then sacked the haciendas of Nonogasta. According to a
"notable" from Chilecito, the members of the montonera, among whom
were not only "bandits" but also "men recognized as good landowners,"
had risen up "like fanatics under the popular influence of Chacho," pro-
voked as well by "unjust persecutions on the part of legal authorities."[1]
Later that year, the people from the villages of Famatina, Pituil, and Campanas in the north of the department, and Vichigasta in the south, refused
to acknowledge all legal authority. Not only did they not recognize the
governor of the province but they also did not accept the subaltern authorities who had been appointed by the Unitarians in charge of the department. These villages recognized only their own local authorities who,
apparently, had the approval of Chacho.[2] And in November and December 1862, elections in the department resulted in a new gaucho mobilization. The department was to have elected representatives to the provincial
legislature, who would in turn elect a new governor. People from those
villages rose up and attacked Chilecito again.[3] In March 1863, a montonera
occupied Chilecito, inciting what some Unitarians saw as "a scandalous
revolution in the department."[4] The Federalist took various members of
the wealthiest families prisoner and requested money in exchange for their
lives.

In 1865 and 1866, gauchos from the valley became the target of the recruitment effort launched by the national government for the war with Paraguay, which predisposed most of the inhabitants of Famatina to rebellion. The occasion arrived in 1867, when the gauchos of Famatina yielded to a rebellion led by Felipe Varela. It was then that political violence in the valley reached its highest point in the history of the struggle between Unitarians and Federalists in La Rioja. A protagonist of provincial political life since the 1830s alleged that the rebellion of 1867 gave rise "to montoneras of the worst character that the provinces have produced."[5]

Political strife in Famatina was partly a consequence of the larger processes of state and nation formation. Yet, conflictive social relationships between landlords and gauchos that, in some cases, were at work since colonial times, also fueled party struggles. Patterns of land ownership, labor and commercial relations, competition for mineral resources, and the ethnic differentiation between notionally white landlords and equally notionally Indian gauchos, all accounted for the form that political turmoil took in Famatina.

Although the scale and intensity of the conflict in the 1860s was exceptional, Famatina's agrarian and ethnic divide had shaped the political life of the province since independence. Specifically, it had limited the capacity of the Famatina elite to cultivate a large following in the valley, and thus, to compete for power in the province. The prominent families of Famatina, like the Ocampos, Brizuela y Dorias, and Dávilas, had formed part of the Riojan elite since colonial times and had led the process of independence in the region. As a result, in the first revolutionary decade, they emerged as the local heirs of colonial power and their men became governors of the province. But their prestige and power began to diminish when the cattle ranchers from the Llanos entered the political life of the province, bringing with them larger followings. In 1821, Don Nicolás Dávila, one of the largest landowners in Famatina, was elected governor thanks to the support of Juan Facundo Quiroga. Probably aware of the new sway of the Llanos, Dávila took several measures (some of them illegal) to limit Quiroga's influence, but he did not succeed, and the first clash between Famatina and the Llanos followed. In March 1823, in the battle of "El Puesto," Quiroga defeated Dávila and killed the governor's brother, Don Miguel, who became one of the first and most legendary victims of political fights in La Rioja.[6]

Famatina was not the only place where party struggles, agrarian conflicts, and ethnic divides intertwined. This phenomenon was repeated in other departments of La Rioja and, as certain evidence also suggests, other provinces of the Andean interior. A notable case, as we will see, was the department of Arauco, where agrarian and ethnic tensions had limited the political strength of Unitarian landlords, and in the 1860s, fueled the political violence of the Federalist montoneros.

Famatina

In the decade of 1860, the department of Famatina was economically key in the province of La Rioja, and Chilecito, the administrative head of the department, surpassed the province's capital as a commercial center. This was reflected in the estimated value of all land properties in the department and the corresponding real estate taxes, which represented the most important resource for the provincial treasury.[7]

The wine produced in the haciendas of the valley was the main source of income for the department. Most of the wine was converted into *aguardiente* (brandy) to be sold in Tucumán and Córdoba.[8] The second most lucrative economic activity was mineral extraction, particularly silver. This silver went into the hands of Chilean merchants who traded in the valley or found its way into the commercial houses of Córdoba. The silver's price was paid in imported goods, either for the miners' own use or for resale in the valley by the commercial houses of Chilecito.[9] Production of wheat flour and corn was also important. Since this production, particularly that of wheat, exceeded the province's demands, the surplus was sold principally in Córdoba, which was also the major market for dried fruits from the valley.[10] Finally, the other significant source of revenue for the valley's producers was the cultivation of alfalfa fields. These were rented to cattle drivers who were headed toward the mining markets of Chile's Norte Chico, or the owners used them to fatten their own cattle, which were sent to the same market. The alfalfa fields also allowed valley proprietors to maintain the mule teams they used in commercial transportation throughout the interior, an activity considered among the most profitable in the region.[11]

In the middle of the nineteenth century, Famatina was the most populated department in the province (see table 1). The 1,378 families counted in the census of 1855 made up a total of 8,579 inhabitants, predominantly *castas* and Indians. The valley's population had undergone notable growth during the first half of the nineteenth century. In 1806, the parish of Angui-

TABLE I Population of the Department of Famatina, Nineteenth Century

Year	1806	1855	1869
Inhabitants	4,034	8,579	10,668

Sources: "Informe de Josef Nicolás Ocampo," Anguinán, 16 May 1806, adjoined to Padrón del Curato de Anguinán (Famatina), Archivo del Arzobispado de Córdoba, legajo 19, 2: unnumbered pages; "Censo General que Manifiesta el Número de Habitantes de la Provincia de La Rioja, levantado el 26 febrero de 1855," *Registro Oficial de la Provincia de La Rioja,* 1: 124–25; and *Primer Censo Nacional,* 421.

nán (later the department of Famatina) had a population of 4,034, which more than doubled in fifty years.[12]

The Valley Society

In colonial times, Spaniards appropriated the valley's best lands and most of its scarce water supply for agricultural production and, to a lesser extent, cattle raising. This process, which meant the development of the haciendas, took place primarily in the areas of Chilecito, Nonogasta, and Sañogasta, in the center and west of the valley. For their part, the original valley inhabitants were located in *reducciones* (reductions) founded on the worst lands with little water. This process of *reducción* led to the establishment of the villages Vichigasta, Malligasta, Tilimuqui, Anguinán, Famatina, and Pituil, known collectively as "*los pueblos.*"[13] In addition, at the end of the seventeenth century, a demographic fall in the indigenous population combined with the relocation of natives from properties now claimed by *encomenderos* (encomienda owners) led to the virtual disappearance of some villages. This process left vacant lands and water resources, which Spaniards acquired through *mercedes reales* (royal grants).[14] Thus, social differentiation in the valley had clear spatial dimensions: los pueblos were mainly the residence of the poor peasants, while the areas of Chilecito, Nongasta, and Sañogasta were the seats of Spanish notables. This process of the notable families appropriating the best lands and water would continue even after independence.

The *Registro de Contribución Directa del Departmento Famatina* of 1855 helps in reconstructing the patterns of landownership in the valley as well as approximately outlining the distribution of wealth.[15] A little more than a third (38.5 percent) of the valley's families had no properties.[16] The landless already constituted a significant proportion of the valley inhabitants at the beginning of the nineteenth century. In 1806, a report on the parish of Famatina noted:

> In this parish there are many vagrants and shiftless people, many mestizos, mulattos and sambaygos and free blacks, without lands nor waters, with which to work and raise themselves from the idleness that possesses them.[17]

As a consequence, the castas made up the bulk of the peones who worked in vineyards, transport, and mining.[18]

Who, then, were the landowners of Famatina? The poorest proprietors owned little if any water, which barely sustained small orchards or plots of corn or wheat.[19] On occasion, these properties included small vineyards whose production was for self-consumption. Vichigasta, to the south, was a typical village of this type of labrador.[20] These labradores must have suffered a precarious existence. In 1865, a law that regulated property tax exempted "farms whose value does not exceed one hundred pesos, when their owners have no other means of subsistence."[21] The law recognized that properties valued at around 100 pesos barely guaranteed the survival of their owners, and therefore, property taxes would be an additional hardship. If the poorest labradores are added to those who were landless, it is possible to conclude that almost two-thirds (61.43 percent) of the valley's population lacked sufficient water and land to secure its own subsistence.[22]

The proprietors immediately above the poorest labradores, although still smallholders, owned more water, and so, cultivated larger orchards or corn and wheat plots, marketing a portion of their production to the notables of the valley.[23] Some of these labradores also had small alfalfa fields, which permitted them to maintain some work animals such as burros or mules.[24] Pituil, in the north of the valley, represented an average village of this type of smallholder.[25]

The smallholders, like the landless, engaged in other activities to complement agriculture. Families emigrated seasonally to nearby forests where they collected algaroba, used to produce food and alcoholic beverages as well as to feed goats or any work animals they might possess.[26] These peasants also worked as peones in the valley's agriculture, driving cattle to the mines in northern Chile, or as workers in those same mines. Small-scale, independent mining, which the mineral richness of the department permitted these labradores to practice, was another crucial alternative.

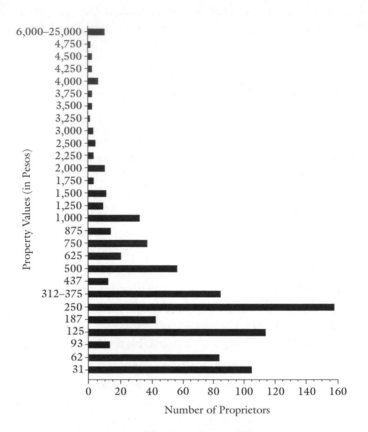

FIGURE I   Proprietors of the Department of Famatina, 1855.
Source: Registro de la Contribución Directa del Departamento Famatina, 1855, AJP (LR)

The medium-sized labradores, who might have been either successful landowners of Indian origin or from impoverished Spanish families, cultivated fruits, wheat, and corn on a greater scale than the above-described groups, primarily because they controlled greater amounts of water.[27] They also maintained medium-sized vineyards and alfalfa fields that they rented to cattle traders en route to Chile or used to fatten their own cattle. A key distinction between them and the smaller labradores was their need (indeed, their ability) to hire peones.

To complete the portrait of the landowners thus far mentioned, it is important to know that a large number of them were of indigenous origins, and a little over one-third of all the properties of the department were actually *tierras comunales* (communal lands). In some villages, like Vichigasta or Pituil, most of the proprietors had *derecho al pueblo* (the right to the villages' lands), which is to say, they were comuneros. Yet, in practice—and at times legally—these properties were considered private.[28] Thus, each individual and family enclosed their lands, separating them from the holdings of their fellow comuneros, and worked it with full usufruct of its yield; comuneros sold properties to each other or to outsiders of Spanish origin, entered into legal disputes over land and water rights with other comuneros, and bequeathed their property in wills.[29] Although these proprietors in general had no legal title to the properties, their property rights derived from their standing as *indios originarios* (descendants of the area's original inhabitants), a category that, by the mid–nineteenth century, implied no special status and was only used legally to legitimate land possession.[30]

Based on value, the larger landowners controlled half (50.9 percent) of the rural real estate in the department.[31] The nucleus of this sector, what could be called an elite, was made up of proprietors whose names were always preceded by the qualifying "don," which even in the mid–nineteenth century connoted "noble" origins—that is to say, whites with a certain fortune. These landlords came from the thirteen families of Spanish origin who had formed part of the regional elite since the conquest, in some cases, or the end of the eighteenth century in others. In that period, they acquired an important part of the lands of the valley that they would later, in the nineteenth century, continue to augment. According to the register's assessment of these families' properties in 1855, this group possessed a little more than a third (35.4 percent) of the real estate wealth of the department (see table 2). Quite possibly this economic power functioned concretely as a much greater concentration of wealth since, as was common, these families were interrelated.[32]

The wealth of this sector was almost completely vested in haciendas, the oldest and most prominent being located in the center of the valley. The most valuable properties were the Vinculado de Sañogasta, Don Ramón Doria's mayorazgo (estate inherited by primogeniture), assessed at 25,000 pesos; the hacienda in Nonogasta of the García family, assessed at 14,000 pesos; and that of Don Nicolás Dávila, valued at 12,100 pesos. These haciendas controlled large extensions of land and great quantities of water. The Vinculado of Sañogasta, the only property worked by tenants, prin-

TABLE 2 Families of Large Landowners in Famatina, 1855

Family	Real Property (in pesos)
Dávila	29,975
Brizuela y Doria	25,000
Gordillo	24,875
García	24,500
San Román	20,250
Ocampo	13,625
Isaguirre	8,500
Angel	7,250
Del Moral	5,250
Villafañe	3,125
Soaje	3,125 *
Noroña	2,500
Iribarren	1,370 *
Total	166,220

* Iribarren and the Soaje brothers had their most important properties in Vinchina, respectively valued at 10,017 pesos and 9,300 pesos.
Source: Registro de la Contribución Directa del Departamento Famatina, 1855, AJP (LR).

cipally produced wheat and, to a lesser extent, corn. The other haciendas were worked directly by their owners, with wine production being the main source of income.[33] Wheat, corn, and alfalfa also made up an important part of the production of these estates, the latter being used to fatten the cattle—belonging either to the haciendas or outsiders—that was sold in the mining centers in the Chilean Norte Chico. Those families who were more oriented toward commerce in cattle had grazing ranches in the neighboring department of Vinchina, on the road to Chile.[34]

These families' mule teams grazed in the alfalfa fields as well. Commercial transportation, in the service of merchants and producers from the province or other areas of the interior, was one of the most lucrative businesses in the region. The possession of cargo animals permitted the notables to market not only their haciendas' products in neighboring provinces but also the produce of other proprietors in the valley. One of the primary goods that the landlords sold was flour ground in their own mills, from wheat harvested on their haciendas or bought from the labradores. After selling such products in other regions, the notables loaded their livestock with goods from overseas or regional products, which they later sold in the valley at a high rate of profit.[35]

Finally, the landlords exploited the department's mineral resources. In the 1820s, for instance, the wealthiest landowners were involved in mining operations, some of which employed more than seventy workers.[36] By the 1860s, however, the biggest mine—like others, striking in its inefficient and rudimentary operations—had no more than thirteen workers. The value of mining-related investments suggests that landlords sunk more into agriculture and cattle raising than the production of gold or silver.[37]

Landlords and Gauchos

The precariousness of subsistence agriculture often made labradores economically dependent on landlords. Labradores, like the tenants of the Vinculado de Sañogasta, found it difficult "to cover their yearly expenses" without resorting to the sale of future harvests, from which the landlords milled flour. But while this practice allowed labradores to survive during the planting season, it left them "no surplus whatsoever" after the harvests.[38]

Salaried workers were also frequently dependent on the haciendas. According to an 1806 report, the many Indians who worked for Spaniards received a minimum part of their woefully small wages in cash. *Lienzo*, a rough cloth, made up the bulk of their payment: Indians paid their tribute to the Spanish crown in lienzo, and the landlords valued the cloth at double the market price when distributing it among their workers. It was, concluded the report, through this "abusive" mechanism that hacendados guaranteed *jornaleros perpetuos*—a permanent labor force.[39] Similar practices continued into the 1860s, laying the ground for dependency and conflict between landlords and workers.

The trial of the peon Solano Andrada from the village of Tilimuqui for the murder of Don Manuel Pazos, an affluent proprietor, revealed much about social relations in the valley.[40] Despite the deference that Andrada showed to Pazos as his *patrón* and employer of more than five years, on numerous occasions Andrada had abandoned his work, through which he was to repay his debt to Pazos, and returned to Tilimuqui. Pazos would then go and look for him personally, forcing Andrada to return; or resorting to the surest method, Pazos would inform the justice of the peace that Andrada was a fugitive, and the official would apprehend and return him to Pazos. In these cases, the justice of the peace intervened to "settle differences" between a patrón and his peon, which is to say that he would "legally" stipulate the amount of debt and work required to cancel it.

But Andrada and Pazos had conflicting perceptions of the debt. According to a witness, Pazos had gone to look for Andrada on the day that the latter murdered him "so that [Andrada] would come and pay him what he [Pazos] claimed he owed according to his accounts, and said Solano Andrada denied it, saying that he did not owe it."[41] Pazos's insistence inspired a violent response that ended in his death. Another witness testified that "he heard [Andrada] say that Don José Manuel Pazos was charging him a debt that he did not believe he owed and that he bothered him so much, trying to get him to pay the debt, that things got so bad that he had to kill him."[42] "So that Pazos would leave him alone," Andrada stabbed him and then cut his throat. Searching for an explanation, the victim's son suggested that aggression was the inevitable response when a hacendado pushed to the limit the natural repugnance that Indians and castas felt for work. It was well known, he concluded, that "what is not left to the [peon's] arbitration, breeds discontent."[43] That this belief was taken as a true and inescapable part of employer-peon relations speaks to the daily strains on those interactions—partly generated by workers' indebtedness.

The large landowners continued to expand their properties in the nineteenth century. They bought land in los pueblos; both the names of the sellers and values of the land sales imply that those relinquishing land and water rights were mainly the indios originarios who formed part of the sector of small proprietors.[44] It is likely that the origin of these sales lay in the conjuncture of two factors: on the one hand, impoverishment and indebtedness may have forced small landowners to mortgage and ultimately sell their properties, a process that may have been accelerated by the fact that this land was no longer sufficient to sustain an increasing number of families, as the demographic growth in the valley indicates. On the other hand, since the beginning of the 1830s, the Chilean mining centers had become a significant market for the larger landowners, and therefore, their interest in acquiring land was heightened.

In the valley, agriculture relied on only one source of water: scant supplies flowing down from the sierras. The value of a piece of land varied according to the amount of water that irrigated it, which highlights the importance of water supplies.[45] Under these conditions, competition for water was a serious source of discord in the valley. Confrontations could arise between villages that shared irrigation ditches or proprietors from the same community.[46] But disputes also pitted small- and medium-sized proprietors against the landlords. Illustrative is the 1864 disagreement between José Luis Moreta, a poor labrador, and the hacendado Don Vicente Gómez.[47] Gómez denounced Moreta before the justice of the peace "for constant theft of water from him [Gómez] and other inhabitants of San Miguel." The justice then forbid Moreta to irrigate his property. In response, Moreta brought his own lawsuit, during the course of which he was accused of not being owner of the water he used. He replied that "he had no title whatsoever, but that he had cultivated an orchard with the irrigation runoff and drainage from the farm of a señora [of the Ocampo family] who at the time of her death permitted him to redirect the drainage of said farm, and that this was the right that he possessed."[48] Nevertheless, Moreta was obliged to discontinue the irrigation of his orchard. Many of the poorest labradores depended in part on the job market, but a significant portion of their subsistence came from the fruits produced in their orchards, particularly in the months before the harvest, when wheat and corn were most scarce. Thus, the loss of access to the excess water threatened Moreta's means of existence.

For the landless as well as the poorest landowners, mining offered an alternative way of securing a livelihood. Peasants from los pueblos found employment from the beginning of the nineteenth century in the mines that the notables of the valley had opened in the Cerro de Famatina.[49] But mining in the valley also permitted peasants to avoid wage work. The mineral abundance of the department of Famatina allowed poor peasants to work the rich, surface veins of the *cerro* (hill) directly, engaging the entire family unit in independent, small-scale mining. The *pilquineros*, as they were called, spent weeks in the cerros, returning to their adobe huts below, where women and children helped to process the extracted minerals to be sold in bars of silver to merchants.[50] For the local elite, the pilquineros were unwanted competition, occasioning the loss of a good part of their earnings. Pilquineros not only clandestinely mined veins that belonged to the landlords but also appropriated the most accessible, virgin deposits of the surfaces whose exploitation required no investment. This was not a minor consideration, especially in view of the inefficiency of mining enterprises and dearth of capital among local elites. In the opinion of a member of that elite itself, the mines of Famatina in 1868 were no more than narrow gaps scratched out of "some rich eruption worked on the surface and abandoned at the first sign of deterioration."[51] The surface veins that the pilquineros appropriated, then, represented prize opportunities for the elite as well.

This competition could take very personalized forms, as Segundo Bazán—a gaucho from the town of Famatina who, to earn his livelihood, cultivated wheat, sold meat, and tried his hand at mining—would find out. In 1869, Bazán was accused of stealing cattle and turned in to the authorities in Chilecito. There, as he testified, "some gentlemen, Don Adolfo Giménez, Don Elías Cabral, and Don Felipe Viscarra, came to the jail and they proposed that, if he [Bazán] would allow them to work a mine that he had found, they would see to his release."[52] A fuller appreciation of the blackmail to which those well-known merchants of La Rioja and Chilecito submitted Bazán comes from the comments of an expert who visited the region in the 1860s. According to his report, most of the region's silver was extracted by pilquineros.[53] The portion that the notables lost, then, was appreciable.

Finally, a brief reference to the forms that political power took in the valley uncovers another dimension of the relations between landlords and gauchos. Social differentiation underway since the colonial period established the powerful families of the areas around Chilecito and Nonogasta: it also created a clear geographic divide politically. In the nineteenth century, the departmental authorities, members of the most influential families, resided in Chilecito. This generated a particular experience of the functioning of power in the valley for the inhabitants of los pueblos—one fraught with confrontation and resistance. Gauchos were personally touched by the power of the landlords. For example, as justices of the peace, landlords handed down judgments and executed sentences on local matters. The landlords were responsible as well for tax collection, which won them a certain amount of gaucho hostility.[54] Less frequently but no less significantly, in those instances where the emergent state ordered peasants drafted into the national militia (such as in 1855)[55] or international conflicts (1865), it was the landlords who served as recruiters.

Unitarians and Federalists

A look at the social composition of the parties in the valley will assist in understanding the relationship between social tensions and the form political conflict took. First, let us examine the Unitarians. Late in 1862, residents of Chilecito signed a petition containing an exhaustive list of the most prominent members of the valley's Unitarian Party. The petition, written when Federalist montoneros threatened the village, asked for the protection of San Juan Governor Domingo F. Sarmiento, whom the signers considered the "natural agent of the National Government."[56] As an official who intervened on behalf of the petition asserted, Chilecito was the "only bulwark of the Liberal party" in the valley; Sarmiento concurred, writing to Mitre that the signatories were "what exists there of our party."[57]

Who, then, belonged to the Unitarian Party in the valley of Famatina? Of the total thirty-seven signatures on the petition (see table 3), the families Dávila, Gordillo, and Soaje were each represented by four, and the Del Moral family contributed three. The García, San Román, Iribarren, and Noroña families each accounted for one signature. Thus, at least nineteen of the thirty-seven signatories came from the richest, most prestigious families within the group of large landowners. These families of Spanish origin were part of the local elite since colonial times. The remaining signatories were also prominent figures in the valley, whether so defined by their wealth, family ties with landlords, positions as distinguished officials in the department, or a combination of these possibilities. Such was the case, for example, with Francisco Plaza, a wealthy hacendado, and Joaquín González and Manuel Serrey, who besides being a hacendado and doctor respectively, both married into the Dávila family. On the other hand, José Linares and Crisólogo Chaves had no fortune, but their positions as commanders elevated them in the local society.

Most of the signatories had properties in the central part of the department, in Chilecito, Nonogasta, and San Nicolás. In addition, these landlords and prominent figures had accumulated, or would accumulate, state employment and offices in the department in the 1850s and 1860s, just as their forefathers had done in the colonial period and during the first half of the nineteenth century. According to the national government official who supported the petition, Chilecito was "the meeting point of old Riojan society that had survived the ravages of [Facundo] Quiroga or that had returned from Chile [after the fall of Juan Manuel de Rosas], such as the señores Dávila, García, San Román, Iribarren," who were "the most noble and cultured in the province of La Rioja."[58] Indeed, the Famatina elite's Unitarian militancy, which had grown throughout the 1820s, persisted into the 1860s.

TABLE 3   Unitarians in the Department of Famatina, 1862

Name	Real Property (in pesos)	Occupation	Position	Village
Barros Casale, Domingo	2,500	Mine Owner		Corrales/ Famatina
Chaves, Crisólogo			Commander	
Dávila, Domingo	7,500	Hacendado	Departmental Justice	San Nicolás/ Chilecito
Dávila, Nicolás	12,725	Hacendado		Nonogasta/ Chilecito
Dávila, Pedro	937			Sañogasta/ Chilecito
Dávila, Tito				
Del Moral, Prudencio				
Del Moral, Sebastián			Justice of the Peace	Chilecito
Del Moral, Tristán				
García, Samuel			Justice of the Mines	Nonogasta/ Chilecito
González, Joaquín		Hacendado	Commander	Nonogasta/ Chilecito
Gordillo, A.				
Gordillo, José O.				
Gordillo, Santiago			Tax Collector	
Gordillo, Uladislao	4,000	Mine Owner		Chilecito
Guzmán, José	1,500	Hacendado		Los Sar- mientos
Guzmán, José Manuel		Merchant		Los Sar- mientos
Iribarren, Manuel A.	10,670	Hacendado	Tax Collector	Chilecito/ Vinchina
Larrahona, Pedro		Mine Owner	Departmental Justice	
Linares, José María			Commander	Chilecito
Noroña, Miguel		Merchant	Departmental Justice	Chilecito
Plaza, Francisco A.	1,750	Hacendado		Chilecito
Rivero, Manuel		Tailor		Chilecito
San Román, Marcial	750	Hacendado	Commander	Chilecito

TABLE 3   Continued

Name	Real Property (in pesos)	Occupation	Position	Village
Serrey, Manuel		Doctor		Chilecito
Sierra, Santiago		Merchant		Los Sarmientos
Soaje, Camilo	3,125	Hacendado		Chilecito/ Corrales
Soaje, Eliceo	9,500	Hacendado		Chilecito/ Vinchina
Soaje, Fermín				Chilecito
Soaje, José Paciente				Chilecito

Note: I did not find any information on the following persons who also signed the petition: Martín Carrión, Amadeo Chirino, Amaranto Conde, Mauricio Díaz, José González, Blas Linares, and Carmen Jose Lozada.

Sources: "Vecinos de la Villa de Famatina (Chilecito) a D. F. Sarmiento," Famatina, 23 October 1862, in *Mitre-Sarmiento,* 167–68; and *Registro de la Contribución Directa del Departamento Famatina,* 1855, AJP (LR).

FEDERALISTS

Next, let us explore the social composition of Federalism in the valley. While no single document like the Unitarian petition exists, I have drawn from a variety of sources to make an enumeration of the key Federalist montoneros in the valley during the 1860s. First of all, they showed consistency in their political affiliations: of the seventeen people I identified as leaders, seven participated in at least two rebellions, and several in three. For example, Esteban Cabrera, José Santos Castro, and José Manuel Carrizo, along with Carlos Angel and Clásico Galíndez, all led Federalist gauchos in the rebellions of 1862, 1863, and 1867.

I found social indicators for ten of the seventeen leaders (see table 4). Of those, only Carlos Angel belonged to a prominent family in the valley.[59] Clásico Galíndez, who came from an elite family in the neighboring province of Catamarca, should also be considered an influential figure. Although not a proprietor, Galíndez was a well-known merchant who had done business in the department since the 1850s.[60] Of the remaining eight leaders, six were medium-sized landowners and two were smallholders. In general, then, the social status of the Federalist leaders was much lower than that of the most distinguished members of the Unitarian Party. Fur-

TABLE 4   Federalist Montonera Leaders in the Department of Famatina, 1860s

Name	Village	Occupation	Real Property (in pesos)
Angel, Carlos	Corrales	Mine Owner	750
Cabrera, Esteban	Famatina/Los Sarmientos	Labrador	935
Carrizo, José Manuel	Pituil/Famatina	Labrador	1,000
Carrizo, Pedro	Pituil	Labrador	312
Castro, José Santos	Chañarmuyo/Angulos Antinaco	Labrador	1,000
Galíndez, Clásico	Famatina	Merchant	
Maza, Rosa	Campanas	Labrador	750
Moreno, Rosario	Famatina	Labrador	500
Olmedo, Cesario	Famatina	Labrador	500
Sarmiento, Casto	Famatina	Labrador	375

Note: No information was found on the social origins of the following individuals, who led montoneros in the years indicated: José María Suero (1862), Emilio Alvarez (1862), Antolín Díaz (1862), Tristán Díaz (1862, 1863), Valeriano or Balerio Miranda (1862, 1867), Calaucha (1862, 1867), and Pedro Peñaloza (1867). Apparently, Tristán Díaz, José María Suero, and Pedro Peñaloza were from the Llanos, and the first two were active in the valley as emissaries from Chacho, charged with mobilizing federal troops in cooperation with the leaders of Famatina.

Sources: Francisco S. Gómez to Angel Vicento Peñaloza, Rioja, 29 December 1862, cited in *El Famatina,* 14 February 1863; Domingo Villafañe to Ignacio Rivas, 12 June 1862, AGN, X–2–2–2; "Parte Policial [procesados por traición a la Patria]," *La Regeneración,* 1 September 1867; "José Manuel Noroña solicita acreditar los robos de que ha sido objeto por los montoneros de Varela," 1867, AJP (LR), juzgado de paz, N–17; and *Registro de la Contribución Directa del Departamento Famatina,* 1855, AJF (LR).

ther distinguishing themselves from members of the Unitarian Party, most of these Federalist leaders had never occupied administrative positions in the department. Even in the 1850s, a period of relative calm in which the Federalists' political sway in the province was evident, only Galíndez and Angel filled political positions. The others would take posts only in those exceptional moments when the rebels controlled Famatina.

Equally significant, the *Registro* of 1855 listed five of these Federalist leaders as comuneros, while we know that another, Esteban Cabrera, who had obtained land by purchase and not because he was an indio originario of the village, was nonetheless categorized as Indian.[61] Therefore, six out of the ten Federalists were of indigenous origin, in contrast to the overwhelmingly white, Spanish composition of the Unitarian Party. The Federalist leaders differed from the Unitarians in their geographic origins as

Positions	Status	Rebellions
Governor	White	1862, 1863, 1867
	Indian	1862, 1863, 1867
	Comunero	1862, 1863, 1867
	Comunero	1862
	Comunero	1862, 1863, 1867
Customs Agent	White	1862, 1863, 1867
		1867
		1867
	Comunero	1867
	Comunero	1862

well. Nine of them were proprietors and/or residents of the old Indian villages in the north of the department. Of these, five were landowners in the village of Famatina, while two owned land in Pituil and the other two had properties in Angulos, Chañarmuyo, Antinaco or Campanas. These Federalist leaders appeared to be distinguished members of these villages, although they were not the richest. It is possible that some of them belonged to families that had become "bosses" or "governors" of Indian communities in the colonial period and still existed as such in the 1820s.[62]

Let us turn now to the gauchos who were mobilized and filled the lowest ranks of the montonera. I identified fifteen montoneros who participated in Federalist rebellions in the valley during the 1860s, but found the occupations of only ten. Of this group, four were labradores, three worked on haciendas (one as a peon and two as ranch hands), two were miners, and one was a shoemaker. None of these montoneros were landowners.[63] Many of the rebels—seven—were married, which suggests that they may also have had children.[64] Concerning the geographic origins of these gauchos, most—eleven—came from the old Indian villages in the north and south of the department; only one came from Chilecito. Some of them showed consistency in their political affiliations. Four of the fifteen montoneros participated in more than one of the several mobilizations that the valley witnessed in the 1860s.

Political affiliation and party identity were significant points of reference for the inhabitants of the valley in their everyday life, and during moments of relative peace, they shaped, on individual bases, relations between neighbors. For example, a witness who testified against a gaucho from Malligasta, Casto Olivera, claimed that he was "of bad habits, continually appearing drunk in the streets, insulting and mistreating certain neighbors, one of them being Don Santiago Sierra, now deceased, whom he fiercely stabbed, fleeing afterwards to the fort of Andalgalá."[65] This could have been a mere neighborhood rumble, if we did not know who the protagonists were. Olivera was described in the trial as an "obstinate montonero." In support of their characterization, witnesses declared that he was the "man of confidence" of the Federalist leader of Famatina, Esteban Cabrera. They alleged that during the rebellion of 1867, Cabrera sent Olivera to persecute "all the most notable residents" of Chilecito and take some prisoner. Don Santiago Sierra, whose title bespoke his Spanish origins and a certain fortune, belonged to a family of well-known merchants from Los Sarmientos, a town neighboring Malligasta, Olivera's home. In addition, Sierra had been one of the signatories of the Unitarian petition in 1862, and afterward, aide to a Unitarian commander of the department, José María Linares. It was in this capacity that Sierra found himself in the battle of Cuesta de Miranda, where, following the Unitarian's defeat, he was pursued in a bloody chase and finished off by montoneros.[66]

The Agrarian Component of Political Conflict

But to what extent were party identities and political rivalries shaped by landlord-gaucho relations? One of the ways to approach this question is to analyze some of the concrete forms that political struggle took in the valley and the behavior of the rebels during the mobilizations. We can begin with the manner in which the gauchos used the space created since late 1861 by the larger political process to address some of the problems that marked their relations with the landlords.

Political mobilizations affected the competition between landlords and gauchos for the valley's mineral wealth. Although Chacho signed a peace treaty with the national government in June 1862, a nearly permanent mobilization of gauchos gripped the valley over the next few months. And in December 1862, Don Samuel García, a Unitarian hacendado, mine owner, and justice of the mines in the department, wrote to the provincial government about "the need to take action to diminish, even if it is not possible to eradicate, the ill that miners known as pilquineros bring to mining, with their destructive methods of working whatever veins they find."[67] Still, García reminded the government that the situation required delicate treatment. His report cautioned that owing to "the state of demoralization of the masses, their lack of respect for all government mandates and the impossibility of bringing them to obedience . . . , any reforms intended to curb the bad habits of these classes of society, calls for extreme precaution."[68] In a province where the state, with its inadequate resources and institutions, could barely prop up its police powers, the Federalist montoneras seemed to work on the pilquineros' behalf.

Federalist rebellions were also an opportunity to do away with deference. The conduct of Cansio Olmedo, a "poor peon" from the village of Famatina, is revealing. During the rebellion of Felipe Varela, Olmedo appropriated animals belonging to Don Felisísimo de la Colina, a hacendado from the department of Arauco. Not content with his spoils, Olmedo pursued the hacendado and his sons with the intention of killing them, but they managed to escape by taking refuge in the neighboring hills.[69] The peon's daring, however, did not stop there. He then demanded of the hacendado's wife a ransom of 300 pesos, "and since she did not have [it] he threatened to drag her to the headquarters [of the montonera] on the back of a horse, as was the custom."[70]

In that society, a woman on horseback "belonged" to the man who rode the horse. It left no doubt that the man protected the woman at the same time that he proudly displayed her. Indeed, it was a public acknowledgment if she was that man's wife, of their relationship. But when a peon and the wife of a hacendado so appeared in public, the significance was different. As Sarmiento observed in his depiction of the outlaw in *Facundo*, it not only showed the audacity of a man formidable enough to have stolen a woman but also had the consequence of publicly offending the woman's family.[71] A gaucho who witnessed the event understood it this way, later declaring that " 'Lame' Olmedo behaved shamelessly with the wife of Don Felisísimo."[72] Olmedo's intention was to defile the honor and respectability of the de la Colina family, and thus, turn social relations upside down. But why did Olmedo do that? When he was brought before the court, accused primarily of cattle theft, Olmedo tried to avoid his responsibility by contending that he was simply following his officer's orders. One of the hacendado's sons rejected Olmedo's strategy, saying that if the theft of livestock had been ordered by a superior, what explained the persecution at gunpoint of his father and brothers, and the contribution that the defendant demanded of his mother? According to de la Colina, "Olmedo committed those robberies because he wanted to do it, because he served the rebels willfully and spontaneously, because he has been one of their agents in los Sauces, and finally . . . , Olmedo is known as a very obstinate montonero."[73] Olmedo's conduct, in other words, was the result of his spontaneous, consistent, and widely known identification with Federalism.

The analysis of the victims of the montonera also suggests some of the meanings of Federalist mobilizations in the valley. In July 1867, when the rebellion led by Felipe Varela had been contained, the official newspaper of La Rioja published a list of twenty-seven Unitarians throughout the province who had been killed on various occasions by Federalist montoneros (see table 5). Of these, sixteen were from the valley of Famatina, which gives some sense of the intensity of the rebellion in that department. The Famatina victims were of a specific social background. The majority—twelve—were members of the group of large landowners: the Gordillo family lost three members to montoneros, and the Noroña family lost two. The remaining important families—the Dávilas, Ocampos, Del Morals, Soajes, San Románs, and Iribarrens—each suffered the loss of one member. Other distinguished figures in the region ended up on the list: Commanders José María Linares and Crisólogo Chaves, as well as the rich landowner Don Fernando Vega. Further, such social selectivity was accompanied by a definite political stance: most of the family names that had appeared as signatories on the Unitarian petition of 1862 reappeared as victims on the 1867 list, as did particular individuals. Seven of the victims in 1867 had signed the petition. This consistency in political and social origins among the victims implies that the montoneras provided a forum within the political arena for some form of resolution of the tensions between landlords and gauchos.

How the deaths occurred and the life histories of the victims are also significant. Many of the victims were slain individually or in small groups, rather than in formal battle. In most cases, the evidence indicates that the victims were known to the montoneros and a particular target of their violence. This individualization of political violence reflected the personalized way in which the notables exercised power and related to the gauchos. Thus, Don Manuel Iribarren, Don Marcial San Román, and Don Teófilo Carreño were attacked by a group of gauchos in the village of Malligasta; after intense resistance, they were stabbed to death.[74] Commander

TABLE 5   Victims of the Montonera, 1867

Name	Department	Real Property (in pesos)	Position	Petition of 1862 Signatory
Arias, Balbino	Costa Baja		Recruiter	No
Bazán, Fermín	Costa Baja		Commander	No
Carreño, N. (hijo)	Vinchina			No
Carreño, Teófilo	Vinchina	500	Tax Collector	No
Castellano, Camilo	Vinchina		Recruiter	No
Chaves, Crisólogo	Famatina		Commander	Yes
Conde, Amaranto	Famatina			Yes
Dávila, Tristán	Famatina/ Vinchina	2,416	Governor	No
Del Moral, Sebastián	Famatina		Justice of the Peace	Yes
Gordillo, Gaudioso	Famatina	250		No
Gordillo, José M.	Famatina	562		No
Gordillo, Justo	Famatina			No
Herrera, Galo	Costa Baja		Tax Collector	No
Iribarren, Manuel A.	Famatina/ Vinchina	10,670	Tax Collector	Yes
Linares, José María	Famatina		Commander	Yes
Lozada, Carmen José	Famatina			Yes
Noroña, José N.	Famatina			No
Noroña, Rodrigo	Famatina	4,000		No
Ocampo, David	Famatina			No
San Román, Marcial	Famatina	750	Commander	Yes
Soaje, Manuel	Famatina/ Vinchina	517*		No
Vega, Fernando	Famatina	4,000		No

*The Soaje brothers' property in Vinchina was valued at 9,300 pesos.

Note: I did not find any information on the following victims: Celestino Barcala, Vicente Barros, Eladio Cedrón, Casimiro Guzmán, and Casto Poblete.

Sources: "Las Víctimas de la Montonera del '67," La Regeneración, 18 July 1867; Registro de la Contribución Directa del Departamento Famatina, 1855, AJP (LR); and "Vecinos de la Villa de Famatina (Chilecito) a D. F. Sarmiento," Famatina, 23 October 1862, in Mitre-Sarmiento, 167–68.

José María Linares, who according to his fellow Unitarians was "cruel and bloodthirsty with the montoneros," was relentlessly pursued by montoneros, and then captured, humiliated, and finally lanced publicly in the Federalist camp.[75]

Colonel Don Tristán Dávila was also one of the victims. The way he met his end was not unusual and shows that he, too, was known to the montoneros. In May 1867, a group of montoneros attacked Dávila and others in the midst of a Unitarian meeting. Wounded, Dávila managed to escape and hide out. But a few days later, a group of montoneros attacked his house, killing him in his chambers. The leader of this party was José Manuel Carrizo, a medium-sized labrador and comunero from Pituil who would be singled out repeatedly in the 1860s as head of the Federalist montoneras.[76]

Dávila's history and the very fact of his death were particularly representative of the form that the struggle between Unitarians and Federalists had taken in La Rioja during the nineteenth century. Since colonial times, his family had been one of the wealthiest and most influential within the group of Famatina's landlords, and his father, Don Miguel Dávila, killed by Facundo's troops in the battle of "El Puesto" in 1823, was one of the first and most legendary victims of party struggles in postindependence La Rioja.[77]

True to his family's political affiliation, Tristán began his political career in 1830 when he followed General Lamadrid into battle against Facundo. Then, in the 1840s, he took part in the northern coalition against Rosas and was subsequently forced into exile in Chile until 1852. During the 1860s, his family origins and Unitarian militancy would turn him into one of Mitrismo's most distinguished allies in La Rioja, where he was interim governor of the province in 1865 and 1866.[78]

As a prominent proprietor in the valley of Famatina, like other landlords, Dávila's relations with the gauchos seemed to be somewhat problematic.[79] In November 1865, barely two years before his assassination and only months after La Rioja's contingent for the Paraguayan war had revolted, Dávila's wife wrote from their estate about the difficulty in finding workers:

> I do not have one single peon; Paschi has come by but I can't make him go out and work for anything, he says that you turned him over to the contingent and *forgave the debt he owed you,* and he's afraid that

they'll call him up again, and nobody wants [to] hire himself to the house for fear that they'll get taken away.[80]

Two phenomena appear to have encouraged the gauchos' hostility toward Dávila. First, his role in the gathering of the contingent, to which he even acceded his own peons, generated distrust among the valley's workers. Second, one of his former workers disputed the legitimacy of his debt to Dávila and tried to avoid becoming dependent on the landlord. Davila's uneasy relationship with the gauchos, therefore, was the consequence of both long-term, conflictive social arrangements specific to the valley and the larger, twin political processes of party struggle and state formation. But while the workers' antagonism in 1865 only took the form of avoidance, in 1867, during the rebellion led by Felipe Varela when party strife generated mass mobilizations and created a moment of generalized war in the valley, the gaucho resistance escalated to include assassination.

Famatina and the Andean Interior

In other departments of La Rioja, like Arauco, agrarian conflicts were also intertwined with political struggles. Arauco was, in many ways, similar to Famatina. Its population of notional Indian peasants sold their harvests in advance to rich, notional white landlords and merchants.[81] Likewise, during the first half of the nineteenth century, rich landlords had bought land and water in some Indian villages, turning the plots formerly owned by small proprietors into larger alfalfa fields.[82] And, as in Famatina, water was not only crucial for agriculture but also a source of tension. In this respect, the conflict between the Del Morals and Chumbitas is telling.

The Del Morals, some of whom owned land in the neighboring department of Famatina and had signed the Unitarian petition of 1862 as well, were important landowners of Spanish origin. The family had identified with Unitarianism since the 1820s, and like the Dávilas, lost some members to the violence of Facundo and other Federalists.[83]

The Chumbitas were a large family of Indian origin whose predecessors had been "governors," or caciques, who ruled the village of Aymogasta in the late eighteenth century.[84] In the nineteenth century, some of them continued to play key roles in local public life. The "Indian" Orencio Chumbita built the village church in 1830, and in the 1840s, he was commander of the local militia, a renowned Federalist militant, and a personal friend of Chacho.[85] In the 1850s, Orencio's son, Don Severo Chumbita (whom his rivals called "the Indian Chumba"),[86] also became the commander of the department as well as one of the most important Federalist leaders in the province, participating in four rebellions in the 1860s. Don Severo was a well-to-do labrador whose property in Aymogasta situated him above the majority of the labradores of his department.[87] His authority and capacity to mobilize people was also strengthened by an important network of kinship relations that united him with the rest of the villagers of Aymogasta and the Indians of other villages, like Machigasta.[88] In addition, Don Severo may have also been well related with those who claimed to be of Spanish descent; he was compadre with one of them, and as we will see, they occasionally shared their social life. Yet, differences were never completely erased, as Daniel Del Moral would make clear in a letter to the governor of the province on January 2, 1862.[89]

A few days earlier, on December 22, 1861, Severo had invited Daniel Del Moral to a "dancing and drinking party." Although Del Moral felt that the invitation "diminished his dignity," he finally decided to attend. At the party, Del Moral described to other guests

> the disorder in which we live with respect to the water and I told him [Severo] that he authorized this evil and that this exposed us to a struggle among neighbors, because of his extreme tolerance [of disorder], and I demanded the necessity of fixing the *marcos* [that measure and regulate the quantity of water that each owner must receive].

Severo declined responsibility, but the exchange did not end there. According to Del Moral,

> While heatedly talking about these matters [Severo] was encouraged by a fool to impose fear on me. . . . [T]his bothered me and I told him [Severo] that he had always been and still was a protector of rogues and then he grabbed me and kept me down where I was seated and punched me several times, then, the highway robber Mercedes [Chumbita, Severo's uncle] rushed toward me, from my back, with a dagger in his hands, trying to kill [me] by treason, as he usually does. . . . [S]ome women rushed and protected me, holding his arm, while he imperiously shouted to them, "let me finish with this rogue from San Antonio [Del Moral's estate]." [I]t was then that the "great chief" [Severo] gave the order to arrest me.[90]

Daniel ran, mounted his horse, and escaped toward San Antonio, where he mobilized some twenty men "first, to protect myself from my personal enemy, and then, to attack him; I found one of his partisans and sent him with my threats to [Severo] Chumbita, that he should be aware of my hostility." Later, friends on both sides of the conflict managed to appease the contenders. Yet, Daniel exclaimed, "for their disgrace, I am still alive and I can persecute them until I finish with them, to guarantee my existence."[91]

As the national political process unfolded, local conflicts deepened, bringing more violence to Arauco. Two months after the rumble in the party, national troops occupied La Rioja, and Chacho (and with him, Severo Chumbita) rebelled against Mitre's government. The troops from Buenos Aires burned many Federalists' homes (including Severo's) in the villages of Machigasta and Aymogasta to the ground. In spite of the peace agreement with the Unitarians signed by Chacho in May 1862, conflicts and resentments did not disappear: some of the few Unitarians of Arauco had been only too willing to cooperate with the national troops during the repression.[92] In August, one of those Unitarians claimed that Juan Simon Chumbita (Severo's cousin) and others had repeatedly attacked and tried to kill him, "insulting me and giving me the title of Unitarian Savage"; another quoted Severo as alleging that several people, including the Del Morals, "were the cause of his ruin" and "would pay with their lives."[93]

In March 1863, Chacho launched his second rebellion, and once again, Chumbita followed him. As the commander of Arauco, Severo ordered Don Daniel Del Moral and his brother Don Honorato to give his troops two horses and save their alfalfa fields for the horses of the montonera, but according to Chumbita, they stubbornly refused twice. His uncle Mercedes, as a captain in the montonera, pursued and arrested the Del Morals and their cousin, Francisco Sotomayor. Then, at dusk on March 18, Mercedes, his montoneros, and the prisoners took the road to the city of La Rioja; barely a league south of Machigasta, by a long algaroba tree, Mercedes ordered the party to dismount, and he and his men cut the throats of the Del Morals and Sotomayor, leaving their corpses in the fields nearby.[94] Another Del Moral brother, Don Pastor, managed to escape from Mercedes, but was later captured and executed by the montoneros.[95] In June, when taken prisoner by Unitarian troops, Mercedes said that Severo had given the order to kill the Del Morals, and that when Chacho was told of their deaths, he sanctioned them by saying that "it was well done, now they had less enemies." Immediately after his interrogation, Mercedes was lanced and his throat was cut at "the same site where he immolated those victims."[96]

The deaths of the Del Morals and Sotomayor led Sarmiento to reflect on the nature of political violence in the Andean interior, especially in La Rioja. In *El Chacho* (written in 1866, a year before Tristán Dávila, another Del Moral, and other Famatina landlords were killed by the montonera), Sarmiento wrote that the Indians of San Juan and La Rioja had been reduced since colonial times to inhabiting arid, barren lands, from which they could not eke out "their necessities."

> *To these causes of distant origin is due La Rioja's eternal rebelliousness,* and its most recent—that of Chacho. For a half century, members of the Del Moral family have fallen victims of *the sordid resentment of the dispossessed.*
>
> *Their grandfathers diverted a stream to irrigate their lands, leaving those of the Indians dry.* . . . In the time of [Facundo] Quiroga this family, along with the [O]Campo and the Doria [Dávila] families, was the target of montonera persecutions. Five [*sic*] of its sons have had their throats cut in the last uprising [of Chacho] . . . while the gentlewoman escaped to the woods to save herself from *Indian revenge.*
>
> *How can we explain, without these antecedents,* the spontaneous, fervent participation in the uprising of Chacho, of not only los Llanos and los Pueblos of La Rioja, but the *laguneros* (Indians from the lagoons) of Guanacache, the inhabitants of Mogna and Valle Fértil, and all the inhabitants of San Juan spread throughout the desert?[97]

In the lagoons of Guanacache, too, as Sarmiento indicated, small- and medium-sized proprietors of indigenous origin—from whose ranks would come some of the Federalist montoneras' leaders in the 1860s—confronted big ranchers of Spanish origin. As governor of San Juan, Sarmiento had seen how the ranchers, eager to expand their holdings, attempted to push gauchos from their land yet only managed, according to him, "to swell the ranks of Chacho."[98]

These conflicts were kept alive in the collective memory of those in the Andean interior, and some testimonies allow a glimpse of the ways they were interpreted. In 1921, stories recalling of the deaths of the Del Morals still underscored the ethnic and social connotations of party struggles: because of their "ancestry" and "wealth," the Unitarian Del Morals had fallen victim to the montoneras.[99]

Folklore also sheds light on how the relationship between party and agrarian conflicts was represented. One of the most revealing pieces is a story collected in Los Sarmientos—an old Indian village in the valley of Famatina—that has Facundo Quiroga as one of the protagonists. In the tale, "a *paisano* [countryman] went to sell Quiroga a *media* of wheat, a media in those days being a 'half load.' When the deal was struck, the paisano filled a sock [in Spanish, also a media] with wheat and presented it to Quiroga, ignoring his friends' dire warnings of the punishment he would face. Quiroga, having to admit that the paisano was in the right, paid for his sock as if it were a half a load."[100] The story, a "trickster tale"[101] (a genre that repeatedly featured Facundo as one of the protagonists), is a gaucho comment on the sale of future harvests, a practice that embodied their dependency on the landlords and, as a large landowner recognized, "left them no surplus whatsoever."[102] The trick allowed the gaucho to come out on top once a deal had been made, and thus, the clever use of words became a weapon to negotiate the sell of the harvest with the landlord and minimize the fragility of the gaucho's domestic economy. Here, the trick also has partisan connotations provided by the specific role Facundo plays. In this local adaptation, Facundo is neither the fool nor enemy of the trickster, as is usually the case with victims in this type of tale. To the contrary, the Federalist caudillo approves the gaucho's cunning because he was "in the right."

This sanction of gaucho cleverness is a constant in this genre as long as it features Facundo as victim. In another tale, for instance, Facundo's approval is presented in an even more celebratory tone: "Admiring the ingenuity and initiative of the man, Quiroga gave him an ounce of gold."[103] And it is possible that these types of stories actually gave Facundo a special reputation: various chroniclers who have left us with a negative portrait of the caudillo nonetheless acknowledged that "his specialty was to reward with his indulgence acts of cleverness, ingenuity or personal valor."[104] In popular representations, then, everyday forms of resistance by gauchos take on Federalist connotations. Given the nature of political affiliation in Famatina, however, the presence of Facundo in this tale should be read in a more local, yet partisan, manner as well. He who approves gaucho resistance here is not only a Federalist caudillo but also the leader of the troops that murdered Don Miguel Dávila, one of the most legendary victims of the struggle between Unitarians and Federalists in La Rioja. Hence, we can imagine that when the story was told in the valley, the audience could also read it as a comment on the wealthiest of Famatina landowners, the Dávilas.

A slightly different version of this tale was collected in the neighboring valley of Catamarca (where small proprietorship and subsistence agriculture also abounded), which suggests that Facundo's role in the representation of the agrarian connotations of Federalism extended to other areas of the Andean interior.[105] Other pieces of folklore from Catamarca make a clear connection between gauchos' agrarian experience and Federalism. In the valley of Catamarca, as in other regions dominated by subsistence agriculture, gauchos suffered periods of scarcity before their harvests. The hunger that gripped them during those times was personified as a "bad man" named Tanico, who carried a big knife in order to threaten people with death. To combat Tanico, the gauchos would prepare a stew, itself personified as General Cachilico, the person who "gave life." But this cyclical conflict had partisan connotations. A popular song, "To General Cachilico," narrates the seasonal vicissitudes of gaucho survival and begins like this:

> They tried to banish
> The General Cachilico
> A man so Federalist
> Just like the savage Tanico.[106]

Tanico is characterized as "savage," meaning Unitarian; Cachilico is labeled a Federalist. In Catamarca, gauchos also identified Federalism with their subsistence, while they blamed hunger and death on Unitarianism.

THE LLANOS, A SEMIDESERT plain located in southern La Rioja, is broken at its center by three parallel mountain chains that run north to south, forming what are known as the three coasts. The western chain creates the Costa Alta of the Llanos; the center, the Costa del Medio; and the eastern, the Costa Baja. The plains surrounding the three chains extend beyond the limits of the province of La Rioja into the western part of the province of Córdoba, the north and east of the province of San Juan, and the northern portion of the province of San Luis.

During the colonial period, the villages of the Llanos of La Rioja made up the parish of Los Llanos; after independence, it became the department of Los Llanos, which was subsequently divided into two departments in 1847. The western area became the department of Costa Alta de Los Llanos, and included the villages of Tama, Malanzán, San Antonio, and Guaja, located in the Costa Alta and Costa del Medio. The eastern department, Costa Baja de Los Llanos, principally included the villages of Catuna, Olta, Ulapes, and Chepes.

According to estimates made in 1806, the population of the parish of Los Llanos was 3,886 inhabitants, including 264 Spanish families, "the remaining families being known as '*naturales*' because of their low birth." Among this second group were the few Indian tribute payers of the parish, the inhabitants of Olta, and the castas and slaves, who were the majority.[1] The population increased nearly threefold during the first half of the nineteenth century, and by 1855, the departments of Costa Alta and Costa Baja combined were home to 10,594 people; the estimate for 1863 was 11,000 inhabitants.[2]

Since colonial times, the Llanos was the only part of what was to become the province of La Rioja dedicated to cattle raising. The cattle raised there, which fed the city of La Rioja and much of San Juan, along with the daily production of hides, fats, and cheese, were the principal source of income for the population of Los Llanos. The region's limited agriculture primarily involved subsistence production, and only exceptionally bountiful harvests were marketed.[3]

In the arid climate of the Llanos, access to water and pasture were crucial to cattle raising. Natural sources of water, already few and far between, dried up during years of low rainfall. Thus, the survival of a herd depended on a criador's ability to construct reservoirs (*represas*) and "buckets" to preserve water.[4]

Livestock raising determined the rhythm and pattern of colonization in Los Llanos. From the early eighteenth century until about 1850, the criadores populated the three Costas without venturing too far out onto the most arid plains, since streams and springs running down from the sierras provided the only source of water for their animals. This meant that the space occupied by the most important criadores was limited, and land was available for meager agriculture and smaller-scale livestock raising throughout the nineteenth century. In 1806, an ecclesiastical report noted that in the parish of Los Llanos, "there are many . . . lands."[5] This clearly set Los Llanos apart from the other parishes of La Rioja, such as Anguinán (Famatina), where lands were quite scarce. It also explains, to some extent, the attraction that Los Llanos held for the poor from other parts of La Rioja as well as the neighboring provinces, who migrated to Los Llanos beginning in the late eighteenth century. That migration was at least partially responsible for the province's demographic growth in the first half of the nineteenth century.[6] Furthermore, the availability of land accounted for the relatively harmonious relationship between large criadores and labradores, and even legally landless workers, facilitating the establishment of vertical relations of solidarity.

The region's aridity put limits on the growth of the cattle-raising industry. Fragmentary information from the first half of the nineteenth century allows an approximation of the magnitude of livestock raising in Los Llanos. The most optimistic estimates located between 20,000 and 30,000 head in the region.[7] Evidence for the second half of the century is roughly consistent with these figures. In 1860, the livestock in the two departments of the Llanos must have been close to 38,000 head. The scale of these figures bears some relation to those of the First Agricultural and Livestock Census (which should serve as a maximum); in 1888, the census reported 29,212 head of cattle in the department of Rivadavia (formerly Costa Alta), in comparison with the 18,300 estimate in 1860.[8]

Even at their most generous, the approximations speak to a notable poverty in the Llanos. Martín de Moussy, who traveled through the region in the 1850s when cattle raising was undergoing a modest expansion, observed that the ranches in the Llanos "were far from having the importance of those of the Pampa," where, according to his calculations, a square league of natural pasture could feed up to 3,000 head of cattle. In contrast, the properties of this arid region, "infinitely less rich in pasture and water, had no more than a relatively small number of cattle on a large expanse."[9] The disparity that so struck the French geographer becomes clearer if we compare estimates of the head of cattle in two littoral provinces with different ties to the Atlantic market. In 1837, the province of Corrientes had about 466,590 head of cattle, while in 1840, Buenos Aires had 3 million.[10]

Labradores and Landless Workers

Approximately 40 percent of the population of the department of Costa Alta possessed neither land nor cattle.[11] Still, it is possible that the portion of the population without access to land was less than this estimate suggests. In the Llanos of La Rioja, not having registered, taxable property, or even legal possession of property (squatting was a possibility), did not imply having no access to land. Such was the case with the labradores, or agriculturalists, a social sector with diffuse limits that included some of those proprietors who occupied the lowest ranks of the Tax Registry as well as other inhabitants whom the fiscal documents left out.

Who were the labradores, and what were the defining characteristics of agricultural production in Los Llanos? In the Llanos in 1855, there were 621 criadores and 760 labradores.[12] The latter produced corn and, to a lesser extent, wheat—crops that depended on rain in the summer. When the summer rainfall was heavy, the labradores utilized natural depressions that collected water and retained humidity. This allowed corn planted in December to mature with the summer rain and be ready for harvesting in March. Wheat, by contrast, was planted at the end of the summer rains, in March or April, growing slowly during the dry winter months and coming to maturity as the first summer rain fell again, in November or

December. These plots of land, called "swamp" or "stubble" fields, were small and could not be cultivated every year, depending as they did on seasonal rains.[13] Swamp or stubble fields had little value, which may explain why they were not included in the tax registry.

Destined to feed family units, these crops were marketed only in exceptionally good years, when they were in excess of immediate needs. Even so, the scale and instability of this type of agriculture did not meet the minimum needs of most of the labradores. To secure their subsistence, these families had to turn to the labor market, with diverse strategies that allowed them to take advantage of the few opportunities that the Llanos economy offered. The case of the Quintero family, of Costa Baja, is instructive. When he was fifty years old, the head of the family, Bernabel Quintero, defined himself as a labrador. As for his sons, José Angel, a twenty-seven-year-old bachelor, was a muleteer; Mateo, twenty-five and also a bachelor, identified his occupation as "labrador and other common labors"; and Facundo, a minor still without a chosen occupation, worked with his father and brothers.[14]

As their occupations suggested, the Quinteros planted "their swamp" and simultaneously labored for rich proprietors, almost all of them criadores. Their work included maintaining pastures where livestock was enclosed, preparing orchards, planting the stubble fields that the criadores had for their consumption, and even participating in the construction of housing. They also worked in cattle raising, whether caring for the animals or retrieving free-roaming cattle that had strayed. In the case of the latter, it was in the criador's interest to give the Quinteros one animal for every three that they recovered. The animals that the Quinteros received as payment served as the start of a small family herd, although it was difficult to enlarge it since some of the animals would surely be sacrificed for food in times of scarcity.[15]

Labradores could easily accommodate themselves to the needs of the cattle economy, which neither needed nor could maintain a year-round workforce. The labradores provided for some of their needs through subsistence agriculture, and worked in cattle ranching according to the seasonal demands of the criadores. Reinforcing this complementarity between criadores and labradores, some of the latter may have lived as *agregados* (squatters) on the properties of the former. This type of arrangement, dominant in other cattle economies, appeared not to have been so common in Los Llanos, though there is evidence that it existed.[16]

It is possible that many of these labradores were migrants (or their descendants), usually from neighboring provinces, who settled in Los Llanos at the end of the eighteenth century and during the first decades of the nineteenth. According to the evidence from the end of the eighteenth century, this group was largely made up of ex-slaves and mulattoes.[17]

The group of workers without land or livestock included peons, muleteers, and to a lesser degree, artisans of various types, such as saddle makers and weavers. These workers, who at the beginning of the nineteenth century constituted an important proportion of the society of Los Llanos, found a principal market for their labor in cattle ranching.[18] Nevertheless, that market offered only limited opportunities. During a good part of the year, caring for cattle, most of which roamed free, required few hands; and branding and roundups, which did require extra workers, were seasonal tasks.

Finding work, then, appears to have been a major problem for the peons and ranch hands of Los Llanos. Domingo Montivero, a *péon jornalero* (day laborer) of Ambil, said that "he knew how to work to make his living, but only if he could get a job."[19] One response to the lack of work was migration. Some peons went to nearby provinces like San Juan, Córdoba, or Santiago del Estero, while others went as far as the mines of the Norte Chico in Chile.[20] Most of the workers lived in such poverty that it was considered exceptional when a peon owned a workhorse.[21]

The difficulties that peons, *jornaleros* (day laborers), and labradores encountered in securing their subsistence were notorious. A dearth of continuous or stable work in agricultural production periodically exposed them to hunger, and cattle rustling was one of the ways that this sector responded to this seasonal experience. Peons and labradores robbed cattle and, on rare occasions, horses. In 1835, Ramón Flores of Costa Alta declared that of "all the robberies he had seen," in which he and his accomplices had rustled forty-five animals over a long period of time, he had stolen thirty-nine head of cattle and only six horses. Flores himself testified that the main objective of the robberies was to gather food.[22] A jornalero from Costa del Medio, also accused of cattle rustling, explained that he "made use of the animals out of necessity."[23] The scarcity that threatened workers and labradores was known to the authorities, who sometimes found "necessity" a sufficient reason to moderate sentences meted out to rustlers. In some cases, the penalty was simply to pay the value of the animals consumed.[24] Some prosperous members of the region explicitly recognized the seasonal hardship of the workers and labradores, as did Don Hipólito Tello, a rancher from Los Llanos and governor of the province in the 1840s, when he "slaughtered cattle and distributed it among the poor."[25]

Land Tenure

The ways of holding land dedicated to cattle raising in the Llanos of La Rioja appear to have been unique in what today is Argentina. *Mercedes* (land grants, initially from the Spanish Crown and later from the first independent governors to distinguished inhabitants of the region) were subdivided over generations among heirs of the original ranch owner. Although this subdivision implied the transfer of property rights connected to the original grant or ranch, the piece of land itself remained physically undivided, being converted into a property of common rights. In other words, the descendants of the original owner shared proportional rights to the use of the facilities, waters, and fields of the ranch or grant, and although mostly of Spanish origin, became, as they called themselves, comuneros of the merced or ranch.[26]

The number of comuneros making up a ranch or merced varied. While the merced of Atiles was the property of only four comuneros, that of Tama, the most highly subdivided in Costa Alta, was home to seventy-five proprietors.[27] What each of these criadores possessed was not a property with fixed physical limits but rather a title to "*acción y derecho* [rights] to the common fields and waters"of the grant or ranch. The title gave the comunero the right to raise a certain number of cattle using a certain proportion of the facilities, grasses, and waters that were held in common by all the proprietors. The comuneros knew what proportion corresponded to each person and the economic benefits that could be derived from that portion, variables that were reflected in the monetary value of each right that made up a merced.[28] The values of these rights within a single ranch or merced also varied, so that, for example, while some comuneros of Merced de la Ediondita had rights taxed at 31 pesos, the richest of them, General Peñaloza, had a title worth 500 pesos.[29] It is difficult to know what each right represented in terms of quantities of land (or grassland) and water, and therefore, number of animals. For instance, judicial and notary records only acknowledge that a right was sold "according to accustomed use."[30]

The status of comunero did not necessarily imply usufruct rights to all the resources of a merced. If several proprietors built a reservoir, for example, only those comuneros could then use it.[31] Valuable orchards, due to the number of trees and availability of water, and cornfields, because they provided a subsistence crop, were also exempt from common rights, and as such, considered individual properties.

While these proprietors had access to the use of communal property, the titles to this right were considered private property; comuneros transferred them in sales to other comuneros or outsiders. In the same way, individual titles were bequeathed, even to heirs who were not among the comuneros of a merced or ranch.[32] No less significant, the provincial state considered each comunero an individual taxpayer responsible for taxes on real estate property (the contribución territorial) in proportion to the value of one's rights.[33] In addition, the most important part of the wealth of a comunero—livestock—was private property. In the same fashion, care of the animals was also the work of individual owners, not the comuneros as a group.

Notwithstanding, this form of land tenure implied a communal management of pastures, water, and facilities.[34] It is hard to know in any detail, however, how this aspect of everyday life actually functioned. Documents make reference to the execution of these questions "according to use and custom," but do not explain the distribution of responsibilities among comuneros, their respective roles, or the obligations necessitated by this form of property. All of these aspects would reveal much about the type of social relations that this communal property generated.

Yet, we do know that the majority of these merced or ranch proprietors descended from the same Spanish ancestors. The case of the merced of Tama, for example, suggests the importance of this phenomenon. There, of a total of seventy-five proprietors, seventeen comuneros shared the name of Romero, and another fifteen, Sanchez.[35] These two last names alone accounted for almost half the proprietors of that merced. Mercedes and ranches, therefore, linked comuneros through a dense web of kinship ties in addition to those created through the communal management of the administration of grasslands, water, and structures.

Another distinctive characteristic of landholding in the Llanos of La Rioja was the geographic dispersion of the rights of many proprietors. While 62.5 percent of the proprietors in the department of Costa Alta held possessions in only one merced or ranch, the remaining 37.5 percent had rights in two or more mercedes or ranches, and some proprietors had rights in as many as eight different places.[36] These proprietors shared in the use of, for example, two mercedes with comuneros who were not necessarily related to one another. Thus, General Peñaloza had a right to the communal fields and waters in the merced of Guaja, the use of which he shared with ten comuneros. Ten other comuneros shared rights to water and pasture with him in the merced of La Ediondita. In this way, Peñaloza participated in the exploitation of the two mercedes, along with twenty other individuals. Some of those twenty comuneros, in turn, had rights in other mercedes in which Chacho did not have interests, thereby tying them to additional comuneros. This form of landholding and management of resources implies an invisible, almost infinite web of relations between comuneros in Los Llanos, the influence of which on social practices is difficult to estimate.

Finally, the dominance of landholding through such rights meant that *estancias* (ranches) held as exclusive property, not by comuneros but by a single owner, were few. Although in other cattle-ranching economies of the Río de la Plata, estancias were the most common type of property ownership, the registry of 1855 only included nine such properties in the department of Costa Alta, and the majority of those were in the hands of the wealthiest proprietors. These ranchers, however, could also have rights in land grants—titles that might, in some cases, have a greater value than their ranches.[37]

The Proprietors

Up to this point, we have explored those groups—labradores and landless workers—that were not among the proprietors of Los Llanos. Now, we turn to the landowners in the department of Costa Alta, utilizing information from the *Libro de Registro* (see figure 2). Based on the type of economic activity they engaged in, two distinct groups emerge. Most of the proprietors, 352 of the 409 included in the document (or 86.07 percent), were criadores—which roughly corresponded to the 345 hacendados in Costa Alta reported in the provincial census of 1855. They held properties dedicated to cattle raising and were owners of "rights to a ranch" or the lands of a merced, as well as corrals, reservoirs, watering holes, and buckets.

A second group (only 13.93 percent), smaller and heterogeneous, came entirely from the poorest of the proprietors, and participated in the labor

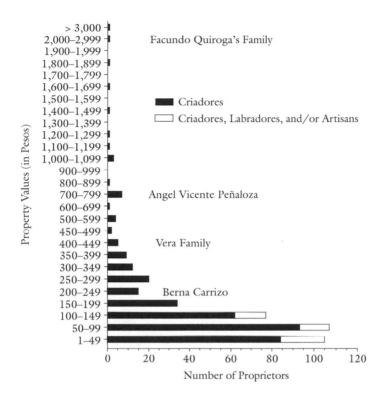

Property Values (in Pesos)

> 3,000
2,000–2,999   Facundo Quiroga's Family
1,900–1,999
1,800–1,899
1,700–1,799
1,600–1,699
1,500–1,599   ■■ Criadores
1,400–1,499   ☐ Criadores, Labradores, and/or Artisans
1,300–1,399
1,200–1,299
1,100–1,199
1,000–1,099
900–999
800–899
700–799   Angel Vicente Peñaloza
600–699
500–599
450–499
400–449   Vera Family
350–399
300–349
250–299
200–249   Berna Carrizo
150–199
100–149
50–99
1–49

0   20   40   60   80   100   120

Number of Proprietors

FIGURE 2   Proprietors of the Department of Costa Alta de los Llanos, 1855. *Source: Libro de Registro de las Propiedades Territoriales del Departamento de la Costa Alta y del Medio de los Llanos,* 1855, AJP (LR).

market generated by cattle ranching at the same time that they engaged in artisanal production or cultivated their own fields. For example, José Antonio Yacanto, the owner of an orchard taxed at thirty-one pesos, defined himself as a "foreman," and José Blas Montaña, who owned an orchard of prickly pears, said that his occupation was "labrador and *telero* [weaver]."[38]

Nevertheless, the distinction between the majority, who were criadores, and this group composed of labradores and artisans, should not be taken as a rigid categorization. In some cases, proprietors who according to the census did not have property devoted to cattle raising, did participate in that activity. Pedro Antonio Guzmán, who owned only a house and an orchard in Malanzán taxed at sixty-two pesos, worked in "pasturing and raising cattle, although on a small scale, and he also worked at times in agriculture." [39]

The Criadores

Who, then, were the criadores? The poorest of them lived in adobe huts, had small orchards, and used their lands to raise cattle.[40] They could have from five or six to thirty head of cattle, as well as some horses and other livestock such as goats.[41] The social distance between these criadores and the labradores and landless workers was quite small. Within just one family, some members might define themselves as criadores, while their brothers might consider themselves jornaleros.[42] Given that the number of their livestock was not large, these criadores could not live exclusively from ranching, and so worked for the richer landowners. They might care for others' cattle and receive a portion of those animals as compensation; or they were simply employed as forepersons.[43] Other criadores combined ranching with small-scale marketing or mule driving.[44] Their limited stock of animals also impelled some toward cattle rustling. At times, they tried to brand other people's cattle with their own symbol; on other occasions, they avoided sacrificing their own animals for food by consuming those of the richest criadores.[45]

Some of these smallholders were "people of color," either freed slaves or their descendants. This was the case with Bonifacia Villacorta and her descendants. Villacorta had been a slave, but in the early 1820s, she was freed. A short while after, she gave each of her three illegitimate children, still slaves, a cow so that they could begin to form their own herds. Despite their status, slaves in the Llanos of La Rioja were considered "absolute proprietors" who "knew how to negotiate and make contracts." Once they owned cattle "branded with their own mark," slaves could utilize the animals in order to free themselves.[46] As judicial documents in a case involving Villacorta attested, "Even a slave has his fortune, and through it, frees himself, as has come to pass with the . . . illegitimate children of [Villacorta], who have been freed, and have means to make a living."[47]

Situations like Villacorta's (in addition to the migration and settlement in Los Llanos mentioned earlier), would explain the significance of the free population "of color" in La Rioja in the nineteenth century. The census of 1814 showed that "people of color" represented 43.2 percent of La Rioja's population. This group was made up of slaves, 7.6 percent of the province's population, and *libertos* (freed slaves), 35.6 percent of the total, making the latter the most numerous socioethnic group in the province.[48] Therefore, it is possible to suggest that a good portion of the small proprietors had their origins in the "peasantization" process affecting ex-slaves, who were integrated into the cattle economy of Los Llanos as small producers.

The middle-sized proprietors combined cattle ranching with livestock marketing or the small-scale marketing of other products.[49] Their properties generally consisted of adobe huts or houses, orchards, stubble fields of corn for their own consumption, and lands set aside for cattle. It is difficult to know the exact size of their herds, but they probably ranged from 200 to 400 head.[50] The forebears of some of these proprietors (some of them of Spanish origin) had settled in the region during the 1820s and 1830s, attracted by the availability and low price of land. They could acquire property via purchase, simple occupation, or a merced from the governor in return for their service in the many political conflicts of the time.[51]

Other members of this middle group belonged to the region's oldest Spanish families, who had settled in the Llanos at the end of the seventeenth century. Over time, however, as family properties were subdivided through inheritance and the regional economy stagnated, some members of these families had fallen into relative poverty. Such was the story for the Peñaloza family, many of whose members were to be found in this sector.[52]

The participation of the middle-sized criadores in the public life of the Llanos was crucial. They frequently acted as legal representatives for their impoverished neighbors, or occupied positions such as commander of the militia or justice of the peace. In addition, some of them played key roles in various political struggles. Members of the Vera family, for instance, were among the most active Unitarians in the 1860s. By contrast, Federalist leader Berna Carrizo was also part of this sector. Carrizo was one of Peñaloza's closest confidants, and during the second rebellion of Chacho in 1863, he served as governor of La Rioja. In 1866, this Federalist chief, at the head of a montonera, tried to depose a Unitarian governor, an endeavor that ended in his capture and execution.[53]

Finally, there were the largest landowners.[54] The richest proprietor was Don Diego Moreno, whose mercedes, "las Salinas" and another unnamed, were assessed at 3,500 pesos. Following him were Facundo Quiroga's siblings and children, who registered as one single taxpayer, held properties valued at 2,161 pesos.[55] Among the other large landowners was Don

Paulino Orihuela, a longtime political figure in La Rioja whose properties in Atiles and Malanzán were valued at 1,657 pesos. And far from the richest criadores but still among the largest was then Colonel of the Argentine Confederation Don Angel Vicente Peñaloza, whose two "right[s] to waters and communal fields" in the mercedes of Ediondita and Guaja were taxed at 750 pesos.

These proprietors belonged to the oldest families of Spanish origin in the region. The Peñaloza family had bought land in the early 1700s, while Don Prudencio Quiroga, Facundo's father and a native of the province of San Juan, had moved to the neighboring Llanos, acquiring property between 1776 and 1780.[56]

By the mid–nineteenth century, the properties of big landowners were composed of houses, corrals, orchards (which could have a high value depending on the water and trees that they contained), cornfields for subsistence, and lands for cattle. In addition, they included reservoirs to water cattle, which increased the productivity and worth of the estate.

How many head did a large landowner own? According to the 1806 parish report, only "very few" had "some cattle." The richest proprietors in this regard were

> Don Nicolás Peñaloza, who is said to have up to 5,000 head; Don Prudencio Quiroga, in San Antonio, 2,000; Don Clemente Galván, in Ambil, some others; Don Cayetano Ontivero in Catuna . . . up to 5,000; in Chepes the widow Casilda Flores has 1,000 head; in Colosacán Pascual Quintero 3,000; in Solca Don Juan de la Vega as much as 1,500; but all of these have their cattle roaming free, or wild.[57]

The richest proprietors in the early nineteenth century, including Don Nicolás Peñaloza, Chacho's grandfather, and Don Prudencio Quiroga, Facundo's father, both residents of Costa Alta, owned head of cattle that numbered in the thousands. The sparse, fragmentary data from the second half of the century, however, indicate that the richest owners of the 1850s or 1870s had fewer head in their herds, which rarely went beyond 1,000. Indeed, it was not exceptional for a large landowner to have only several hundred during this period.[58] It is possible that the figures used here for estimating average numbers of cattle underrepresent the stocks of these large ranchers. Still, we should remember that nineteenth-century observers also noted the low productivity of Los Llanos ranches, which had a "relatively small number [of cattle] in a great extension of land."[59]

What capital did these herds represent? By an optimistic estimate, a large Los Llanos ranch's total capital value, including buildings, reservoirs, lands, and livestock, would rarely exceed 10,000 pesos.[60]

These are, to be sure, rough estimates, but it is clear that some of the wealthiest families of Los Llanos did experience decline in the first half of the nineteenth century. This was due to two factors. The regional economy itself was stagnant, if not in decline, as suggested by the availability of land and its low value. At the same time, the division of rich properties among several heirs had led to an intense fragmentation of land. Take the case of the Peñaloza family. At the beginning of the century, Don Nicolás Peñaloza owned mercedes in Atiles and La Ediondita, where as seen earlier, he had as many as 5,000 head of cattle.[61] He also had fourteen children from two marriages, thirteen of them married with children of their own.[62] As a result, in the *Libro de Registro* of 1855, these mercedes were no longer the property of one owner. Atiles was home to four comuneros, and La Ediondita had been divided among eleven others. Such subdivision affected the value of the properties belonging to these heirs as well. Of the eight descendants of Don Nicolás in 1855, only two belonged to the group of largest landowners. The others were considered small- and medium-sized proprietors.[63] With the exception of Facundo's fortune, a similar pattern emerged in the Quiroga family.[64]

Nevertheless, this same group of families produced Facundo, General Tomás Brizuela, Governors Hipólito Tello and Lucas Llanos, and Chacho, all Federalist leaders who controlled the province between 1820 and 1863. Some of these ranchers, notably Facundo and Chacho, became political actors on the national level. Like Rosas and Urquiza, they were members of prominent, prosperous families in their region who began their careers as commanders of rural militias, later becoming caudillos with authority and influence in their province.

A full appreciation of caudillismo in La Rioja and the interior, however, should take into account the differences between the roles and trajectories of Facundo and Chacho, on the one hand, and Rosas and Urquiza, on the other. Although all could be included in the category of large cattle ranchers, there were crucial discrepancies in their social origins. Let us take the case of Chacho. In the mid-1850s, the wealth of Los Llanos's richest ranchers, including Peñaloza, would not have exceeded 10,000 pesos, even by the most generous estimate. In the littoral cattle economies linked to the Atlantic market, this fortune would have placed them in the lower ranks of the small-sized proprietors. Based on estimates for the same period, the value of land and animals belonging to a small sheep rancher in Buenos Aires was around 10,000 pesos.[65] The situation of the big proprietors of Buenos Aires was quite different, of course. Juan Manuel de Rosas, who was among the richest ranchers in the province of Buenos Aires, owned some 300,000 head of cattle, which together with his lands and urban real estate, was worth more than 4 million pesos.[66]

Facundo's circumstances illustrated the limitations of simple categorizations like large rural proprietor. At his death, he possessed a substantial fortune, but during the execution of his will, it became clear that Facundo had never inherited anything from his father and that all his property was joint, having been earned since his marriage in 1817.[67] This is to say, Facundo had accumulated his fortune during eighteen years of married life, a period that coincides, almost exactly, with his entire political career (1818–1835). The properties that his wife and five children inherited were in the province of Buenos Aires, where Facundo had transferred most of his interests. His fortune there totaled 200,000 pesos, 144,000 (or 72 percent) of which was invested in provincial bonds earning 15,000 pesos in interest annually.[68] Facundo's will also stipulated that his properties in other provinces had not been divided. It is evident that among these properties was his possession in Los Llanos, which according to the 1855 tax registry, had still not been divided, belonged to his heirs, and was worth 1,000 pesos.

While this property did win Facundo a place among the richest ranchers in Los Llanos, ranching was an insignificant part of Facundo's total fortune. It clearly did not allow him to accumulate such wealth, even taking into account certain privileges that, given his political power, Facundo had in the La Rioja economy.[69] We can only attribute his impressive accumulation to his political career. We should include as part of that career the legendary "contributions" that Facundo exacted from his defeated political enemies, his cooperation with commercial groups in Buenos Aires (with whom he tried to exploit mines in Famatina, for instance), and his links to the provincial government of Buenos Aires, whose bonds paying 6 percent at the time of his death in 1835 were the main source of his capital accumulation. This was well known in the political circles of the day, and gave Sarmiento the occasion to say that in Buenos Aires, Facundo "played" (*especulated*) with "the ups and downs of the public funds."[70]

W HEN ONE OF MITRE'S personal envoys traveled through
Famatina and Arauco in 1863, he called the inhabitants of
"the small agricultural villages" gauchos, or "country people."
That is, he used the word in a denotative sense: gauchos were all those
who lived in the countryside, whether they depended on subsistence agriculture, or worked in cattle raising or mining businesses, as was the case
in those Riojan departments.[1] This descriptive sense is more evident if we
note that the majority of those "small agricultural villages" were old Indian
reducciones, and even in the second half of the nineteenth century, their
inhabitants were characterized as Indians as well as gauchos.[2] Thus, used in
this manner, the word included different ethnic categories: in the La Rioja
of the 1860s, an Indian could also be a gaucho. In a similar fashion, those
who lived in the countryside and were of African descent (and in La Rioja
there were many) could also be viewed as gauchos, although individually
they might be referred to as "a man of color" or "criollo."[3]

The word was also used in this denotative sense by some inhabitants of
the countryside when they wanted to introduce themselves to an urban
and learned audience. When he corresponded with other influential figures in national politics, Chacho defined himself as "a gaucho [who] only
knows about country matters," while referring to his followers as "the
people of my class," thereby indicating not the class origins of his clients
but the simple fact that they were, like him, inhabitants of the countryside.[4]

When urban dwellers used the word in this way, however, it did carry
a class connotation. Thus, they referred indistinctly to gauchos or the

masses.[5] The meaning of the latter was twofold: on the one hand, it recognized that gauchos formed the most numerous group in the province. On the other, "masses" also referred to those who occupied the lowest position in an organization—for example, a militia commander referred to the soldiers that occupied the lower ranks of his troops as the "masses of the squadron."[6] Therefore, when masses was used interchangeably with gauchos, it also meant that they were at the bottom of society. Indeed, it is in this geographically and socially denotative sense that I have used gaucho throughout this book to mean "poor inhabitant of the countryside."

Many times, although not always, this class connotation was also associated with a cultural one, and both had a derogatory meaning: the inhabitants of the countryside were not only poor but rustic and ignorant as well. A lawyer and prominent Riojan politician indistinctly called a group of political rivals gauchos, or "drunk riffraff"; most of them were labradores, but the group also included carpenters, shoemakers, brickmakers, muleteers, masons, and wageworkers, and the majority were illiterate.[7] Of course, this characterization was influenced by political confrontation. Yet, under other circumstances, when this same lawyer wanted to positively portray the behavior of country people, he could not help but refer to their "simple spirit," reminding his peers that "ignorance does not reason."[8]

To refer to their neighbors, the inhabitants of the countryside used several terms, including paisano and gaucho, in the sense already mentioned.[9] Most of the time, though, they used the word in another way: gauchos were those involved in cattle rustling or any other type of crime, even assassination. In other words, gaucho was equivalent to rural bandit. The case of Eugenio Sosa, a married and illiterate muleteer from the province of Córdoba, allows us to understand this meaning. When, in 1872, the authorities of Los Llanos asked him "what reasons had forced him to establish his residence in this province, leaving his home and not having here neither family nor properties to take care of," Sosa responded that years earlier, while he was drinking with another individual, "they fell out . . . and he stabbed the other to death."[10] This crime forced him to flee to Los Llanos, where he began a wandering life sustained by cattle rustling. This trajectory gave Sosa a certain reputation. Hence, when a labrador from Los Llanos charged that Sosa had stolen his horse, he also asserted that Sosa "was a gaucho that people feared because of his deeds."[11] This meaning of the term was so extended that people from rural areas even used it as a verb: *gauchar* an animal was synonymous with "stealing" it.[12]

In the 1860s, provincial authorities and national government officials also used gaucho as a synonym for bandit, although the reasons for this were completely different from those of the country people. An officer of the national troops, for instance, communicated to his superior that in his military operations in La Rioja and other provinces of the interior, he would treat "with great moderation the honest and hardworking neighbors, but not the gauchos, because you know that it is always necessary to treat them differently, and you know that these provinces are covered with this type of people." [13] In this case, the labeling of the majority of rural inhabitants of the provinces as gauchos or bandits was the product of their Federalist affiliation and participation in the rebellions against the authorities. In calling the rebels gauchos, their political involvement was criminalized. This is even more evident if we take into account that during the 1860s, the Unitarian authorities began to use the word bandit as a synonym for Federalist; later, the Federalists themselves appropriated the term and used it in a contentious tone.

The conflicts of the 1860s also linked the term gaucho with montonero, the name given to Federalist rebels. Thus, the authorities indistinctly referred to rebels as montoneros or gauchos. But what did montonero mean? Since the beginning of the civil wars, in the provinces of the interior, a montonero was one who rebelled for political reasons against the departmental, provincial, or national authorities. On some occasions, revolutionary and montonero were synonymous.[14] It is in this broad sense of a "rebel against the authorities" that I use montonero here.

It is nonetheless essential to point out that the Unitarians' intention of controlling the provinces of the interior, along with the resistance that the process of state formation generated, slightly changed the sense of the word in the 1860s. During that period, montonero usually referred to those who rebelled against the national authorities in particular. This meaning was given to the word even by those who had been montoneros. When Santos Guayama, a legendary leader of Federalist mobilizations, was co-opted by the Taboadas brothers, from Santiago del Esteo, for electoral purposes, he did not accept the label of "rebels and against the national government" flung at his troops, remarking that "he was not montonero because he was serving [the government of] the nation." [15]

The meaning indicating disobedience and rebellion against national authorities generated some apparently absurd uses, yet it also reflected the degree of political discipline and centralization that the national state was achieving in the provinces of the interior. In January 1874, the national government attempted to manipulate the election of national representatives in the province of La Rioja on behalf of Nicolás Avellaneda. With this in mind, the national government requested the assistance of the provincial governor, who nevertheless chose not to comply. The national government retaliated by encouraging and informally supporting a rebellion organized by the Riojan Avellanedistas against the government of the province. Thus, when a Llanisto was asked about the purpose of the rebellion that he had joined, he responded that they wanted "to overthrow the [provincial] government because the governor was a montonero and the rebellion was for the nation." Likewise, another rebel, an illiterate carpenter, explained that they aimed to overthrow the governor because "the government [of the province] had rebelled against . . . the national flag." [16]

The repression that the state-in-formation unleashed on the provinces of the interior, particularly in La Rioja, also associated the term with that experience. As one Riojan elite remarked, the gauchos of the province preferred to be called anything but montoneros because they had learned that for the authorities, "he who carries the name of montonero is a beast that must be quartered in the very moment he is caught." [17] Another member of the Riojan upper class incorporated this phenomenon into a satiric gauchesque poem aimed at the rebels. His verse relaid the experience of a Chachista gaucho whose main concern was to receive an amnesty in order to save his own life; at the same time, he advised his friends, "Toribio the saddlemaker" and "Rufo the butcher," that if necessary, it was "much better to flee than to be montonero." [18]

The word *montonera* originated in the Banda Oriental during the wars of independence. According to one version, the groups of gauchos who followed the caudillo Jose Gervasio Artigas were called *montones* (literally, piles or crowds).[19] In the provinces of the interior in the 1860s, the word *montonera* made reference to mobilizations—whether on the departmental, provincial, or national level—that rebelled against the authorities. Montoneras, then, were groups of mobilized gauchos that ranged from as little as six rebels up to four thousand. The word, understood in this way, was used by authorities and elites—who called a political rival *estaba montonereando* or *había levantado una montonera*—as well as gauchos—who spoke of *andar en montonera* or *formar montonera,* knowing full well that it implied the crime of rebelling against authority.[20]

The Caudillos and Their Followers

In addition to their personal capacity to mobilize, leaders like Chacho and Felipe Varela also counted on the help of lesser caudillos. Indeed, a good number of the gauchos who joined mobilizations did so on behalf of intermediate Federalist leaders, who recognized the leadership of Chacho or Felipe Varela and put their followers at their service. I identified thirty-three politically active Federalist leaders in the province in the 1860s (see tables 4 and 6, including the corresponding notes).

Most of these middle-rank leaders rose from or operated in Los Llanos (fourteen) and Famatina (seventeen), while the remaining two were from Arauco and Guandacol. Firmly committed to their Federalist militancy throughout the 1860s, two-thirds (twenty-three) of these leaders participated in at least two Federalist rebellions, many (thirteen) in three mobilizations, and some even in four. Among them were some old Federalist militants, like Lucas Llanos, governor of the province in the 1840s and Peñaloza's close confidant since the end of that decade, as well as newcomers who joined the party after its defeat at Pavón, like Aurelio Zalazar, who began his rapid but brief political career in 1865 as leader of a rebel contingent of Riojano gauchos recruited for the war against Paraguay. Moreover, seven of these thirty-three leaders lost their lives in the 1860s as a consequence of their political participation in favor of Federalism.

What was their social background? Given the geographic, social, and economic diversity of the province, it is convenient to take a regional approach to this question. Los Llanos was home to four criadores, one merchant, two labradores (one of whom was also a mule driver), and a peon. Half of these leaders, in short, came from the most stable sector of Llanisto society: the criadores. In the case of Don Lucas Llanos, his political trajectory and hints as to his personal fortune suggest that he was among the richest criadores in the department of Costa Baja and, in general, Los Llanos.[21] Berna Carrizo's situation was different. Governor of La Rioja in 1863 during the second rebellion of Chacho, this old Federalist lead a montonera in 1866 that tried to topple the Unitarian governor, a movement that culminated in Carrizo's own capture and execution. Although Carrizo raised livestock, he was in the lower ranks of medium-sized proprietors, far below the richest criadores of that department (see figure 2). Although as criadores, both Carrizo and Lucas Llano occupied positions in the upper echelon of Los Llanos society, this does not seem to have

TABLE 6   Federalist Montonera Leaders from All Departments,
Except Famatina, 1860s

Name	Department	Occupation	Marital Status	Age	Rebellions
Andrade, Crisólogo	Costa Baja	Merchant	Married	30	1863, 1867, 1868
Carrizo, Berna [1]	Costa Alta	Criador			1862, 1863, 1866
Chumbita, Severo	Arauco	Labrador	Married		1862, 1863, 1867, 1868
Flores, Ramón	Costa Baja	Criador	Married		1865, 1867, 1868
Guevara, Carmen [2]	Costa Alta	Labrador	Married	30	1865
Gutierrez, Elías	Guandacol	Muleteer	Married	32	1867, 1868
Llanos, Lucas [3]	Costa Baja	Criador	Married		1862, 1863
Luna, José Jacinto	Costa Baja	Criador	Married	50	1863, 1867, 1868
Nieto, Indalecio	Costa Baja	Labrador/ Mule Driver	Married	32	1865, 1866, 1868
Zalazar, Aurelio [4]		Peon	Married	30	1865, 1867, 1868

[1] Executed in 1866

[2] Died in combat in 1865

[3] Died in prison in 1863

[4] Executed in 1869

Note: No information was found on the social origins of the following individuals, who also participated as leaders in rebellions during the years indicated: Apolinario Tello of Costa Baja (1862, 1863, 1867, 1868); Juan Gabriel Pueblas (1862, 1863, died in combat) and Fructuoso Ontiveros (1862, 1863, died in combat), both from the province of San Luis, but operating principally out of the Llanos of La Rioja; Gerónimo Aguero (1862, 1863, 1865, died in combat); Sebastián Elizondo (1863, 1867, 1868); and Santos Guayama (1867, 1868, 1869). These last three, all natives of the province of San Juan, were politically active in La Rioja, mainly in Los Llanos.

TABLE 7 Montoneros, Province of Origin, 1860s

La Rioja	58
San Juan	5
Córdoba	4
Catamarca	1
San Luis	1
Tucumán	1
Chile	3
Total	73

TABLE 8 Montoneros, Department of Origin, 1860s

Costa Alta	12
Costa Baja	9
Llanos *	6
Total Llanos	27
Famatina	14
Arauco	8
Vinchina	3
Guandacol	3
Total	55

*While I do not have reliable information on which department they came from, I know they lived in Los Llanos.

TABLE 9 Montoneros, Occupation, 1860s

Labradores	30
Artisans	9
Peones and Wageworkers	8
Muleteers	8
Estancieros *	3
Miners	2
Butcher	1
Foreman	1
Honey Collector	1
Military	1
Criador	1
No Occupation	1
Total	66

*A herder who cared for cattle in a remote area of a big hacienda.

TABLE 10   Montoneros, Marital Status, 1860s

Married	36
Single	27
Widow	1
Total	64

TABLE 11   Montoneros, Age Range in Years, 1860s

16–20	6
21–25	15
26–30	22
31–35	3
36–40	8
41–45	3
46–50	8
51 and over	1
Total	66

TABLE 12   Montoneros, Education, 1860s

Cannot Sign	58
Can Sign	14
Total	72

Sources (tables 6–12): "Causa criminal contra José Antonio Manrique, José Desiderio Fernández, José Naranjo, Juan de las Rosas Paredes, José Antonio Reinoso y David Ibañez por delito de sedición," 1865, AJP (LR), criminal, M–#8; "Causa criminal contra Eugenio Sosa y Rosa Quintero," 1872, AJP (LR), criminal, S–#5; "Causa criminal contra Santiago Montaña por cuatrero," 1871, AJP (LR), M–#16; "Causa criminal sin carátula," 1865, AJP (LR), B; "Causa contra Francisco Argañaraz, Angel Mariano Riveros, Javier Gómez y José Ocampo, por suponerselos reos de falsedad en la causa seguida a Crisólogo Andrade," 1871, AJF (LR), penal, legajo 5; "Causa contra Tomás González por sospechas de montonero," 1869, AJP (LR), G–#11; "Don Elías Salinas solicita se le indemnicen los perjuicios ocasionados por los montoneros," 1869, AJP (LR), civil, S–#17; "Don Elías Salinas denuncia a Don Jacinto Luna como rebelde a la autoridad nacional," 1869, AJF (LR), penal, legajo 4; "Causa contra Crisólogo Andrade por suponersele participación en el delito de rebelión y otros crímenes," 1870, AJF (LR), penal, legajo 4-; "Causa sin carátula en Archivo Paunero," 7–26–8–2359; "Causa criminal contra Toribio, Ramón y Blas Gaitán (hermanos), Carmen Alvarez y Eliceo Zalazar, por partícipes en la última rebelión en esta provincia," 1867, AJF (LR), penal, legajo 2; "Causa criminal contra los reos Nicolás Páez, Dolores Clavero, Pedro José Carrizo y Paulino Rivero por partícipes en la última rebelión," 1867, AJF (LR), penal, legajo 2; "El Segundo Jefe del Ejército del Interior contra Eusebio Arguello, Casto Olivera y Bonifacio Carrizo por el delito de rebelión," 1867, AJF (LR), penal, legajo 2; "El Comandante Principal de Famatina contra José Sigampa por complicidad con la rebelión y otros delitos," 1867, AJF (LR), penal, legajo 2; "Causa criminal contra Domingo Díaz y Alejandro Flores por complicidad en la rebelión encabezada por Felipe Varela," 1867, AJF (LR), penal, legajo 2; "Don Felisísimo de la Colina contra Cansio Olmedo por indemnización de daños y perjuicios causados en el año 67 en la montonera que asoló la provincia," 1869, AJP (LR), criminal, O–39; "Causa contra Florentino Vega, Vicente Contreras y Manuel Escalante por atribuírseles participación en la rebelión encabezada por Felipe Varela en esta provincia," 1868, AJF (LR), penal, legajo 3; "Causa criminal seguida de oficio contra los reos presentes Don Manuel Vicente Bustos (et al.), 1865, AJF (LR), penal, legajo 1; "Causa Criminal contra Indalecio Nieto," 1872, AJP (LR), N; "Causa criminal contra Agustín Molina, por rebelión," 1872, AJF (LR), penal, legajo 5; "Causa criminal contra Toribio Urrutia (chileno) por participación con los rebeldes encabezados por Felipe Varela," 1867, AJF (LR), penal, legajo 2; "Causa criminal contra Francisco González por rebelión y otros delitos," 1864, AJP (LR), criminal, G–8; "Causa criminal contra Elías Butierrez por atribuírsele el crimen de rebelión," 1868, AJF (LR), penal, legajo 3; "Causa criminal contra Jose de los Santos Echegaray Carrizo por participación con la Rebelión encabezada por Felipe Varela," 1867, AJF (LR), penal, legajo 2; "Causa criminal contra Adrian Guzman por suponersele cómplice en un asesinato perpetrado en la sierra de Catamarca y haber andado con Guayama en la última montonera," 1870, AJP (LR), criminal, G–#66; "Causa contra los autores y complices del conato de revolución contra las autoridades legales de la provincia," 1869, AJP (LR), criminal, B–#34; "Sucesión de Don Lucas Llanos y Desposoria Arias," 1911, AJP (LR), Registro Juicios Sucesorios, LL–#24; "Juan Llanos por sí y sus hermanos contra la testamentaría de Don Hipólito Tello por cobro de pesos," 1871, AJP (LR), civil, LL–#4; and "Libro de Registro de las Propiedades Territoriales del Departamento de la Costa Alta y del Medio de los Llanos," 1855, AJP (LR).

been a necessary factor in these caudillos' capacity to mobilize. This is even more clear with regard to Indalecio Nieto, Carmen Guevara, and Aurelio Zalazar, two labradores and a peon respectively; all held the lowest social rank, and at least two of them were illiterate.[22]

As noted before, Famatina's leadership shared a fairly consistent social diversity. Only two leaders were prominent members of the valley's society. Most were middle- or small-sized labradores and comuneros from the Indian villages of the department. The case of Severo Chumbita, from the department of Arauco and one of the most important Federalist leaders in the province, was roughly equivalent to that of the leaders from Famatina. Of the twenty intermediate leaders for whom we have information on their social background, no more than five were members of the most prestigious and/or wealthiest families in the province, or even their departments, which implies that in the La Rioja of the 1860s, a prominent social position was not essential for political leadership.

Rather, these leaders emerged by demonstrating their political and military capabilities in party struggles. They had certain qualities that enabled them to mobilize and lead large groups of gauchos in war (such as inspiring confidence and obedience among the followers), critical skills that were recognized by their peers from the countryside, regional Federalist leaders like Peñaloza and Felipe Varela, and even urban politicians. This recognition, in turn, helped these caudillos make alliances and gain support, and to participate in political operations of regional importance. Aurelio Zalazar, an obscure and simple peon in 1865 when he led a Federalist uprising, rose to the rank of colonel just two years later during the rebellion of Felipe Varela. None of this, however, prevented his being captured and executed by the national government in 1869. According to a member of the Unitarian elite of La Rioja, such meteoric careers, albeit short, had an explanation:

> In the Argentine provinces one needs neither riches nor talent and education, nor other antecedents but the valor and audacity of the children of the countryside, to move and take control of the destinies of the country. [Many] have begun more or less like Zalazar, apprenticing themselves in the rebellions that they have led with more or less success, but always with audacity and with daring.[23]

Yet, personal qualities alone did not guarantee these intermediate Federalist leaders a following. The gauchos wanted to know for whom and for what cause they were being mobilized. In the case of Peñaloza at least, the evidence suggests that, in part, the gauchos gave their loyalty to an intermediary precisely because they knew it was aiding Chacho, whom they considered the consummate leader. When the montonera of the Riojan Federalist leader Carlos Angel besieged the city of La Rioja in early June 1862, a situation developed that demonstrated how the gauchos' loyalty toward Chacho imposed limits on the intermediate leaders' authority and capacity to mobilize. Although Peñaloza's subordinate, Angel disregarded the peace treaty that Chacho had just signed in Los Llanos with the national government, and instead decided to besiege the Unitarian troops and their allies in the city. When Chacho, in Los Llanos, discovered what had happened, he ordered Angel to lift the siege. Angel not only disobeyed Chacho's order but also apparently concealed news of it from his troops. Nevertheless, rumors circulated among the gauchos: "Angel's soldiers were dismayed when they discovered that the general (for the masses of La Rioja there was no general other than Peñaloza) had ordered the suspension of hostilities. . . . [B]efore the demoralization of his soldiers led to an open rebellion."[24] Angel had to renounce his plans and put an end to the siege. This was not the only occasion when an intermediate Federalist leader ignored an order from Peñaloza, and the gauchos, on realizing it, disobeyed and followed the will of Chacho.[25] In other instances, only a public proclamation by Chacho on behalf of the intermediate leaders could draw a good number of followers to those caudillos.[26]

Who were the followers? The records of the criminal trials brought against the gauchos who participated in the Federalist rebellions contain information that allows us to reconstruct the social profile of those who occupied the lowest ranks in the montonera (see tables 7 through 12). Just how representative is this sample?[27] The 66 rebels for whom I have information on their occupation, for instance, would have represented as much as 13 percent of the 500 gauchos the authorities estimated Zalazar mobilized in 1865, or as little as 1.6 percent of the 4,000 Federalist soldiers who followed Felipe Varela into battle in Vargas in 1867.

The vast majority of the montoneros were from the province of La Rioja, while the rest hailed from the bordering provinces, especially San Juan and Córdoba; three were Chileans, although two of them had settled in La Rioja. The largest group within the Riojan montoneros was that of the Llanistos, followed by those who lived in the valley of Famatina. The remainder lived in the departments of Arauco, Vinchina, and Guandacol.

Almost all of these montoneros had an occupation. The labradores, who mainly depended on subsistence agriculture, formed the largest group, trailed by artisans (from saddlemakers to shoemakers), muleteers, and wageworkers. Only one montonero said that he did not have any occupation, while another defined himself as a criador, suggesting that he possessed some cattle, and therefore, a higher social position.

While a significant proportion of the montoneros were single, most were married, an indication that they also had families. More than half were between twenty-one and thirty years old, which roughly corresponds with the largest group within the adult population of the province of La Rioja.[28] In terms of their education, the vast majority were illiterate.

In short, most of the rebels lived in certain departments of the province, almost all had an occupation, and the majority were married and probably had families. This implies that except during mobilizations, gauchos and montoneros led stable lives and were far from criminal or marginal characters. Even Sarmiento, as director of the war in the interior and governor of San Juan, confirmed that after Chacho's defeat in Caucete, "only fifteen among more than one hundred prisoners taken did not have somebody who asked for their release and who testified that they were honest people, which demonstrated that all of them were well-known people who had families."[29]

Internal Workings of the Montoneras

The organization of the montoneras was similar to that of the provincial militias, which since 1853 had been called the National Guards. Thus, a popular song from San Luis equated being a follower of the Federalist caudillo Juan Saá with being a member of the National Guard: "I do not care about Urquiza / I am also a Federalist / I am part of Don Juan's people / of the National Guard."[30] Some gauchos, as a consequence, interpreted their participation in the rebellions as military experience. A worker from Los Llanos said that his involvement in the montonera led by Sebastián Elizondo in 1868 was "the only time he was in the military service."[31] The montoneros called themselves "soldiers" or "troops," and one montonera leader referred to his followers as "his military men," a characterization also shared by those who did not participate in the rebellions.[32]

As with the National Guard, the montonera was a hierarchical, top-down organization. The distribution of positions and responsibilities was based on similar criteria to that of the militias. As we have seen in relation to the leaders, rank was determined according to the social position or influence that an individual had at the local level, or the military or political skills that a person had demonstrated in other episodes of partisan conflict. Sometimes the assignment of those positions was simply a result of the circumstances of a struggle, during which leaders of a rebellion could press some individuals to accept a higher military rank.[33]

Once a person had achieved a certain position, his rank was supposed to be respected by the leaders of future mobilizations. That is, during the organization of a montonera, those who had participated in earlier rebellions would approach the leaders and offer their assistance with the expectation that they would maintain their previous rank. The leaders of a new montonera, however, could choose to ignore these past achievements, in which case the individual either had to accept the new rank given by the leaders or not join the rebellion at all.[34]

This hierarchical organization was also manifested in the so-called councils of war. These ad hoc, oral trials were used to judge both political enemies and members of the rebellion. In terms of the latter, the councils tried those rebels who did not follow their superiors' orders or broke the routine discipline expected from any soldier; punishment could include the death penalty. Elías Gutiérrez, one of the leaders who rebelled with Felipe Varela, "tried" and sent to the firing squad one of "his soldiers" because he had looted two houses without proper authorization from his chief and "attacked a lady with a knife."[35] As well, during the rebellion of 1865, Aurelio Zalazar executed two of his montoneros because they looted two houses in the Llanos.[36]

The montoneros were aware that different ranks meant various levels of authority and responsibility. In this respect, the workings of written orders within the montonera are illustrative. When the leaders of the montonera ordered their followers to carry out a specific operation, from expropriating cattle to executing a political rival, they usually did it in writing. The written order had two functions: first, it helped the person in charge overcome any problems associated with the operation, which was especially useful in convincing one's peers and subalterns to obey. Second, and more important, in the event that a rebellion was defeated and there was a legal suit, the written order cleared subordinates of part, if not all, of the responsibility for that specific action. The blame largely fell on the leaders. In fact, when montoneros received only a verbal order, even those who occupied the lowest ranks in the rebellion (the majority of whom were illiterate) pressed their superiors to record it on paper; minimally, they wanted to see the document that, they assumed, contained the order.[37]

The phenomenon of the written order worked not only during periods of generalized war but also in other instances of partisan struggle. A romance that told of the plot to assassinate Facundo Quiroga mentioned that when the Reinafé brothers gave the order to the legendary assassin Santos Pérez, he responded: "I will obey you / but only if it carries the signature / from the hands of your excellence."[38]

This hierarchical chain of command and the different duties it involved shaped the process of organizing rebellions as well. No matter how small or short-lived a montonera was, its organizers always had two main concerns. To begin with, they needed to define their objectives and methods of accomplishing them because, legally, it might greatly affect them in the future if a political friend had been liberated with little violence or the operation had also involved the assassination of some government official. More crucially, the organizers were always careful when deciding on the leader of a mobilization. Most often, this decision involved a delicate process of negotiation. Whoever finally accepted the position of "principal chief" of a rebellion knew that, eventually, he would have most of the responsibility. Symptomatically, one of the rebels involved in a small plot in the Llanos in 1865 used the verb "to head" and the expression "to be guilty" as synonyms.[39] In some cases, when rebels wanted to be held equally responsible, they explicitly avoided designating a leader.[40]

The montonera, with its hierarchical organization, was a key part of the lived experience of the militarization of both politics and the parties for the lower classes, as can be seen in the culture of nineteenth-century gauchos. Seasonal fluctuations in the agrarian economy, for example, were linked in popular music to the military operations typical of the partisan struggles. Borrowing language from those conflicts, some songs referred to the period of hunger before the harvests as a war between Colonel Juan Delgado (hunger), Commander Wheat (the harvest), and Major Cachilico (a stew prepared in the months immediately before the harvest that allowed gauchos to survive). Thanks to Major Cachilico, who leads "the first attack," and the arrival of Commander Wheat, the gauchos "take prisoner" Colonel Juan Delgado, who "must be sent before the firing squad" because he has mistreated them "with a very cruel tyranny." Gauchos also achieved this victory over hunger by consuming fruits that matured in the spring, before the harvest of wheat. This fundamental part of their diet came to life in song as Lieutenant Arrayán, who marched in "the vanguard" with Captain Chalchal and General Penquilla.[41]

The fighting style of the montoneras was that typical of guerrillas (sometimes, both words were used interchangeably).[42] The montoneras rarely confronted the troops of the national government in formal battles. They usually resorted to hit-and-run strategies, with the gauchos vanishing into the nearby woods and hills where they disappeared for weeks or gathered to attack again the next day.[43] Therefore, a good deal of the operations of the national troops were limited to the endless persecution of an always elusive enemy, which exhausted their horses and sometimes left them "on foot."[44]

The Unitarian troops usually found themselves "blindfolded" in the Llanos, without knowing where the enemy was or what direction to take in their own operations.[45] The hostility of the Riojans made it difficult for the national troops to enlist local pathfinders who could lead them through the region or find anybody who could inform them about Chacho's forces. On the few occasions that gauchos offered information, it usually turned out to be false.[46] On the other hand, the majority of the population filled the ranks of Chacho's "secret police," including women and children. They "instructed him with admirable activity about all the movements and intentions of the enemy."[47]

The "war of montoneras or resources," as this type of warfare was called, was one of the ways the rebels tried to enhance their otherwise limited military power and minimize the superior resources, organization, and firepower of the national troops.[48] The poverty and consequent weakness of the montonera was obvious, among other things, in the type of weapons used: they included old swords, knives, clubs, lassos, or even stones, which the gauchos would throw against their enemies. Many rebels also used lances, usually made of a cane with a knife or any other sharp object tied to one of the extremes, which the montoneros used not as a throwing object but to stab the enemy in personal combats on horseback or foot. There were few firearms, and gunpowder and other necessary supplies were scarce (during Varela's rebellion, the montoneros used paper from documents of the provincial administration to make cartridges, which destroyed part of the provincial archive). Yet, the montoneras were powerful enough not only to influence provincial politics but also to challenge the national state, which in turn confronted its own economic, military, and political limitations throughout the 1860s.

Women and Politics

Politics, including the montoneras, were male dominated, and contrary to the *chinas cuarteleras* that marched with the regular troops of the national government, women usually did not follow the montoneros during the military campaigns. Of course, there were a few exceptions. The most notorious was that of Chacho's wife, Doña Victoria Romero, whose legendary courage in marching with her husband "masculinized" her ("she was very courageous, she looked like a man").[49] In the 1840s, in one of

Chacho's campaigns against Rosas, she followed him to Tucumán; and in the battle of Manantial, according to tradition, she not only saved her husband's life but was wounded in the process.[50] As one song recounted:

> Doña Victoria Romero
> If you want me to tell
> came back from Tucumán
> with a wound in her forehead.[51]

But Doña Victoria filled other roles that were at least as important. In 1863, when Mitre's representative visited Chacho in his La Riojan quarters, he noticed that while Peñaloza was playing cards with his officers and soldiers, Doña Victoria was playing cards with other women in the next room. Her social life, too, was essential in building client loyalty.[52] An old gaucho remembered that "she danced very well" and "took good care of the soldiers and because of this they loved her so much."[53]

This aspect of Doña Victoria's political life was far from unique. Other women also participated in creating a consensus around Federalism. Doña Carlota Recalde de Jaramillo and her daughter (who was married to Francisco Alvarez, one of the few Riojan Federalist leaders who belonged to the so-called decent families of the city) were denounced in 1865 for their "strong work of opposition" to the Unitarian government of the province. The two ladies had gone with Alvarez "to the ranchos [the gauchos' neighborhood in the city, made of adobe huts] with the excuse of picking watermelons," but with the real purpose of "working [seducing] the gauchos." "To conquer the gauchos" they had brought with them homemade "cookies and liquors."[54]

In moments of conflict, women's participation could be bolder and take much more militant forms. One notable case was that of Dolores Díaz, who along with other women, was arrested and sent to a concentration camp in Santiago del Estero. According to the Unitarian authorities, like her friends, Dolores belonged to "the scum of the population of La Rioja." She had been "one of the principal agents that the montoneros had in this city . . . contributing with her advice and her words to foment the perverse habits of the gauchos that made up Varela's montonera. . . . [S]he had stored in her own home war articles and she herself had transported them." Dolores, the authorities charged, had "repeatedly participated in the movements of disorder and anarchy" in La Rioja. Her nickname was telling: La Tigra (the Female Jaguar).[55]

Elite women, like Alvarez's wife and her mother, and militants, like Dolores Díaz, were not the only females who engaged in politics. Lower-class women could participate in more massive and, it seems, spontaneous ways. During the montoneros' siege of the city of La Rioja in 1862, for instance, "the servants [maids] of the [decent] houses, the women of the people who are always [identified] with the people of their own class . . . carried the most detailed news to the enemy [the montoneros] . . . and only brought [to the besieged Unitarians] demoralizing news and on purpose, only to make them lose any hope. . . . [I]t was then prohibited the entrance of women to the [Unitarian] quarters." Moreover, when food became scarce in the city, the women who usually sold bread in the streets, "who have marked sympathies for the besiegers," only supplied the montoneros with their precious loaves.[56] In another case, during Varela's rebellion, a female servant attached to a "decent home" went to the headquarters of the montonera and informed the Federalist leaders where a well-established merchant had hidden his wares, thus facilitating its confiscation.[57] Another merchant contended that when his house was sacked in 1867, "ten drunk chinas [mixed blood Indian and black women] came in and insulted my wife, and threatened to beat her because she was a Savage."[58]

Politics were an essential part of women's lives, even if women generally did not participate in military campaigns or other forms of political violence, and was a topic of conversation and gossip. Right after Varela's rebellion, Señora Traverza, a "decent" lady, went to the house of Marquesa Heredia, an illiterate woman, to confront her. Heredia had slandered her by saying that "Señora Traverza had done well with the Federation"—that is, she had been well treated by the montoneros and had benefited from the rebellion.[59] Party struggles also pervaded women's social lives on other, deeper levels. On February 26, 1852, three weeks after Caseros, the news of Rosas's fall arrived in Campanas, a small village in the valley of Famatina. Doña Restituta Izaguirre de Dávila, the wife of Tristán, who had been living in exile in Chile since the early 1840s, informed him that she and other ladies were in the church when they received the shocking news. Her mother had shouted, "Long live the Patria and death to the tyrant!" and "all the ladies went out to the street shouting Viva!" She concluded her letter by asserting, "Thanks to Señor Urquiza we will unite here and soon," and added a significant request in a postscript: "Send me a sky-blue cloth, to make a dress, to use it in the balls that will be organized here [to celebrate]." The gesture connected her to the Unitarian Party, and through it, a political space of national dimensions. As she told her husband: "You see, I am not ashamed of the Patria."[60]

Riojan women's involvement in politics was not unusual in the interior, and may have been the product of several factors, ranging from long-term changes in family structures, to women's participation in the economic life of the province, to larger regional traditions—questions well beyond the limits of this study. Yet, it is possible to suggest (at the risk of falling into a circular argument) another explanation: the way male-dominated politics in a male-dominated society affected their lives. Since independence, insecurity, death, exile, persecution, and other forms of violence had become a permanent part of men's lives. Women, however, were largely spared such ordeals. The very ideology that subordinated them also made their involvement look less political, thereby shielding them from some of the worst aspects of the struggle. In spite of women's participation in the party struggles of the 1860s, only two cases—Doña Carlota Recalde and Dolores Díaz—specifically attracted the attention of the authorities or left a trace in the judicial records (which, in turn, makes it more difficult to study these questions).

At the same time, instability and violence both forced and allowed women to engage in activities that inevitably brought them into the public arena, facilitating their politicization. They began to take charge of family businesses (dealing with workers, partners, and relatives), to attend to the daily unfolding of politics that could affect their loved ones (Tristán Dávila and his wife corresponded across the Andes for almost a decade, and the predisposition of Riojan authorities toward him was a permanent theme), and to assume more active roles in the institutional life of their societies. With respect to the latter, the space created by male-centered political violence allowed for a bolder institutional involvement on the part of women. In May 1867, when the Unitarian governor of La Rioja received word that the montonera would occupy the city for a second time, he and his comrades fled, leaving no authorities in place. The invasion did not take place, and the "ladies of the capital [city] charged with the tasks of government" Señor Lorenzo Pizarro, an old man who was more than seventy years.[61]

Something similar happened in Catamarca, during one of that province's most violent and unstable periods, known as the Night of the Seven Years (1861–1868). In May 1862, Unitarian Governor Correa was deposed by a rival Unitarian faction led by Moises Omill. Correa and his political friends sought asylum in Santiago del Estero, and Omill was immediately sworn in. But seven days later, seeing "the inertia of Correa's party fellows," Doña Eulalia Ares de Bildoza (the wife of one of Correa's political friends) and "other Ladies," followed by a group of lower-class men, initiated "a revolution." Omill fled to Tucumán, and for a day, Doña Eulalia controlled the government. The next day, the "Female Dictator," as a historian called her, organized an election and one of Correa's followers was elected interim governor. Correa then came back a few days later to resume his duties.[62]

I N THE LLANOS . . . the very trees are pro-Chacho," said Colonel Ignacio Rivas, surprised by the support that Peñaloza enjoyed in La Rioja
and especially the Llanos.[1] As the Unitarian officer also observed, "A
proof of Chacho's influence is that the gauchos volunteer to follow him
out of the province [of La Rioja]."[2] Rivas was quick to report as well that
"Chacho is very influential among the ignorant masses of the provinces
bordering [La Rioja]."[3] Peñaloza's large and extremely loyal following allowed the caudillo to wage war and engage in politics not only in La Rioja
but also in other provinces, such as San Juan, San Luis, Catamarca, and
Córdoba. But why did the gauchos follow the Federalist caudillos in general and Peñaloza in particular? This question, simple but fundamental to
the phenomenon of caudillismo, will be the concern of this and the remaining chapters of the book.

Beef, Clothing, and Work

Several immediate material motivations encouraged gauchos to join montoneras and formed an important part of their relations with caudillos. To
begin with, by participating in a mobilization, a gaucho expected to par-
take of his favorite food—beef—a rare treat under normal circumstances.[4]
Since the majority of gauchos depended on subsistence agriculture, beef
was not often included in their diet.[5] Ironically, most gauchos eat beef
only in times of hunger, when they were compelled to rustle cattle. During war, however, the only way to feed large groups of mobilized men
was to kill the cattle found in the places where the troops camped. Thus,

mobilizations gave gauchos the opportunity to eat beef almost daily, and even more, they could do so "legally," or at least under the responsibility of the leaders of the mobilization. This association between a montonera and eating beef was articulated in a popular couplet:

> Captains and Sargeants
> they treat themselves this way
> when they kill fat cows
> they say it is the montonera.[6]

When gauchos joined a mobilization, they also expected to be provided with shoes and clothes by their leaders. This provision, it was assumed, would cover those necessities that the weather and ruggedness of the soil imposed on gauchos during a mobilization; gauchos, in turn, hoped that their new shoes and clothing would survive the campaign so that they could return home better furnished. They considered this provision "a right" and understood that it was the leaders' responsibility. In a poem, one militiaman complained that "twenty-one years I have served / as a captain of the militias / and not even a cotton shirt / in my whole life I have received," which he considered unjust.[7] When this tacit agreement was violated, gauchos usually deserted, but sometimes they rioted or at least threatened to do so.[8]

Gauchos knew that mobilizations generated numerous opportunities to get clothing and other types of goods. Looting was one of them. Most of the time, looting was subjected to the hierarchical organization of the montoneras—that is, it usually took place with the consent of the leaders, and sometimes under their control and supervision, to the extent that looting looked more like an orderly expropriation of goods. Only during combat or moments of generalized violence did looting seem to escape these norms. Another possibility was to appropriate the personal belongings or clothing of their comrades or enemies who died in the struggle. Indeed, one of the gauchos' first reactions when somebody died in combat was to grab his belongings and strip him naked. When the dead was an enemy, it was assumed by all that it was the killer's right to appropriate any goods. Sometimes, however, the form in which death occurred created confusion in the interpretation of the norm. For instance, one of two montoneros that was responsible for the death of a Unitarian officer claimed for himself the clothes and horse of the victim "because it was he who killed him [the Unitarian]," while his comrade "demanded the property because it was he who took him prisoner."[9] In a similar fashion, when somebody received an order to execute a prisoner (usually, by slitting the throat), it was assumed that the ad hoc executioner had the right to appropriate the horse, saddle, and clothes of the victim.[10] Such spoils of war certainly encouraged violence. Yet, they were also considered a legitimate means of rewarding those who had to perform unpleasant tasks. On one occasion, when a Federalist gaucho dying from his wounds asked "to be finished off" to avoid pain, one militiaman volunteered for the task, requesting in exchange "the very nice bolas that he [the wounded] had." The dying man agreed, and his throat was immediately slit by the militiaman.[11]

Another material incentive to join a mobilization was the monetary reward that the leaders of the montoneras offered gauchos. According to one observer, Facundo and Chacho's troops were made up of "the very needy that speculating with their interest, accepted to be hired for sums of money."[12] In effect, in the limited job market of the interior's regional economies, the montoneras offered gauchos a good opportunity "to work" and supplement their income. This method of mobilizing gauchos was not the patrimony of Federalism; it was also used on behalf of Unitarianism. Octaviano Navarro reminded Mitre of the importance of paying back wages to the National Guards who had so efficiently campaigned against Varela. The payment of their salaries, he said, "will encourage our masses and it will predispose them to serve with the same enthusiasm [in the future] since they will know that they will be appropriately rewarded."[13] Commander Irrazábal, too, was aware of the significance of these material rewards since, as one of his soldiers remembered, "he paid [his troops,] giving them clothes, blankets, money and everything they needed."[14] Actually, political struggles in general, of which the montoneras were only one expression, had become, at least since the 1820s, an occasional source of employment for the lower classes.[15] Thus, in 1851, the two parties that competed in the legislative elections of the province of Santiago del Estero accused one another of buying votes (for one real each) in the rural departments.[16] And in La Rioja in the 1860s and 1870s, the competing parties in several elections would offer from three to eight pesos for each vote.[17]

Yet, conceiving of mobilizations as work was not the only way gauchos viewed politics and their relation with the caudillos. Other aspects of popular political culture appealed to them as well. When a montonero was questioned about the content of "the promise" that the leaders of the montonera made to some of the gauchos that would later participate in the second rebellion of Chacho, this illiterate labrador responded that the Federalist caudillos Juan Gabriel Pueblas and Fructuoso Ontiveros made them

> the offer of ten monthly pesos for each soldier, but that this had not been honored yet, [they also promised them that in the villages they would invade in the provinces of Córdoba and San Luis] that they would take [prisoner] all the employees [of the government] and they would execute them and that they would place their own authorities, with the promise that the last soldier would be "class" [promoted] after the invasions.[18]

Here, the "promise" was an "offer of a salary": a monthly payment of ten pesos to each montonero, which in those days was a good deal. In 1865, for instance, the soldiers of the national troops stationed in La Rioja and the peons hired by the provincial administration did not earn more than six and seven pesos, respectively, per month.[19] Other Federalist leaders could not offer more either: after the first rebellion of Peñaloza, Carlos Angel intended to pay his gauchos "four or five pesos," which he himself acknowledged "was not much."[20] Besides just a salary, however, Pueblas and Ontiveros made the gauchos a political offer, too. They promised to execute the Unitarian officials of the rural departments (*"los empleados [del gobierno]"*) and replace them with "their own authorities"—that is, Federalist officials. Finally, after the campaign, those gauchos who participated in the montonera would be promoted from soldiers to noncommissioned officers ("class") of the National Guards. This offered material as well as political benefits for the gauchos: on the one hand, their salaries as officers would be higher than the ones they received as soldiers; on the other hand, it also implied a position of more power and recognition at the local level.

The relative importance of the monetary offer and other such motivations for gauchos would be evident a year later, when the rebellion for which they had been mobilized was defeated. A few days after Peñaloza had been assassinated, Pueblas gathered his gauchos, proclaiming that "Peñaloza is dead . . . and that those who want to follow him should come forward: that he is heading to Indian territory, and like two hundred [men] decided to follow him."[21] Even in defeat, when monetary promises could not be fulfilled and most likely did not look attractive (a few days later, Pueblas himself would die in a skirmish with Unitarian troops), many gauchos still followed this Federalist leader, which suggests the significance of personal and political ties between caudillos and followers.

Still, to be more precise about the relationship between politics and money in popular political culture, it is necessary to analyze the limitations that the Unitarians encountered in applying this method of mobilization to La Rioja and other provinces of the interior, where the majority of the gauchos sympathized with Federalism and its leaders. During the first rebellion of Chacho, one of the few Unitarians of Los Llanos informed a political friend that

> the men I am gathering . . . I do not trust all of them, but I want to prevent them from join[ing] the montonera and to enlarge the forces of Chacho, thus I must tell you that I have more prisoners than the force that I can trust, and even the latter drive me crazy, telling me about their necessities, and we cannot pay them anymore because we are running out [of money] . . . , our pockets cannot provide clothing and pay the troops [anymore], as we have done until today. It is important to take into account that my soldiers do not steal, thus all their necessities are covered by my pocket and if I do not do this, we will soon have no soldiers.[22]

In spite of the fact that the Unitarian chief paid gauchos in clothes and cash, he found himself in the ackward position of having "more prisoners" than people "that I can trust" because the Llanistos did not stop manifesting their sympathies for Chacho.

Even when the promise of a salary or the expectation of receiving it prompted the lower classes to draft themselves into the Unitarian troops, the poverty of the provincial and national states, as well as the gauchos' inclination toward Federalism and its leaders, often jeopardized a mobilization. Let us see what happened in Caucete, in the province of San Juan, in June 1862. According to a Unitarian commander, the gauchos from the village were "willfully serving" in the militias, although they "had not received any salary yet." Nonetheless, he maintained that "the spirit of insubordination" was already brewing in that village. Several isolated, but increasingly frequent, incidents arosed his concern. For example, one of his soldiers showed up at a pulpería (tavern) where more than twenty gauchos had gathered and began shouting,

Shit on the savages [Unitarians], I am a son of Peñaloza and I die for him,
and if anybody wants to contradict me, come to the street [to fight]; because
of the savages I am fucked up, for they do not give me even a dime and I
will never take back what I say, not even if they put four bullets in me.[23]

The gaucho's tirade continued through the night. He was taken prisoner
the following morning, and in front of his comrades, received "400 clubs"
(lashes). His frustration was not due to any concrete unfilfilled promises,
which the Unitarians apparently never made, but to the fact that they had
ignored the norm of adequately paying gauchos for their "service." Although this perceived violation motivated the gaucho to publicly articulate his political preferences, the content of his monologue did not seem
opportunistic. On the one hand, the language he used revealed that he saw
himself as a follower of Chacho ("I am a son of Peñaloza").[24] On the other,
as the Unitarian commander observed, Caucete had always been "the focus
of the montonera." In his view, then, the invectives of this gaucho were
yet another display of the political inclinations that those villagers had repeatedly shown (and would show later on).

The commander's unease was also a product of the fact that the gauchos were not only aware of the impact that the articulation between politics and work could have in partisan struggles but they seemed ready to
manipulate it. Thus, in a verse found in several provinces, albeit slightly
varied, a gaucho threatened: "Parrot of the pear tree / if the patria [the
government] does not pay me / I will switch to the montonera."[25] Sometimes, such threats had a tangible effect on political conflicts. The volatility
of the gauchos' disposition as revealed in episodes like the one in Caucete
was used by the Federalists as a weapon. Adopting a language that seemed
to parallel the one in the couplet quoted above, Sarmiento explained that
during Chacho's second rebellion, some Federalist leaders wanted to in-
vade San Juan because they speculated that with the "the discontent of
the [Unitarians] troops . . . not having received their payments, they will
switch to their side."[26]

The role of immediate material motivations in politics provides another
perspective on the looting that often took place during political struggles,
and the rationale for the imposition of forced monetary contributions on
political rivals or other citizens. The leaders of mobilizations usually faced
a good deal of pressure from their own troops, and neither they with
their modest means nor the poor provincial administrations that they con-

trolled or hoped to capture could meet the soldiers' demands. Thus, the solution was either to forcibly tax those who could pay or allow the troops to pay themselves in kind.

Subsistence and Protection

Relationships between caudillos and their followers were largely constructed and reproduced in everyday life, in those situations not directly related to politics. In this respect, the daily workings of the assistance and protection that the caudillos gave the gauchos is particularly telling in terms of the origins of political leadership.

The peasants and workers without land in Los Llanos depended on precarious, low-productivity agriculture as well as a small, seasonally fluctuating labor market. As we have seen, when gauchos periodically confronted serious difficulties in meeting the needs of their domestic economy, they often resorted to cattle rustling to survive. There was another alternative, however: requesting assistance from the better-off criadores. The case of David Ibañez is illustrative. Ibañez, a married worker living in Costa Alta, was arrested in 1865 for his participation in a Federalist plot to attack the Unitarian authorities in that department. During the proceedings that followed, he also admitted to the robbery of two animals. Yet, when he was accused of stealing a third animal, Ibañez denied the charge, arguing that "General Peñaloza had agreed to have an animal butchered and thus they slaughtered a young bull from the hacienda of the Tumaderas."[27] Many other gauchos had gone to Facundo to help meet their basic needs. A Unitarian from La Rioja remembered that Facundo "performed many acts of charity. . . . [M]any poor folk, from near and far, came [to his livestock-filled ranch] to ask for calves for meat," and Facundo responded generously. "With acts of this kind," continued the observer, "[Facundo] secured the loyalty of the common people."[28]

Political struggles and the imperatives of gauchos' material reproduction gave way to complex exchanges in which it was difficult to know who was benefiting more from the patron-client relation. Or so suggested an incident between Ramón Flores, a well-established criador from Costa Baja and leader of various Federalist montoneras in the 1860s, and Bernabé Quintero, a labrador of that department. In 1869, Quintero and his three sons were taken prisoner by the Costa Bajan authorities, who accused them of stealing and slaughtering animals, including some belonging to

Flores. Quintero denied the charges, and in regard to Flores's animals, said that they had been taken and slaughtered

> on orders that [Flores himself] had given, so that part of his cattle might thus be saved. At that time [1866] the deceased [Unitarian commander] Don Galo Herrera had ordered that Flores' livestock be taken. . . . Two animals were slaughtered and two were borrowed, on orders that they later be returned.[29]

In this exchange, the patron benefited not only from the future loyalty he expected to gain from Quintero but in an immediate way as well. The Federalist caudillo used Quintero's difficulties in securing his family's subsistence as a sort of strongbox in which he could deposit and thus safeguard his own property, then under threat from the Unitarians. From the point of view of the labrador, the exchange provided an advance or "credit" in goods that helped him through a period of scarcity. We might also infer that these credits, received from the patron at a delicate political conjuncture, came at a low cost. In addition to receiving two animals as a gift, Quintero still had not returned the other two animals three years later in 1869, contrary to his "agreement" with the caudillo.

Assistance with basic needs not only shaped the gauchos' expectations but also the caudillos' understanding of the patron-client relationship. In July 1862, after the Chacho's first rebellion, during which the Riojan countryside had been devastated, Peñaloza received gauchos in his house daily. The war had left some without a means of subsistence and robbed other families of those members who were able to work. Chacho reflected on the importance of his assistance under these circumstances: "Whoever sees such necessity cannot remain indifferent, unless he has a heart made of bronze and has bid his final farewell to his servants."[30] Assistance, then, was not only a moral obligation for the caudillo; he was also aware that it permanently tested the patron-client relationship.

Protection, too, formed part of the relation between a leader and his followers, and such interventions on behalf of the gauchos covered a wide range of situations. A contested will proceeding gives us an exceptional opportunity to see the daily workings of protection in the Llanos. In 1859, Cruz Sosa, the illegitimate son of the deceased Don Domingo Bazán, criador of Costa Alta, initiated a suit against his father's legitimate heirs. According to the 1855 *Libro de Registro,* the heirs had acciones y derechos in various mercedes assessed at 379 pesos, which placed them among the middling proprietors of the department. In contrast to his half siblings, Sosa was a poor man, so much so that he had no property worth recording. In addition to his work as a shoemaker, he earned a living by collecting firewood in Los Llanos and selling it in the city of La Rioja. This did not suffice to guarantee the subsistence of his family, and his small children collected hay in the countryside, which they would then sell.[31] Sosa, then, was one of the many workers in Los Llanos who had neither land nor livestock. Since he did not have work animals either, Sosa borrowed mules and oxen from Chacho in order to collect and sell firewood and hay.[32]

When Sosa initiated his legal action against his father's heirs, he decided to give the caudillo full authority to pursue the case before the departmental judge. Chacho then transferred this authority to an associate. Sosa's intention in undertaking the suit was to receive that part of the inheritance that, he argued, was his by law. The legitimate heirs maintained that he was not entitled to it, complaining that it was Chacho who wrongly encouraged Sosa to undertake the proceedings.

In fact, Chacho had long been involved in the case. Sosa had sought recognition years earlier, when his father was still alive, as an illegitimate son. On Bazán's death, such acknowledgment would imply that Sosa had certain claims on his father's possessions. Sosa's attempt was unsuccessful. He then went to Chacho, who verbally ordered one of his men to accompany Sosa to interview his father again. This time, when Bazán refused to recognize his son, Chacho's representative intervened and "told the late Bazán that he had been sent by General Peñaloza to see that he bestow a charity on this man."[33]

Bazán once again refused Sosa, who then initiated a legal demand; the caudillo continued to support him. A witness confirmed that "he knew, from the very mouth of the litigant Cruz Sosa, that General Peñaloza campaigned for his [Sosa's] triumph in the complaint."[34] Chacho put at the shoemaker's disposal the influence and power that he wielded among the magistrates and functionaries of the provincial administration. Later, a labrador would say "that he had heard that the General is protecting said Sosa."[35] Tales of experiences like Sosa's circulated among the Llanistos and helped to create the notion that Chacho protected gauchos.

Indeed, protection became a sort of acquired right that gauchos learned to use and manipulate. This was true of Francisco González, an illiterate labrador who participated in at least two Federalist montoneras. In June

1862, after a peace treaty was signed between Chacho and the Mitristas, a suit was filed against González by Ramón Molina, a well-established merchant in the city of La Rioja. Molina had González arrested and brought before the police chief, where he was accused of being among the gauchos who had sacked Molina's house some days before, when the rebellion was in full swing. González denied responsibility for the act, "and concluded by saying that Molina and the chief of police would pay for the damage their accusations had done to him when General Peñaloza arrived [in the city of La Rioja]."[36] Although Chacho was in Los Llanos at the time, far from the city, and obviously would not have known about the difficulties of this gaucho, González's threatening invocation of Chacho's name was effective. Two years later, in 1864, Molina declared "that therefore, fearful of suffering greater damages from the threats of González, he judged it prudent to suspend all complaints until a more opportune moment."[37] This moment presented itself in May 1864, six months after Chacho was assassinated, when Unitarian troops controlled the province. Only then did Molina decide to reopen the case against González.

Sociability

The caudillos developed numerous activities in their daily life that allowed them to socialize with gauchos and other landlords: these activities, in turn, reproduced and amplified the leaders' influence. The very nature of such social events meant that the patron-client relationship also included an emotional attachment between the two parties.

Chacho's social life put him in contact with people from other provinces, facilitated by the fact that the Llanos, a region with its own distinct culture and economy, extended beyond the southern part of La Rioja into the neighboring departments of San Luis, San Juan, and Córdoba. Chacho and his wife were invariably present for the festival of the Virgen de la Candelaria in Olta, one of the most important religious celebrations of the region. Many devotees participated, remaining in Olta until holy week— that is, for nearly two months. When Chacho arrived, he had tents put up for himself, his wife, and his companions, and at night, they also used the tents for dances and meetings. Chacho's visible role in the pilgrimage enhanced his legitimacy as a leader among the believers.[38] On other occasions, the caudillo confirmed his central position in these social-religious activities by assisting in the construction and blessing of small churches in Los Llanos.[39] Chacho was also a central figure in the horse races that were organized in the villages of the Llanos. The *cuadreras,* as these equestrian exercises were known, were considered one of the most significant social events in country life, and provided gauchos an opportunity to get together over several days. The event's prestige drew participants from as far as Mendoza.[40]

The way the caudillos related to the gauchos during these social activities served to make them more attractive to their clients. An observer who knew Peñaloza in the 1840s noted "one of the secrets of his uncommon popularity." Although Chacho's strength and valor were outstanding, there was something else that "in the eyes of his peers elevated him above the others": the familiarity with which he treated his followers. Chacho played cards with his gauchos, and "in those moments there was nothing that distinguished him from the others."[41] Ponciano Roldán, a follower of Chacho, also remembered that Peñaloza "played cards" with his men, "not as a general, but as an ordinary man."[42] The gauchos felt and appreciated Chacho's intimacy with them in other subtle ways—ways intended to erase the distance between the leader and his followers. As a political friend commented, Chacho spoke "in that style that makes him more gaucho and more ignorant because he wants to, and shows off that way."[43]

While Peñaloza carefully cultivated his own image, it is also true that this intimacy was possible because the upbringing and customs of the caudillos were not far removed from those of the gauchos. In fact, while Los Llanos society did exhibit clear social differentiation, this did not necessarily imply a great cultural gap between the caudillos and their followers since the "wealth" (that is, the less-crushing poverty) of the better-off criadores still provided for no more than a rustic lifestyle. Chacho, and other caudillos like General Tomás Brizuela, lived in nearly as precarious, poorly constructed adobe huts as their followers.[44] Their dress was that of the countryside, and according to urban observers, in appearance they were hardly distinguishable from gauchos.[45] No less crucial, most of the richer criadores of Los Llanos read and wrote with difficulty—with the exception of Facundo, who had a higher than average level of education—and it was not unusual if they were illiterate. This was the case with Chacho, who like nearly all his clients, could neither read nor write.[46]

The narrow lifestyle gap between the richest criadores and the gauchos appeared to be sanctioned in certain social norms. Nearly all proprietors carried the title of "Don," which in that society implied noble origins. The fact that even those who periodically suffered from want would appropriate such a title indicates that in Los Llanos, there was a degree of amplitude in using this term that in most regions (including other departments of the province) still served to scrupulously mark and legitimate social and ethnic status. In the eyes of the notables of the department of Famatina, for instance, this practice in Los Llanos connoted an unacceptable "devaluation" of the status of "noble." While Famatina's elite would recognize the "noble" origins of Chacho, who used the "Don," they would nonetheless underscore that Chacho's was a sui generis nobility "since in Los Llanos there are no wretches; there everyone is a 'Don.'"[47]

This shared cultural background facilitated a sense of community and belonging, reinforcing solidarity between caudillos and gauchos. This was clear in Peñaloza's self-perception:

> I am a gaucho. I understand nothing but the ways of the countryside, where I have my gatherings, and the people of my class, I don't know why they love me nor why they follow me: I love them, too and I serve them with everything that I have, doing for them what I can.[48]

In speaking of himself as a gaucho, and referring to his clients as "people of my class," the caudillo pointed not to his social origins but to the cultural community to which he and his followers belonged: rural La Rioja.

But there was something more linking caudillo to client, which emerges despite Peñaloza's studied ingenuousness. "They love me," he said, and "I love them, too." This affection was not lost on the Unitarians, who either admired the "adoration" that Chacho's followers felt toward the leader, or were outraged that the popular sectors of La Rioja lived "blinded by their affection for that loutish gaucho."[49] The caudillo's sociability with gauchos, and the mutual ties that arose from that experience, generated one of the fundamental components of the client-patron relation: an emotional attachment.

Caudillismo and Party Identity

In 1867, during the course of a judicial investigation in La Rioja, a merchant from the neighboring province of San Juan was asked if he knew which individuals had taken part in the rebellion led by Felipe Varela, a question that prompted the sweeping response that he does not know who in particular took part in the montonera, but as is generally known and he himself knows *almost*\ all Riojans must have taken part because they are known and reputed as montoneros.[50]

The "almost" was inserted later, probably at the insistence of the Unitarian officials conducting the investigation. In the 1860s, those describing La Rioja could not help but point to the rather homogeneous political sympathies of its people. Certainly, such assessments tended to stereotype Riojans, bespeaking a unanimity that even leaders like Chacho knew did not exist. Yet, and in spite of evidence indicating the capacity of a few Unitarian leaders to mobilize some followers, it is clear that Federalism was pervasive and dominant among gauchos. Indeed, Federalism transformed the province into a stronghold for the party defeated at Pavón.

Riojan gauchos were aware that to be Chachista or Chachino also meant being Federalist and engaging in the struggle against the Unitarians. Actually, Chacho's relation with his followers was one of the meanings that Federalism took on at the local level. This integration of caudillismo and party identity helps clarify the continuity of the gauchos' political militancy in the 1860s. Eleven of the fifty-eight lower-rank montoneros from La Rioja had participated in at least two Federalist rebellions. A notable case was that of Santiago Montaña, a harness maker from Costa Alta, who confessed that he had joined montoneras led by Aurelio Zalazar and other rebels "only twice, and with Peñaloza, he had gone an infinite number of times."[51] It appears, then, that while he had been active politically throughout the 1860s, his participation had taken place under at least two Federalist leaders, who as far as we know, were not personally related to each other.[52]

Federalist Gauchos, Unitarian Leaders?

The articulation between Chachismo and Federalism was also evident in the difficulties encountered by some actors, who did not belong to that party, in their attempts to establish political relations with the gauchos. Even Chacho's death did not mean that gauchos were available for any leader, whatever their political affiliation might be. Instead, those with political ambitions had to negotiate gauchos' support within the traditions and symbols, and therefore the meanings, imposed by Federalism. In the

La Rioja of the 1860s, Federalism as a political identity that maintained captive the loyalty of most gauchos. This critically affected the ability of those elites identified with Unitarianism to conduct politics and govern. To see how this phenomenon concretely worked in political practice, let us examine the barriers that the Dávila family from Famatina ran up against in mobilizing and controlling gauchos. The details of several episodes illustrate this fundamental aspect of La Rioja politics in the nineteenth century.

In 1862, the officers of the national troops sent to La Rioja could not hide their disappointment on discovering the political incapacity of their local allies. Colonel Sandes, for example, wrote to his fellows that Commander Exipión Dávila had joined the national troops with his contingent, "a group made up of . . . seven men!"[53] In the same tone, another officer of the national troops, whose operations had succeeded in momentarily dislodging Chacho from Los Llanos, sent a message to all the Riojan Unitarians, especially Tristán Dávila, cousin of Exipión, to "see if now that Peñaloza is gone they can do something about this rebellious population."[54] After three months of battling Peñaloza, however, the national government decided to negotiate an agreement with Chacho that included entrusting him with the tranquillity of the province. One of the arguments in favor of leaving Chacho in place was that the national government could not depend on people like Tristán Dávila. Dávila, although recognized by the officers of the national troops as "the best of our friends [in La Rioja]," had barely managed to pull together 20 men in June 1862, when some 600 montoneros besieged the city of La Rioja.[55]

The limitations faced by the Dávilas was no passing political phenomenon. In 1867, the problem surfaced again. During the rebellion of Felipe Varela, when Exipión Dávila was ordered to mobilize the militias of the department of Arauco, he largely failed in his mission. After Felipe Varela retreated in defeat toward the north of the republic, Exipión Dávila was indicted in August 1867 as an accomplice in the rebellion. According to the charges, soon after the rebellion started, Dávila had "turned over" the Arauco militias under his command to the Federalist leader of the department, Severo Chumbita. Dávila did not deny the allegation, and he publicly accepted the facts of the case. Nevertheless, he argued that the circumstances under which he had been forced to take those actions absolved him of responsibility.

In January 1867, with Felipe Varela at the head of rebel troops on the march from San Juan, Dávila had received orders from the Unitarian governor to mobilize the Arauco militias and march with them to the city of La Rioja. Dávila was a hacendado in the department of Famatina, but apparently it was not the first time he had been designated commander of the Arauco militias. Once in the city, on orders from the governor, he informed the gauchos that he would no longer be their leader; the government had decided to put them under the direction of Commander Pablo Yrrazabal. This decision initially produced discontent, and then strong resistance, among the militiamen. Some of the gauchos even went to the governor's office to openly declare that they refused to obey the new commander.[56] Why? Although the judicial proceedings do not make the causes clear, the correspondence of an observer is more revealing: the militiamen said that "they would die rather than obey a commander like Yrrazabal, who assassinated General Peñaloza."[57] More than three years after the death of the caudillo, these gauchos remained Chachistas. They displayed their allegiance publicly and used it as a basis for political action, challenging the orders of the Unitarian government. The government, finding "no way to make itself respected" and fearing "that the uprising would take a new turn and go so far as to topple the authorities," ordered the militias to return to Arauco to guard that department and Famatina.[58]

Dávila was again ordered to take charge of the militias, march toward Arauco, and once there, mobilize other militias. Afterward, following orders, the Unitarian commander decided to march toward Famatina to put down a Federalist montonera in that department. In a move that revealed his mistrust of the militias, before setting off, Dávila "asked" the gauchos about their "disposition" toward fighting against the Famatina montonera. Apparently the response was positive, and he began the operation.[59] Once in the countryside, but still far from the montonera, Dávila met two Unitarian acquaintances who had newspapers and news from the city of La Rioja. The papers, read before the officers of the militia, reported that a Federalist uprising had deposed the provincial government on February 2, and that Los Llanos had declared its support for Felipe Varela.[60] According to Dávila, "This news, which could not be hidden from the troops, produced a complete demoralization in them, since they all had decided sympathies for the Federalist party. . . . From that moment they began to disband."[61] These militiamen had already demonstrated their political inclinations before the Unitarian governor himself. But while their protest had been clear and firm, it had also been specific and limited. They rejected one Unitarian commander, Yrrazabal, but were willing to accept Dávila. This later shift in behavior showed their capacity to understand political processes, for when they received news that the regional balance of power had changed, they decided to up the level of action. They began to desert, and many volunteered their services to the Federalist Party.

Under these circumstances, Dávila decided to avoid a confrontation with the montonera of Famatina and return to Arauco. Yet the desertions escalated during the retreat. Realizing his inability to control the militiamen, Dávila disarmed some of them and let them go, "suggesting to the gauchos that they should not join the montonera."[62] He arrived in Arauco with his diminished troops even as the desertions continued. Trying to salvage part of his forces, Dávila decided to march toward the province of Catamarca to join the Unitarian troops and authorities that still remained there. Once again, before beginning the operation, he "asked" the remaining militiamen if they were willing to accompany him to the neighboring province. The responses seemed to him sufficiently ambiguous to warrant calling off the journey.[63] He then received an ultimatum from the new Federalist governor of the province instructing him to turn his troops over to the Federalist caudillo of Arauco, Severo Chumbita.[64] Encountering hostile forces at every level, Dávila negotiated the operation with the son of the caudillo. Some of the militiamen, it seemed, felt betrayed by Dávila and "wept" over his decision. But as one of the gauchos from the militia who testified in the case against Dávila remembered, when the Unitarian commander handed over his troops, Chumbita's son had told them, " 'Whoever wants to follow my father, follow him,' without obligating any of them." The militiamen responded, "as did this witness, that they would follow him with great pleasure."[65] And so, Dávila left the command of the militias in a move that won him the favor of the Federalists, who allowed him to return home.

These difficulties in mobilizing gauchos stemmed not only from the Unitarians' own political limitations but from the gauchos' unyielding politicization. They were Federalist and, even in 1867, Chachistas as well, which defined their manner of participating in political struggles. Thus, when he was imprisoned and accused of "complicity" in the Federalist rebellion, Dávila gave his version of the events by way of excusing himself, and concluded by calling on "the opinion and judgment of impartial men who know what it is to lead National Guards in La Rioja."[66]

The Federalist rebellion of 1867 would claim many victims among the

Unitarians, especially in the department of Famatina. Barely three months after Exipión Dávila had handed over the militia under his command, his cousin, Colonel Tristán Dávila, and members of the Gordillo and San Román families, close relatives of the Dávilas, were all assassinated by the montonera.[67] The political misadventures of the Dávila family did not end there. Unitarians since the 1820s, the family nevertheless fell into disgrace with the national government in 1867. By early 1868, the Dávilas could no longer count on the support of the national troops stationed in the Andean provinces. The army now backed another faction of Unitarians, one that had dislodged Cesáreo Dávila from the governorship in an armed conspiracy in 1867.[68] Even though politically orphaned, the Dávila family still coveted control of the government, and in April 1868, they organized a successful local rebellion that temporarily deposed the Unitarian governor.

The Dávila family had to introduce innovations into their political practices to compete for power. Searching for support for the rebellion that would reseat Don Cesário, the family courted several Federalist leaders. A Unitarian from La Rioja, showing disgust with the Dávilas' new political line, commented at the time that the family "now calls itself Federalist, believing that it will thus attract the masses."[69] This maneuver to create an independent political base implied negotiations between leaders. One of the Federalist leaders approached by the Dávilas was Severo Chumbita, the caudillo to whom Exipión Dávila had turned over the militia one year earlier. Exipión's past actions surely facilitated the new accord, but now it was Chumbita who had ulterior motives, of recent origin, in accepting the rapprochement that the Dávilas proposed. Chumbita was a fugitive from federal justice because of his participation in the defeated Federalist rebellions, and Don Cesario Dávila had promised pardons for Chumbita and other Federalist leaders if he reclaimed the government.[70]

But the Dávilas could not rely on negotiations alone; the Unitarian family also had to accept and publicly use certain Federalist symbols from the popular political traditions of La Rioja. Another local Unitarian expressed repugnance when Don Cesario Dávila, after the revolt that returned him to the governorship, appeared in the city of La Rioja:

> At that time Don Sesario [sic] entered the plaza . . . all of them with their red cap, their red shirt . . . they had unanimously shouted "viva General Taguada [for Taboada], viva the future vice president Don

Manuel Taguada, viva the president of the republic Don Justo José Orquisa [for Urquiza]," all the families Gordillo and San Román, the Indian Chumba, all had shouted "viva the federation." . . . These indecent men did all of this, to grab what they wanted they have become Federalists.[71]

There is no evidence that the Dávilas persisted in their Federalist militancy. The rapprochement and public displays of enthusiasm were simply a product of an opportunism that was neither exclusive to nor characteristic of Argentinean politics in the nineteenth century. Yet the significance of the episode lies in how local political traditions defined the context of the operation and put certain limits on the maneuver. The request for support could not be made in the language of Unitarianism, nor with its symbols. Nor could the request be articulated purely in the name of the Dávila family (for example, asking lower-class Riojans to support the "Dávila Party," "Dávilistas," or the "Party of Famatina"), a language that would have taken the operation out of the context of the Unitarian-Federalist conflict and, given the contradictory partisan traditions of the Dávilas and most lower-class Riojans, would have presumably enhanced the effectiveness of the appeal (this type of more purely personalistic and familial language and appeal would become more common in provincial politics from the 1870s on, when Unitarianism and Federalism disappeared as political forces). Instead, the request had to be conducted with the symbols and language imposed by popular political traditions, which had specific meanings that did not easily include the Dávila family. One witness to these disagreeable scenes testified that even in Federalist garb, the Dávilas "get nothing but the few [men] that they have in the plaza by force of money, of the few *Riojanos* that are with them, most are forced."[72]

The political identity of the gauchos, then, was so deeply rooted that this attempt to manipulate them had obligated some members of the local Unitarian elite to abandon, at least temporarily, their own political traditions. This maneuvering had a high political cost: in the process, the Dávilas alienated other members of the elite and increased the mistrust that the national government felt toward the family.

Deep-rooted Federalism also accounts for the radicalism with which some montoneros interpreted their political affiliation. Thus, a song that told of the military successes of Felipe Varela's rebellion in 1867 finished with a quartet that declared:

As a distinctive symbol
a sash red and strong,
with the word in the forehead,
Federalist until death.[73]

This vow to dress in "a sash red" and remain "Federalist until death" was, at least in some cases, more than a manifestation of a creative popular culture or a verbal display of political commitment. Santiago Salcedo, a Unitarian, recalled that in the Rebellion of 1867, his unit had taken a nearly unarmed group of montoneros by surprise. In that critical situation, trying to save their lives, some of the gauchos appealed for the clemency of the Unitarian commander, crying, "Don't kill me. I know Colonel [Ricardo] Vera!" With death imminent, however, other gauchos were more resolute. They proclaimed, "Kill me, for I am Federalist!"[74]

THERE MUST BE some truly great quality in the character of that old gaucho," Sarmiento admitted in his ambiguous reflections on Chacho, whose assassination he allegedly ordered.[1] As Sarmiento's commentary in 1866 suggested, there was something unique, ultimately mysterious, about those individuals who had achieved the status of caudillo, a quality that could be seen in the attraction that the persona of some leaders exercised over the gauchos.

The distinctive personality of these leaders was an essential component of the first explanation of Latin American caudillismo proposed by Sarmiento himself in his *Facundo*. Yet, this question has been largely neglected by modern historiography. Scholars' reluctance to consider this aspect of caudillista leadership has to do with common understandings of the phenomenon of personal magnetism or attraction, which social scientists have also referred to as charisma. The concept of charisma carries a sense of emotional involvement and manipulation, and consequently, it is associated with irrationality and political incapacity on the part of the followers. On the other hand, because of its emphasis on the persona of the leaders, the phenomenon of charisma has been considered too exceptional and idiosyncratic to allow for valid generalizations. Thus, because of the explanatory limitations of this concept, historians have usually preferred to simply note the phenomenon without attempting to systematically explore its workings.

Nevertheless, a few social scientists have bucked this trend, calling into question the idea that charisma irradiates from the persona of the leader;

instead, they propose that it should be seen as a reciprocal relationship between leaders and followers. "One has charisma," James C. Scott argues, "to the extent that others confer it upon one; it is the attribution of charisma that establishes the relationship."[2] Here, followers are a fundamental part of the equation since it is their "cultural and social expectations that exercise a controlling or at least limiting influence over the would-be charismatic figure."[3] John Charles Chasteen, too, maintained recently that the charismatic leadership of the caudillos must be analyzed relationally: the charisma was in the eye of the beholder who projected their own values onto the strongman.[4]

If charisma is conferred on one, if charisma is indeed "in the eye of the beholder," then the historian should try to reconstruct the beholder's gaze—that is, we should look for the charismatic appeal among the followers who are projecting their social and cultural expectations. In short, the study of charisma should be similar to the study of the followers' perceptions and representations of the leaders.

This approach requires paying close attention to the culture of the followers. Since the charismatic relationship involves the hopes of the followers, the phenomenon of charisma, Scott says, is culturally specific: "What is charismatic for one audience is not compelling for another, what works in one culture, falls flat in another."[5] This relation between leadership and cultural specificity has also been recognized by Clifford Geertz, who contended that in order to understand the charismatic figure and what he/she means, it is necessary to study the symbols and conceptions that prevail in his/her society.[6] In his exploration of Queen Elizabeth's charisma, for example, Geertz showed that she "became a moral idea" in the British political imagination: Elizabeth was "Chastity, Wisdom, Peace, Perfect Beauty and Pure Religion as well as Queen, and being Queen she was these things."[7] Similarly, by studying cultural representations of the caudillos, it is evident that the caudillos were more than party or military leaders in the gauchos' minds. These popular portrayals touched on a wide array of significant and specific experiences in postindependence, rural Argentina: "Everything stood for some vast idea and nothing took place unburdened with parable," and thus, caudillos also became a "moral idea."[8] The study of caudillos' charismatic appeal, then, reveals as much about the leaders as it does about the culture of their followers. The cultural specificity of the phenomenon has also been remarked by Chasteen, who appropriately categorized caudillos as "culture heroes."[9] And it was the role of gauchos' values in the construction of the charismatic appeal that explains, to some extent, the emotional attachment between the caudillos and their followers, a tie that included sentiments of admiration, obedience, and even fear on the part of the gauchos.

The study of popular depictions of Facundo and Chacho highlights the role of oral culture in the formation of the nation as well. In the rather poor and largely illiterate society of the rural interior in nineteenth-century Argentina, representations of caudillos mainly took place by necessity in the realm of oral culture.[10] Different genres, like jokes and speeches, featured the caudillos as protagonists, but most of the portrayals took the form of songs and stories. This repertoire was part of a politicized oral culture whose pieces circulated throughout the provinces, putting people from different regions in contact with politics and political protagonists, and in the process, helping to define a political space of national dimensions in the mind of the audience. In this way, nineteenth-century Argentinean oral culture, with its emphasis on caudillos, played a fundamental role in the slow process of nation formation.

Throughout this book, and in this chapter, folklore is crucial to the study of popular politics. Here, I rely especially on the *Colección de Folklore de la Encuesta Docente* (CFED, or the Folklore Collection Gathered by Teachers), an exceptionally rich collection, probably unique in Latin America and comparable to the Federal Writers' Project of the Works Project Administration (WPA) in the United States. It is made up of hundreds of dossiers containing songs, tales, testimonies, proverbs, superstitions, and so forth, gathered in 1921 throughout the country, especially in rural areas. At the time, most of the informants were over seventy, eighty, or even ninety years old, and because of their educational level and experience, they really belonged to the nineteenth century; in some cases, they had been protagonists of or eyewitnesses to the phenomena under study. The use of folklore, of course, raises methodological questions that will be explored in the course of this chapter.[11]

Politics, Caudillos, and Oral Culture

Politics occupied an important place in the oral culture of the provinces of the interior in the nineteenth century. This can be seen in many of the songs that remained in the collective memory of the provinces in the early twentieth century. For example, among the thousands of pieces collected in 1921, some 250 songs had a strictly political content, and many of those were principally concerned with the caudillos and their political lives. In terms of the caudillos from La Rioja, several collections of popular songs have recuperated eight songs about Facundo and twenty-one about Chacho.[12] The geographic location of the songs collected reveals the extent of their circulation. Songs that have as their protagonists Riojan caudillos, for instance, appear not only in the province of La Rioja but also in Córdoba, San Luis, San Juan, Catamarca, Tucumán, Salta, and Jujuy. The collection of 1921 also preserved a good number of stories featuring caudillos as protagonists: twenty-two concerning Facundo and thirteen about Chacho were collected in the provinces of La Rioja, Catamarca, and San Juan.

Testimony from some of the caudillos' contemporaries suggested the importance of such songs and stories in political life. In 1862, an observer noted that after Chacho had successfully resisted the Porteño troops, the gauchos were simply raising the power and prestige of Peñaloza in the provinces of the interior "by singing the glories of the general."[13] And General José María Paz remembered that in his campaigns in the province of Córdoba toward the end of the 1820s, besides confronting Facundo on the battlefield,

> I also had a strong enemy to combat in the popular beliefs about Quiroga; when I say popular I am speaking of the countryside, where those beliefs had taken root in various parts and not only in the lower classes of society. Quiroga was taken as a man inspired, he had well-known spirits that penetrated everywhere and obeyed his mandate . . . and a thousand other absurdities of this type.[14]

The beliefs that circulated in the form of stories and songs, and the resulting perceptions that they generated among the rural population of Córdoba, were key elements of the gauchos' loyalty to the Riojan caudillo.

Oral culture, as Paz recognized, was a political dominion, a space where the struggle between Unitarians and Federalists was waged. Humor was also used as a weapon in this conflict, and Unitarian and Federalist leaders became the protagonists (as well as targets) of jokes. In the 1840s, a Unitarian from Santiago del Estero named one of his horses Juan Manuel (a reference to Rosas, and another way of placing the Federalist caudillo in the camp of the barbarians, the enemies of civilization).[15] When Catamarca was occupied by Unitarian troops from Buenos Aires in 1862, a poor black defiantly called a dog passing by Bartolo (short for Bartolomé Mitre, the Porteño leader of the Unitarian Party), an insolence that cost him 500 lashes.[16] And after the death of Chacho, in 1863, a poem of Unitarian origins played with the religious connotations of the sky blue and red colors that identified the Unitarians and Federalists, respectively:

> Peñaloza died
> he went straight to heaven
> but as he saw it was sky blue
> he went back down to hell.[17]

But in spite of its contentious nature, oral culture seems to have been dominated by Federalism. Thus, a quick review of the 205 songs collected in 1921 that explicitly referred to the conflict between the two parties shows that two-thirds of them were Federalist.[18] And if we consider the presence of leaders of both parties in those songs, the predominance of Federalism is even more pronounced: of the total number of positive depictions of leaders from both parties, more than four-fifths concerned Federalist caudillos. The names Urquiza, Facundo, Rosas, El Chacho, and Felipe Varela were most often evoked. Among the rarely mentioned Unitarians were the Taboadas, General Lavalle, General Paz, General La Madrid, Mitre, Sarmiento.[19] Although these references do not necessarily reflect the amount of support each party enjoyed, they certainly reveal the predominance of Federalism in the oral culture; and this, in turn, signals the pervasiveness of this partisan identity among the illiterate, the main users of oral culture.

This predominance is further suggested by the positive identification of some Federalist caudillos with the popular art of composing songs. In two versions of the same story, when prisoners held by Rosas and Felipe Varela composed two eventually famous (and at least in one of the cases, much admired) songs, the Federalist leaders rewarded them with their freedom in recognition of their ingenuity and creativity.[20]

The more comfortable classes in the small urban centers of the interior also consumed, modified, and added elements to this repertoire. The personal diary of Ramón Gil Navarro Ocampo, a Unitarian as well as a member of the Catamarca elite, gives us a rare opportunity to observe the way in which oral repertoire functioned in the political arena, and how they were consumed and reproduced, thereby generating appropriations and exchanges between the repertoire of one social sector and another.

Sent into political exile, Navarro Ocampo and his family were en route to Chile from Catamarca, accompanied by Juan Lavaysse, a Unitarian from Santiago del Estero who had also been exiled. Crossing the countryside of the province of San Juan one night in March 1846, Navarro Ocampo described how they "sang together the 'Salchichín,' the 'Trágala,' and other songs against the tyrant [Juan Manuel de Rosas]. . . . There were many *guasos* [countrymen] around there who were terrified when they heard us."[21]

Neither the lyrics of the "Salchichín" nor those of the "Trágala" were recorded in his diary. The 1921 collection, however, uncovered one version of the "Salchichín" that circulated, precisely, in the province of Catamarca, and as the young Unitarian noted in his diary, the song's clearly anti-Federalist message denounced Rosas and Juan Felipe Ibarra, the caudillo from Santiago del Estero.[22] Thus, this song that the Unitarian elite from Catamarca sang in the 1840s was still extant in the collective memory of the province in 1921. The lyrics of the "Trágala" were also absent from the diary. And although the 1921 collection gathered six versions of it, none of them were "against the tyrant." To the contrary, they were unequivocally Federalist and Rosista, which implies that the Unitarian elite and Federalist supporters from the lower classes both used the same song but with a different message.[23] In this case, moreover, the evidence leads us to believe that it was the Unitarians who defiantly appropriated elements of a popular Federalist song and changed its meaning.

These songs were only the beginning of a night heavily laden with politics. Juan Lavaysse called together the guasos and addressed a "proclamation" to them, saying that

> the tyrant [Juan Manuel de Rosas] would soon fall, since the grand pharaoh was on the march from the West, . . . Saul and Motesuma [*sic*] from the North, and Richard the Lionhearted was coming from England, and with this entire force against him the tyrant would surely fall. He made them believe, as well, that the family of Rosas would bring forth the Antichrist, and that therefore the tyrant was the enemy of the human race. When Juan [Lavaysse] finished his exhortation, all the guasos shouted "Viva!" and they really believed that they were living in deception, until Juan revealed everything to them.[24]

This speech to the peons and gauchos in the province of San Juan might have appeared incoherent, or at least obscure. In truth, it is not easy to understand the Unitarian's intention in invoking Richard the Lionhearted —and it is impossible to know what effect this had on the gauchos. Other parts of his proclamation are not so difficult to decipher, however. On the one hand, his speech was a convocation of the contradictory figures who formed part of the religious and political cultures of the audience, and whose common denominator was that they were (or better still, had been) in positions of power. Among those on the march against Rosas was the pharaoh, the biblical archetype of tyrannical power. On the other hand, borrowing from the rhetoric used during the wars of independence, Lavaysse invoked Moctezuma. In sermons and proclamations, priests and lay patriots had presented Moctezuma as one of the powerful, legitimate, and even pious monarchs of the Americas, whose defeat at the hands of Cortes had initiated the 300 years of Spanish tyranny.[25] Finally, the Unitarian from Santiago linked the Porteño caudillo with the devil by claiming that Rosas's family would bring forth the Antichrist, making Rosas the enemy of all good christians ("the enemy of the human race").

Lavaysse's choice of religious culture as a vehicle for his message was not capricious. This aspect of popular culture was one of the most fertile terrains to be exploited by any group interested in obtaining the loyalty of the gauchos. But the Unitarians had been expelled from that territory. Because of their nonecclesiastical attitudes and policies, the gauchos saw the Unitarians as an impious threat to Catholicism, a conception that Lavaysse tried to invert: in his proclamation, it was Rosas who was associated with the Antichrist. Still, despite small-scale challenges like Lavaysse's, by 1846 the articulation between politics and religion was a realm securely occupied by Federalism and Rosismo.

Lavaysse's address did not exhaust the repertoire of this politicized gathering in the countryside of San Juan; there was more to come. "We passed the rest of the evening listening to Juan [Lavaysse], the almanac, who told stories about the lives of Quiroga [and] Ibarra."[26] The stories recounted the life histories of two Federalist caudillos: Facundo Quiroga, who had been assassinated eleven years before, and Juan Felipe Ibarra, who after twenty-five years in power was still in control of the province of Santiago del Estero. But how did the Unitarians, whose families had suffered under Quiroga and Ibarra, present these tales of the caudillos? Other entries from Navarro Ocampo's diary that characterized Facundo as "the most barbarous, cruel tyrant of those times" suggest how Quiroga and Ibarra were presented that night.[27] This might also explain why the Unitarians chose to recount the histories of the two Federal caudillos instead of, say, cele-brating the life of a Unitarian notable. Their intention may have been to present an opinion of the caudillos that differed from that circulating among the gauchos. In this area as well the Unitarians faced a difficult task. As a poem of the time went:

> Quiroga gave me a ribbon,
> Ibarra gave me a sash.
> For Quiroga I give my life,
> For Ibarra, my heart.[28]

At least since the 1830s, the gauchos positively associated Facundo with the Santiago caudillo. Thus, stories about caudillos were another oral genre where both elite and gaucho political opinions clashed.

In addition to illustrating how oral culture functioned in the political arena, the entries from Navarro Ocampo's diary point to the relation be-tween oral culture and the process of nation formation. First, when the politicized evening gathering took place in March 1846, the delegation of foreign relations in the province of Buenos Aires served as the only, pre-carious institutional link between the provinces. Years would pass before the provinces would agree to the formation of a national government, and the Argentine Republic would wait still longer. Second, although this meeting took place in the countryside of the province of San Juan, the Unitarian elites and illiterate gauchos invoked the caudillos who governed the provinces of Santiago del Estero and Buenos Aires, and another who had controlled La Rioja for almost fifteen years. While each side perceived these caudillos differently, their common use of songs, stories, and procla-mations evinced a shared political mode that was part of the struggle be-tween Unitarians and Federalists. The group that gathered with Navarro Ocampo in San Juan that night, like those whose names and lives the group invoked, recognized that the struggle encompassed Buenos Aires, Santiago del Estero, San Juan, Catamarca, and La Rioja. The experience of a decades-long conflict, shared by Unitarians and Federalists alike, had de-lineated a common political space in which the struggle took place; here, too, the protagonists experienced the gradual process of nation formation.

It was, of course, possible to detect this process as early as 1829. A Uni-tarian song composed in Tucumán that year denounced Facundo Quiroga as an "infernal vandal." It also referred to the suffering of the Riojan Uni-tarians and encouraged the Tucumanos to assist them:

Let's Go! Let's Go! Let's Go!
brave Tucumanos
to take revenge on the spilled blood
of our brothers.[29]

Riojan Unitarians became the "brothers" of Tucumano Unitarians. Thus, the combination of political conflict and party membership created solidarity and a sense of community between the people of these two provinces.

The idea that the conflict between Unitarianism and Federalism encompassed all fourteen provinces was a consequence of other factors as well. A substantial portion of the population may have become aware of a wider, common geographic space because of their jobs as muleteers or peons; or more important, because of the intense seasonal and permanent migration between provinces motivated by the job market; or because of the availability of land, an extended phenomenon since the late eighteenth century.[30] In the case of the Andean provinces, La Rioja in particular, this "domestic" experience developed along into an "international" one: it was common for gauchos to go to Chile as muleteers or peons, sometimes as fugitives of justice, and since the early 1830s, as miners to work in the Norte Chico. These often dramatic shifts, motivated mainly by the job market, also worked toward the formation and definition of a common political space in the culture of the gauchos.

And there were other cultural manifestations of politics working alongside oral culture in this process. For example, May 25, celebrating the first patriotic government, was a significant date in some provinces. In La Rioja, during public celebrations of that patriotic day, people would shout, "Long live the Argentine Confederation and the Great Rosas."[31] In 1842, to pay homage to the governor of the province of Buenos Aires, the Riojan legislature passed a law that renamed Famatina Hill, the most distinctive and mythologized geographic accident of the province, "The Hill of the Great Rosas." According to the legislature, "Because of its great height [the hill] could be seen from all the departments of the province and from the neighboring provinces," and thus many people would be touched by this tribute.[32] Next, between 1842 and 1844, the government of La Rioja issued new coins with the outline of "The Hill of the Great Rosas" and the slogan "Eternal Glory to the Restaurador Rosas" on the obverse, and the national emblem and words "Confederated Argentine Republic" on the reverse.[33] Such gestures helped to define a common political space (sometimes called the Argentine Confederation); they also shaped the idea that the struggle between Unitarians and Federalists transcended the local level, and included people and public figures from other regions.

Nonetheless, oral culture played a central role in the formation and representation of that political space. The use of oral culture, which recognized that most people were illiterate, was facilitated by two factors: first, that telling stories and singing was an essential part of everyday life; second, that in those fourteen provinces, the majority of the population spoke the same language.[34]

The recognition of a national political space rose not from the project of a particular social sector but, to the contrary, from the conflict that enmeshed both gauchos and well-bred people—a conflict that was communicated orally rather than through written materials. Thus, the perception of a national political space was being slowly shaped by illiteracy and political strife. This perspective, then, takes the process of nation formation out of the exclusive dominion of literacy and the printed manifestations of nineteenth century high culture, like novels and newspapers, and places it in the realm of popular culture and among the illiterate.[35]

Songs and Stories

Certain characteristics distinguish the songs from the stories. The songs, which are in general obviously political and informative, were composed around certain notorious events, although in the glosas (gloss) and romances (ballads) the main characters are identified with certain folkloric archetypes. On the other hand, most of the stories show a clear debt to folklore and substitute caudillos for original characters; in most cases, it is difficult to link the episodes with concrete political events. Similarly, while the presence of caudillos in these narratives is explicit, their political affiliations are assumed.

Nevertheless, the songs and stories circulated together, projecting for their listeners images of actors and events. Thus, in 1921, when eighty-seven-year-old Ponciano Roldán narrated his version of the assassination of Chacho, he ended by saying, "And somebody wrote a few verses for the death of Don Vicente Peñaloza."[36] Providing more details, the song complemented Roldán's explanation of Chacho's murder.

These songs and stories incorporated themes and archetypes that were familiar not only to the oral culture of the Argentine interior but to that of other countries and societies as well.[37] Elements taken from a preexisting repertoire were adapted to the new needs for communication and explanation that political life since 1810 had imposed.

The political life of a caudillo, however, was not automatically adapted to the archetypes and motives of oral culture. For such an assimilation of oral culture and politics to occur, the political actions of a caudillo, his conduct in everyday life, and certain elements of his personality had to coincide, at least to some extent, with the themes and archetypes of oral culture, and with the mentality of that culture's audience.[38] A certain affinity between the caudillos' political life and personality, and the values espoused in the preexisting culture, made some of them "mythogenic" figures whose lives and persons passed into the repertoires of oral culture.[39]

The use of older plots, themes, and archetypes, and the replacement of their original characters by Facundo and Chacho, two Federalist caudillos, was a two-way street process. It gave the cautionary side and moral content of the preexisting repertoire a political identity. At the same time, this substitution of characters put the image of the caudillos in contact with teachings and values that, inevitably, contaminated (in this case, polished and improved) their figures. The process, then, not only politicized the morality expressed in oral culture but also shaped the figure of the caudillos, associating them with the teachings and morality their images helped to transmit. In this process, the caudillos and their party became "a moral idea."

Did the songs and stories collected in 1921 or by other folklorists in the 1920s and 1930s, through which we reconstruct the image of the caudillos in the oral culture of the nineteenth century, circulate during the life of the caudillos, or at least, in a politically significant period after their death?[40] Might they not be a re-creation from a much later period, products of new experiences, especially in the case of the stories? In this chapter, as in the rest of this book, songs and stories are cross-examined with information and insights provided by memoirs, private diaries, correspondence, medical reports, newspapers, criminal and civil trials, and so on, allowing us both to date the themes and archetypes associated with the caudillos as well as to establish a dialogue between practices and representations. For example, Navarro Ocampo's private diary, written in 1846, helped date some of the songs collected in 1921 and revealed how they were used in the mid-nineteenth-century political arena.[41]

Certain differences between the songs and stories also assist in dating the repertoire. The songs' more obvious political and informative content, inspired by notorious events, situates them more specifically in time. But in addition, some songs (the romances in particular) include themes and archetypes that coincide with the themes and archetypes in the stories. Therefore, the specific political information found in the songs serves as a reference to date the themes and archetypes that color the songs and stories as well.

The characteristics of the informants and the way they present the information also suggest that the songs and stories belonged to the nineteenth century and did circulate during the time of the caudillos. As mentioned earlier, most of the informants interviewed in 1921 were more than seventy years old, and many were over eighty or ninety. Gavina Romero, who recounted an anecdote about "the Tiger of Los Llanos," was ninety-five years old in 1921. Her 1826 date of birth would most certainly have assured her the experience and education of a person of the nineteenth century.[42] Another informant began a story that involved Facundo by saying, "I heard my father, who was born in 1830, tell of another event . . ."[43] In the same way, Manuel Antonio Díaz, who was seventy years of age in 1921, explained that he knew of the rebellions of Chacho, in 1862 and 1863, from his father, "who knew the facts and because at that time I was [a] ten year old."[44] And Felipe Paz, from the village of Chamical, in Los Llanos, La Rioja, who was ninety-one in 1921, began his story about the assassination of Chacho with: "I was a soldier of General Peñaloza."[45]

Finally, what was the relationship between oral culture and the printed word? Could it be that some of the pieces collected in 1921 were actually oral versions of songs and stories that had previously circulated in pamphlets, almanacs, newspapers, or popular literature? The scanty research on these problems in nineteenth-century Argentina prevents reaching any conclusion, and the evidence from my own research points in two possible directions. On the one hand, the romance and plot telling of the death of Facundo (in 1835) circulated in print and handwriting throughout the provinces in the 1830s and 1840s, generating numerous oral versions, some of which were collected in 1921. On the other, the songs and stories concerning the death of Chacho suggest how difficult it was for the written word to penetrate and remain in the oral culture. Chacho's death in 1863 soon became the subject of oral culture, and after the 1880s, of the popular criollista literature of Eduardo Gutiérrez and his plagiarists. When the oral versions of 1921 are compared with versions of popular literature from the 1880s and 1900s it is clear that they have different characters and plots. Actually, the oral versions of 1921 followed the earliest rumors and explanations of the death of Chacho that circulated throughout the Llanos immediately after his assassination in November 1863. That is, oral explanations of Chacho's death were apparently unaffected by popular literature. Thus, it seems that the mere existence of the printed word did not imply the modification or contamination of oral culture.

The Power and Authority of the Caudillo

The caudillos, in their day, were perceived as the highest authority. In this respect, popular culture underscored not only their position as political leaders but also distinguished the caudillos as moral authorities and role models in the communities they ruled over. Oral culture integrated well-known motifs from folklore, and invested caudillos with qualities and connotations similar to those that popular classes attributed to kings or patrons in other societies.[46] This association with images of kings stemmed, in part, from the repertoire of preexisting archetypes on which the images of the caudillos were formed, but it could also possibly be the product of three centuries of colonial, monarchical experience, which would have left a model and language through which to define legitimate authority, and the characteristics that holders of that authority should have.[47]

In certain stories, Facundo, hiding his identity, appeared by surprise in various places in La Rioja, although everyone thought he had left the region. These stories attributed to him a special capacity to know what Riojans were doing, and if necessary, reward or punish them. In one story, after the battle of La Tablada (in the province of Córdoba), a group of young Unitarians got together to celebrate the defeat of Facundo. The young men began to sing a popular *vidalita* (a type of folk song) that painted the caudillo negatively when they realized that among them was "an individual in a poncho, with practically the entire face covered by a big hat. . . . The man in a poncho asked them in a polite tone to finish the interesting song." When the song came to an end, "Quiroga (for it was no other in the poncho)" called his soldiers and had the singers shot. "Nobody imagined that the disguised figure was the Tiger of Los Llanos," concluded the story, "for he was thought to be thirty leagues away."[48] Here, using the motif that folklorists have classified as "king in disguise to learn secrets of subjects," oral tradition sought to explain a tragic occurrence: the fact that after the battle of La Tablada, Quiroga did have some Unitarians in La Rioja shot "under the pretext that they had been rejoicing in his defeat."[49] The form the story took spoke of the reach of Quiroga's authority and the control that he exercised over the population of La Rioja. Thus, omnipresence was one of the qualities of the caudillo, which also suggests an appreciation of his power. But this capacity "to learn secrets of subjects" may have been a quality attributed to Federalist caudillos more generally. William H. Hudson remembered that a number of stories about Rosas circulated, many of them

> related to his adventures when he would disguise himself as a person of humble status and prowl about the city [of Buenos Aires] by night, specially in the squalid quarters, where he would make the acquaintance of the very poor in their hovels.[50]

Mediation in the daily conflicts of rural La Rioja was the responsibility of the caudillos. This included interventions in family disputes or conflicts between gauchos and government officials. Sometimes the caudillos proposed solutions, while on other occasions, they made sure that the proper authorities intervened. Conflict resolution and justice, then, were some of the caudillos' duties, and to explain them, gauchos used archetypes clearly drawn from the King Solomon legend. Facundo was portrayed as a Solomon-like figure who used his exceptional wisdom or astuteness to resolve disputes and impart justice.[51]

But the caudillo was the highest authority because he was also responsible, ultimately, for the material and moral preservation of the society. The extent of his authority and the nature of this responsibility were expressed in the language of caudillos and gauchos. Chacho reflected on the dimensions of his own authority:

> I have that influence [over the gauchos], that prestige, because as a soldier I fought at their side for forty-three years, sharing with them the fortunes of war, the suffering of the campaigns, the bitterness of banishment. I have been more of a father to them than a leader . . . preferring their necessities to my own. As an Argentine and a Riojano I have always been the protector of the unfortunate, sacrificing the very last that I had to fulfill their needs, making myself responsible

for everything and with my influence as leader forcing the national government to turn its eyes toward this miserable people."[52]

Peñaloza's authority and status as a caudillo had evolved through the long political experience that he shared with the gauchos since the 1820s, when Chacho had entered into the party struggles as a subaltern of Facundo. His partisan leadership, however, was only one part of his relationship with the gauchos: "I have been more of a father to them than a leader." That is, he had always been "the protector of the unfortunate," putting the needs of the gauchos above his own and sacrificing "the very last that I had." As a father, then, Peñaloza had made himself "responsible for everything."

The kinship language emphasized the nature of the obligation and, especially, affective ties that bound caudillos and gauchos. This explains why references to caudillos as fathers were often articulated in an emotive language. Popular songs defined Facundo, for example, as "a dear father."[53] Likewise, it was said of General Octaviano Navarro, from Catamarca, that "he was beloved by his province, he was the father of said province and his heart was tempered by his very warm soldiers, who beloved him so much."[54]

The authority of the caudillo as a "father" had moral and ideological dimensions, too, as reflected in a story featuring Facundo as the protagonist. Here, the caudillo was going through Tama, a village in Los Llanos, when he decided to stop and join a crowd assembled for a wedding. During the ceremony, the bride refused to accept the man who was to be her husband. She pointed out another man in the crowd and said, "He is the one I love, not [indicating her bridegroom] this one." According to oral tradition, "Quiroga sent his officers to take the girl and hang her from the highest Tala tree and to bring the one she loved to judgment, and give him six shots."[55] It was the caudillo who castigated those who would subvert the functioning of matrimony and the authority of the father to choose a daughter's mate. In this episode, however, the "real" father was absent, transforming the tale into an explicit comment on the caudillo's authority. It was Facundo, the father of all Riojans, who exercised patriarchal authority and did what was expected of any father under the same circumstances. The caudillo was "responsible for everything," including the reproduction of patriarchy. And to fulfill that responsibility, oral culture resorted once again to Facundo's omnipresence, which allowed the caudillo to attend an apparently insignificant wedding.

Clientalism

The stories concerning Facundo and Chacho emphasized that these Feder-alist caudillos appreciated and rewarded the loyalty of the gauchos. There-fore, he who responded when his leader asked for, or needed, help, was compensated beyond what a client would hope for from a caudillo. In one of the stories, collected in San Antonio, the home village of Facundo, in Los Llanos, a peon who, without recognizing the caudillo, helped Qui-roga cross a river and escape when the caudillo was pursued by government officials, was later rewarded by Facundo with "ten oxen and ten cows."[56] Any landless worker or labrador in Los Llanos understood the significance of this compensation: it allowed the peon to begin raising cattle, thereby distancing him from the periodic specter of hunger that was part and par-cel of casual wage labor and subsistence agriculture. In other words, the peon's service to the caudillo was more than amply repaid with an amount of animals that surpassed what the sons of modest ranchers received to start their own ranches. This way of rewarding gauchos appears in stories about Chacho as well: after requisitioning for his troops the "four or five cows" that a couple living in a hut had, "Chacho returned not only the five cows but as many more," doubling the stock of the smallholders.[57]

The poor occupied a privileged and almost exclusive position in the rep-resentation of the patron-client relation, which gave the following a clear social identity. In a story from Los Llanos about the death of Peñaloza, an elderly woman tried to warn Chacho about the fatal event to come, telling him, "Fly from here, I don't want them to kill you, all us poor folk need you." Her warnings were not enough, and Peñaloza died. His death "was felt by all, since he had been so generous in these villages."[58]

In other tales, elements of Chacho's personal history and his special relationship with the poor made him look almost like a saint. "Chacho was a man who had been a priest, and because he liked to sacrifice for humanity he threw off the priest's habit and took up the dress of the gau-cho." With this explanation, one story recounts an episode in which Cha-cho and "other gauchos" went to the house of "a woman who had a good amount of livestock, but she was very tight-fisted, and she had all her ani-mals hidden." When the caudillo asked her "what she had to offer him, chickens, or goats, the woman said nothing." Chacho had her punished, and then the woman admitted that she did have livestock and offered it to the caudillo, who reminded her that "with a man like him, one doesn't tell lies."[59] Here, Chacho's past, which included his childhood experience as a priest's assistant (the priest was Peñaloza's uncle, who was responsible for raising him),[60] and the protection and aid that he as caudillo offered to the inhabitants of Los Llanos, provided the raw material that—articulated through the narrative schemes of the lives of Christ, Peter, and other saints—transformed Chacho himself into a saint and allowed him to comment negatively on the rich. But if Chacho's holy condition was not evident to the world, it was because he "took up the dress of a gaucho."[61]

Patron-client relations also belonged in the realm of party identity. A song composed after the death of Chacho said:

> They say that Peñaloza has died,
> I don't know if it is true.
> Don't get careless, Savages,
> he may rise again.
> Poor Costa Baja,
> such an ill-starred Coast,
> now the star is dead
> that shone on the poor.
> In a place called Olta
> they cut off his head
> ambushing him unawares.[62]

"They" are the "Savages," the Unitarians, who beheaded the poors' protector. This tragic episode in the life of the people of Los Llanos is inscribed in the context of political struggles, giving the protection the caudillo dispensed a clear partisan connotation. To be Chachista or Chachino in La Rioja during the 1860s was to be poor (that is, gaucho) and Federalist, as we have seen.

This perception of caudillismo was not confined to popular culture; the provincial elite understood the phenomenon in the same way. Indeed, they even propagate this definition within the local political culture. Symptomatically, a Unitarian from the La Rioja elite chose the gauchesque literary genre (utilizing the language that the upper classes attributed to the gauchos) to satirize and insult both Chachismo and Federalism. In the poem, a "friend of the Sanctioned Federal Law" related his experience as one of Peñaloza's montoneros, ridiculed the protagonist for the suffering he endured while following the caudillo, and dropped numerous references to the poverty that left him dressed only in a ripped poncho.[63] On the other hand, those few members of the "decent classes" who sympathized with the caudillo were considered a strange contradiction within the local political culture, and their peculiarity had to be explained. These exotic followers of Peñaloza were labeled "Chachistas in frock coat" by their Unitarian rivals.[64]

Death: Heroes and Villains

Throughout the nineteenth century, gauchos recounted the 1835 assassination of Facundo in variations of one lengthy song. Fourteen versions were recorded by folklorists in six different provinces (including La Rioja) in the first decades of the twentieth century. These oral versions were related to an *argumento* (plot) composed in Tucumán in 1835, and to a long romance, apparently written no earlier than 1837, that, like the "plot," circulated the provinces in print.[65] The death of Chacho also became part of the repertoire of oral culture. The 1921 survey recorded five stories and testimonies as well as three songs from La Rioja, Catamarca, and San Luis, all referring to his assassination in 1863. These tragic episodes in the society that Chacho and Facundo led were presented in such a way as to illustrate, once again, some of the motifs that oral culture associated with the caudillos.

In both cases, the popular representations suggested that the tragic end was part of the caudillo's fate, and this fatalist explanation served to confirm that these were truly exceptional figures. Facundo was warned of the coming tragedy in several versions of the song:

> Before the Totoral,
> A woman said to him,
> Watch out, Señor General,
> for today you will lose your life.[66]

Nevertheless, Facundo

> would not make himself believe
> what was about to occur,
> that they would take his life
> without even telling him why.[67]

A story and glosa (gloss) on the death of Chacho evoked the same motifs. The warning was not enough to ward off catastrophe, and the caudillo was assassinated.[68]

The very way in which the stories and songs recounted the concrete events leading to the assassinations, and the way in which they presented the victims and perpetrators, implied a commentary on the nature of the caudillo. Both Facundo and Chacho were figures of heroic proportions, while their assassins were villains whose evil, too, was of exceptional proportions.

The villainous assassin in the songs of the death of Facundo was Santo Pérez, the celebrated leader of the band of gauchos that attacked Facundo in Barranco Yaco and who, in fact, killed the caudillo. But the songs repeatedly told of another of the deaths suffered by Facundo and his group: Quiroga's seven-year-old groom had his throat slit, according to the songs, at the hands of Pérez. As Pérez was about to commit this murder, various people pleaded with him:

> One of the men of the band,
> with a trace of valor left
> said to his superior,
> "don't kill the little creature."[69]

The imminent victim also added his entreaty:

> On his knees the little angel
> begged in the gravest voice,
> that he was an only child
> who would care for his mother?[70]

Other versions of the song gave the child's plea a greater dramatic force:

> His cries to the Virgin our mother
> were such that the very stones
> cried tears of blood at his words.[71]

But his appeals had no effect on Pérez:

> And the assassin Santos
> cut his throat with his own hands.[72]

The villain, whose soul was impervious to these pleas, was possessed of rare malevolence, and the Christian inspiration of the words he ignored implied the source of his evil nature:

> Santo Pérez stood up,
> "I know of no God," he said.

> "If God comes down from the heavens,
> he'll have to fight with me."[73]

Facundo's assassin could only be the handmaiden of the devil. The caudillo, on the other hand, was portrayed as a good Christian:

> Quiroga asks for a truce,
> so that he may confess.
> He wants to prepare his body
> and not meet death like an animal.
> Santos Pérez responds:
> "I will not give you any truce
> The only truce I can give you
> It is the one that can give you a bullet."[74]

Pérez subjected Facundo to what was considered, even during the height of political violence in the nineteenth century, a sacrilege: he refused him the right to confess before dying. Those hearing the song, then, could gather that Pérez denied Facundo not only "this life" but "the next one" as well.[75]

Finally, the devil wins the battle in Barranca Yaco:

> My Sainted Virgin Mary
> endeavors to triumph over sin
> but she cannot defeat Santos
> that criminal possessed by the devil.[76]

The assassination of the caudillo, then, is another episode in the universally recognized war between God and the Devil. But here, the biblical struggle has partisan connotations, too. The portrayal of Facundo as a good Christian evoked the familiar identification of Federalism and its leaders as defenders of the Catholic religion, while the diabolic inspiration of Pérez and his disrespect for Christian values and practices associated the assassin with popular perceptions of Unitarianism. The battle between Facundo and Pérez, the romance suggested, was not only a fight between the religious hero and impious villain but also one between the embodiments of Federalism and Unitarianism.

By emphasizing Pérez's responsibility in the death of the child, the stories sharpened his portrayal as a villain. In this respect, it is interesting to note the workings and impact of this technique. In one version, from La

Rioja, this part of the episode gave the story the tone of a biblical confrontation. Because of the death of the child, it called the gauchos that attacked Facundo "a pack of *Herones*" in reference to Herod, who also murdered innocent children.[77] Another version, also from La Rioja, achieved the desired contrast between hero and villain by declaring that in Barranca Yaco, "Captain Santo Pérez / took the part of evil."[78]

In addition, compared to the "plot" and romance songs that circulated in print in the years immediately following the assassination, some of the oral versions recorded in the twentieth century omitted long passages that told of a trip that Facundo undertook before his assassination and the trial of Pérez in Buenos Aires. These oral versions concentrated primarily on the death of Facundo and the young groom.[79] In 1938, an eighty-year-old inhabitant of a small rural village in the province of La Rioja remembered that the romance song was "very well-known in La Rioja" and "as a youth he heard it sung on many occasions." In his experience, the singers "limited themselves to the death of Quiroga and the groom."[80]

The death of Chacho also became the subject of oral culture. After his defeat at Caucete, Chacho, with very few men, withdrew to the Llanos and sought refuge in a friend's house in the village of Olta. While resting on November 12, 1863, Chacho was captured along with his men by a Unitarian patrol then under the command of Captain Ricardo Vera and Chacho remained handcuffed for an hour. When Vera's superior, Commander Pablo Irrazábal, arrived, he identified Chacho from among the prisoners, lanced him on the spot, and ordered his soldiers to shoot the caudillo. Immediately afterward, Irrazábal ordered his soldiers to behead Chacho and put the head on a pole in Olta's main square. Thus, in the 1860s, Riojan Federalists considered Irrazábal and Vera responsible for the caudillo's death, and during that decade, they repeatedly tried to avenge it, making the two Unitarian officers the specific target of Federalist violence.[81] As with the groom in tales of Facundo's death, however, oral explanations of the "tragedy" of Olta collected in 1921 focused on another figure that participated in the event: Francisco the Miner, a close confidant of Chacho, who betrayed the caudillo.

The emphasis on the role of Francisco could already be detected in one of the first versions about the death of Chacho, which circulated in the Llanos a few days after his murder. On November 20, 1863, the Córdoba newspaper, *El Imparcial,* reported on a rumor in the Llanos concerning Chacho's death, but the editors warned their readers that they "did not believe it." According to the gossip, "a son of the Miner" had assassinated Chacho. The paper explained:

> The Miner is a black, an inseparable compañero of Chacho since the times of [Facundo] Quiroga. He is his [Chacho's] faithful dog, the most loyal of his loyal men. He is his second person. . . . [I]t is hard to believe that the son of this man could be the assassin of Chacho.

The paper suggested that the rumor could be "a trick" on the part of Chacho, who wanted his enemies to believe that he was dead and so be left alone. Finally, the paper reproduced a letter from an inhabitant of the Llanos, dated November 15, informing a friend that "Peñaloza has been killed by his assistants. . . . [O]ne of the assistants people mention is a son of the Miner."[82]

Most of the songs and stories collected in 1921 blamed Francisco himself, not his son. This is not necessarily a contradiction. One of the 1921 versions claimed that "Chacho died quartered by the Miners Francisco and Gregorio."[83] It is possible that Gregorio was actually Francisco's son, and that the reference to their occupation (miner) also worked as a last name, thus highlighting their relationship. The characterization of Francisco in 1921 basically coincided with the one of 1863. He had been "raised by Peñaloza and was a member of his escort."[84] Again, he was one of Chacho's "closest confidants."[85]

How did Francisco betray Chacho? One of the 1921 testimonies alleged that when Chacho arrived in Olta, he posted Francisco as a sentry at a relatively distant spot from Peñaloza's house. But instead of warning Chacho, the Miner led the enemy to the caudillo's hiding place.[86] Another informant that did not explicitly mention the betrayal nonetheless implied the abnormality of events, saying that when the Unitarian troops were approaching, Chacho saw Francisco in the lead, assumed the men were his own soldiers, and carelessly went back into the house.[87]

Francisco did switch sides. A few weeks after Chacho's assassination, Colonel Arredondo informed his superiors that Irrazábal, Vera, and Francisco were at the head of the troops keeping order in the department of Costa Alta.[88] One of the informants cited above, underscoring once more the oddity of events, remarked that "no one knows how Francisco the Miner passed to Irrazábal's side."[89] Yet, a song explained the nature of the betrayal:

Among his own comrades
who, they say, led him to his death,
I will single out one
as the greatest traitor of them all,
who was Francisco the Miner.
The bargain he struck
in that violent death
will last him all his life.
What a way to kill a man
with the greatest affront.[90]

Francisco sold Chacho to his enemies for money ("the bargain he struck"). Felipe Paz, who had been a soldier with Chacho, also remembered in 1921 that "his very own fellows sold out my general Peñaloza."[91]

The song, like the rumor of November 1863, not only referred to the betrayal but also to the fact that Francisco or his son actually assassinated Peñaloza. Again, this does not seem to be in contradiction with Irrazábal's role in the event. The Unitarian commander lanced the caudillo, as described earlier, and then ordered his soldiers to shoot and behead Chacho. And since everything indicates that Francisco was there at the time, it is conceivable that he actually participated in the carnage. As one of the informants testified, Francisco and Gregorio had "quartered" Chacho.

The focus on the Miner(s), then, emphasized the theme of "betrayal," and highlighted both the villainous, Judaslike nature of the perpetrators (and the Christlike character of the victim) and the exceptional circumstances that led to the caudillo's assassination, something already noticed by the editors of *El Imparcial* when they said that the rumor was "hard to believe." This also explains why the spotlight was removed from Vera and Irrazábal, whose role in Chacho's death had been neither forgotten nor forgiven (in the case of Irrazábal, not even in 1921).[92] There had been nothing unusual in their behavior: they had always been enemies of Chacho.

Some of the implications of Francisco's betrayal are clearer in another version. This story conflates Francisco with Irrazábal, who in this version both betrayed and murdered the caudillo. Here, Irrazábal was defined as the "adopted son" of Chacho, so that when he is about to be murdered, Peñaloza says, "My son! How can it be that you would attack me, your father who so cared for you, in this way?"[93] What was apparently a factual relationship of guardian and dependent between Chacho and Francisco is extended in a way that gives the betrayal an additional significance. The son betraying the father was also the client betraying the caudillo. The Judaslike nature of the villain contrasted with the strong Christian character of the caudillo, who had time to make his peace with God:

> General Peñaloza
> had nothing more to say:
> "I ask your pardon, my God,
> now that I'm going to die."[94]

The Caudillos and the Supernatural

In part because of the tragic, inexplicable manner in which the caudillos died, the songs were loath to give up all hope. Thus, the very songs that publicized the deaths of Facundo and Chacho suggested that while the caudillos had been assassinated, the possibility still existed that they lived on or would return to life:

> They say that in Olta
> they have cut off Chacho's head;
> a party of bandits
> caught him by surprise.
> That's what they say,
> I don't know if it's true.
> Man is mortal, this is certain—
> but I don't know if I am persuaded
> unwilling do I search for condolence,
> Our general has died.[95]

Pondering the details of the death and the nature of the victim, the singer of this news was plagued by ambivalence, and vacillated before finally accepting that "our general has died." Such resignation notwithstanding, other songs were more optimistic, attributing to the caudillos, as popular culture was wont to do, immortality. In another version of this song, the death of Chacho is tempered by the reflection that "man is immortal," referring to the caudillo specifically and not humanity in general.[96]

Many songs also told of the possibility of Chacho's resurrection, which took on a precise political cast and served to threaten those who were responsible for his death:

They say that Chacho has died
I say that though this might be true
the *magogos* [Unitarians] better watch out
see if he doesn't rise up.[97]

Supernatural elements were much more important to the image of Facundo than to that of Chacho. The phenomena evoked as examples of Facundo's supernatural powers were many and varied (what General Paz called the "thousand absurdities of this type").[98] In terms of the doubts about his death, they were rooted in Facundo's reputation for invincibility, not only in war (and politics) but also in love and gambling—crucial aspects in a gaucho's definition of masculinity and leadership. In 1829, a gaucho from Córdoba told General Paz:

> Sir, you may think what you like, but years of experience has taught us that [Facundo] Quiroga is invincible in war, in games and (he added in a low voice) in love. There is no battle that he has lost; nor any game; (and again, in a low voice) nor any woman he has desired, that he has not won.[99]

A lengthy romance on Facundo's assassination also registered this quality. Hence, when the caudillo is warned about the plan to kill him,

Facundo thanks the youth
and asks him the question again,
but tells him "the man hasn't been born
who will kill Quiroga."[100]

Some stories indicated that Facundo's invincibility and legendary courage were of supernatural origin. As one tale explained, "some time ago," the inhabitants of Desamparados, in the Fertil Valley of San Juan, said that "whoever could look on the flower of the fig tree would be granted success in all of life's challenges." This "required much courage" because it only appeared once a year at midnight," and "monsters of every description guarded the flower and kept people from looking at it." Nevertheless, "Flora Quiroga, niece of the Tiger of Los Llanos, declared that her uncle was invincible because he had gazed on the fig tree flower."[101] These qualities made Facundo's assassins themselves doubt the reality of their feat:

We have killed Quiroga,
we have his corpse at our side,

but since Quiroga was a sorcerer,
it could be only a bluff.[102]

But how to explain, then, the death of this sorcerer, superwarrior, super-gambler, superlover? The connection that the romance made between the villain and the devil takes on another meaning here. If not even the Virgin Mary could stop Pérez because he was a "criminal possessed by the devil," then Facundo, too, would fall before such a figure.

Facundo and the Tiger

The association of Facundo with the tiger also placed the caudillo in the supernatural realm. In the provinces of the interior, Facundo was known as the "Tiger of Los Llanos," as a famous vidalita from 1829 called him. Composed by his opponents, the vidalita also referred to him as the "Tiger of Atiles," and the "infernal vandal" who steals and kills.[103] But what was the place of the tiger in the culture of the Llanos? What did the "tiger" mean for the gauchos?

O. J. French, an Englishman who traveled through La Rioja in the 1820s, noted the presence of tigers in the province, and made mention of certain "beliefs" and "traditions" that circulated about them. Crossing Los Llanos en route from Córdoba,

> we passed an algaroba tree marked with a cross, which, it is said, commemorates the death of a Franciscan friar, who, having pitched his bivouac for the night, was attacked by a jaguar, and pursued up the tree on which the memorial is carved.
>
> We were more than once disturbed, at night, after our fire was kindled, by the yells and low growls of these animals, which we afterwards tracked through the woods: on one occasion no less than five of them were seen about us.[104]

Tiger attacks and the threat of death in their claws was part of life in Los Llanos. The inhabitants of the region, however, thought that some people were immune to the tiger's violence. The English traveler learned that "the jaguar is believed by the natives not to attack a man who has tasted the animal's blood."[105] Those who could prevail in the battle between man and tiger, would thereafter never fall victim to the tigers.

This belief paralleled another about the "uturunco tiger." In a story that takes place in La Rioja, a peon and his patron had to confront a "man-eating tiger." The peon, a "man of guts," urged his patron to use the same tactic as the Franciscan friar in French's story. He told him

> to climb a tree to save himself, while he [the peon] took on the tiger, because he had the gift to become the uturunco tiger. (The uturunco tiger was a man who covered himself in a tiger skin . . . with which he would acquire an extraordinary strength. He would hide in the hills to rob and kill travelers, concealed in said skin and becoming so dexterous that the entire world would fear him.) [106]

Transformed into a tiger, the peon won the struggle, which led the story-teller to remark that the uturunco tigers "acquired such ferocity that they defeated even the other tigers." [107] Rather than tasting a tiger's blood, in this version the peon triumphed over the animal by acquiring its skin. This capacity to transform oneself into the uturunco was evaluated as a "gift," which made the protagonist different than other mortals. Who would have this gift? The peon was, the story made clear, a valiant man. French's version also emphasized valor, for who but a valiant man could kill a tiger and drink its blood?

An episode recorded by General Paz in his *Memorias* showed how these experiences and beliefs colored the gauchos' interpretation of Facundo's title, the "Tiger of Los Llanos." It concerned the military campaigns in Córdoba. The gauchos who made up the militias of the village of Ojo del Agua deserted en masse just before the battle of La Tablada, which would pit Paz against Facundo. According to Paz, the gauchos took this action because they believed that among Facundo's troop were 400 *capiangos,* a term and concept unknown to the Unitarian general until that moment. Inquiring into the phenomenon, Paz learned from the gauchos' commander that

> the capiangos, according to him, or as the militias understood it, were men who had the superhuman capacity to turn themselves, when they wanted, into the most ferocious tigers, and, well, you see . . . 400 of these fiends attacking the camp by night, would destroy [us] for good. [108]

The capiango was, in certain regions of Córdoba, the equivalent of the legend of the uturunco tiger. Thus, it is possible to suggest that this perception about Facundo's followers was contaminated and shaped by the capacities popular culture attributed to the leader. For the gauchos of the interior, Facundo was not only the "Tiger of Los Llanos" but the "Uturunco of Los Llanos," the "capiango." And these beliefs highlighted the exceptional qualities—particularly valor and courage—of certain individuals who were able to pass a regionally recognized test of heroism: triumphing over a tiger.

While the uturunco carried several positive associations (the valiant peon defeated the tiger and saved his patron), he had negative traits as well. Hiding in the hills to rob and kill, he sowed fear around the entire world. Such features, attributed to the uturunco in the legend, were those that Facundo's opponents emphasized in their famous vidalita. Their portrayal of Facundo was a weapon in a battle for the minds and imaginations of the gauchos, who would recognize the designation of "infernal vandal" not only from the legend but, possibly, in the behavior of Facundo as well. Just as the uturunco made the entire world fear him, Facundo wreaked terror with his personal violence. This violence is ubiquitous in most of Quiroga's stories. Even in stories that ended with a positive message for the gauchos and whose plot lead them into direct contact with the caudillo, the gauchos did not want to face Facundo because of the fear that his violence inspired.[109] And in some of the stories, Facundo's personal violence is, precisely, considered a consequence of being a tiger. For instance, one story that told of a gaucho fainting away because of a heavy-handed joke made by Facundo (who would later reward the gaucho), ended with the observation, "Even in play, the tiger's joke wounds!"[110]

An Oral Genealogy

The stories and songs that told of the exploits of Facundo and Chacho also suggested something of the relation between the two caudillos. One story recalled a famous episode that took place during the battle of Ciudadela (1831), in which the young Peñaloza fought as Facundo's subaltern. While fighting, Chacho took "a lance in the stomach, [then] fastened the wound with a poncho so that his intestines wouldn't fall out." When the battle was over, Peñaloza "laid face down peacefully and when [Facundo] Quiroga asked him what was wrong, he said it was nothing, only a scratch." Yet, "when the wound was examined and its gravity determined, seeing the tranquillity of the man, [Facundo] made him a *comandante*."[111] This story legitimated Chacho's status as a leader and caudillo in two ways. It highlighted his valor and courage, and it showed that the beginning of his political career had been sanctioned by Facundo.

Another story also considered the relationship between Facundo and Chacho. "In the year 1840 [*sic*] the governor of La Rioja committed many abuses," and in reaction to these injustices, Chacho began to challenge his authority. When Facundo found out, he called Chacho before him and asked "why he had done all those things against the government." Peñaloza answered "that he only eliminated the improper things that the governor had done." Then Quiroga proposed his own challenge to Chacho, which if met, would seal their friendship: an arm wrestle. Although the table beneath their arms gave way under their combined force, "neither of the two won." So Facundo proposed a second contest: "they began to fight [man to man], they fought until they were both naked and their backs sweated blood, and neither of the two won." Finally, Facundo "opened a case and took out two knives, and they aimed at each other, Quiroga telling the other not to lament, that if Chacho could kill him that he should do it, and that he [Facundo] would do the same. . . . [I]n the end, neither one wounded the other." Following this third challenge, "Quiroga told Chacho that now they were friends, and he rewarded the other with a position [in the militias] and an escort."[112]

This story was a local variation of tales in which the heroes must perform extraordinary tasks and overcome tests in order to be recognized and accepted as exceptional beings."[113] It confirmed that Facundo authorized the position of Chacho as caudillo, and thus delineated a genealogy of Chacho's legitimacy and authority. Because Facundo enjoyed a reputation as invincible and valiant, Chacho's position as his rival only added to the younger caudillo's status. And Facundo himself sanctioned one of Peñaloza's most notable characteristics: his willingness to struggle against injustice.

Why would his undergoing certain tests legitimate Chacho's position? These particular challenges both underscored the importance of specific values in that society and identified those characteristics that, in the eyes of the gauchos, all caudillos should have.[114] First, physical strength was obviously a positive attribute. Chacho's overcoming such tests in these stories seemed to be more than a projection of gauchos' expectations, since various testimonies confirmed that he was, in fact, of uncommon physical strength.[115] Similarly, in noting his dexterity with a knife, the stories proved Chacho's capacity to defend his honor and his masculinity.

Furthermore, in another story that also followed the structure of the tales of heroes, Chacho faced an additional test: "[Facundo] Quiroga tried to dominate his rival with his gaze, but the stare of Chacho proved the more penetrating"; and in it, Facundo "recognized the character" of Chacho.[116] As certain beliefs suggest, the gaze was culturally relevant for judging the character of persons as well as animals.[117] Various stories about Facundo mentioned in detail his manner of looking at people, implying that it was a recognized facet of the caudillo's personality.[118] In a society based on personal relations, the gaze was one way that clients could make contact with a leader and evaluate his disposition toward them, and vice versa. It would have allowed the caudillo to exercise his authority, too.

A RIOJAN UNITARIAN who first participated in provincial politics
in the 1830s, summarized Facundo's Federalism by explaining that
the caudillo had adopted "the red and black flag, symbol of
'Federation or Death,' synonym of 'Religion or Death,' which he exploited
before the vulgar fanaticism, against the whites, who he called heretics."[1]
This reflection on nineteenth-century politics exhibited a specific sensibility: ethnicity and certain attitudes toward religion—phenomena present
since colonial times and the 1820s, respectively—were crucial in the formation of local political identities.

Ethnic Composition of La Rioja

In 1778, a church register of the parishes of the diocese of Tucumán, a district consisting of the six provinces that today form northwestern Argentina, recorded a total population of 9,721 inhabitants in La Rioja, of which
26 percent were considered either Spaniards or foreigners, 54 percent were
indigenous, and 20 percent were mulattoes (see table 13).[2] Thus, La Rioja
had one of the highest percentages of indigenous people in a diocese where
native peoples, at 36 percent, were far from the majority. The largest group
in the diocese of Tucumán was "mulatto," a generic denomination that
not only included individuals produced by the union between blacks and
whites but also those with mixed African, European, and indigenous
blood, such as the zambos or quadroons. This group, also referred to as
"people of color," accounted for 45 percent of the total population of the
diocese—a figure that encompassed areas, such as the contemporary prov-

TABLE 13   Ethnic Composition of La Rioja's Population 1778–1814

	1778	1795	1814
Spaniards and Foreigners	2,627 (26%)	3,748 (26%)	4,857 (34.2%)
Indians	5,200 (54%)	3,850 (27%)	3,178 (22.6%)
People of Color	1,894 (20%)	6,633 (47%)	6,093 (43.2%)
Total	9,721	14,231	14,095

Sources: Guzmán, "Los Mulatos-Mestizos," charts 1, 3; and *Primer Censo Nacional,* 415.

inces of Tucumán and Catamarca, where the population of color reached 64 percent and 51 percent, respectively. The ethnic composition of La Rioja in 1778, then, was the reverse of what it was in most of the provinces that in the next century, would form the northwest of Argentina.[3]

The 1795 church register of La Rioja would mark an increase in the population and a significant change in the ethnic makeup of the province, which now paralleled the ethnic makeup of the other provinces of the northwest. The total population of La Rioja in 1795 was 14,231, of which 26 percent were Spaniards. The indigenous population, meanwhile, decreased to 27 percent, and those of African descent increased to 47 percent.[4] The absolute and relative increase in the population of color was principally a result of the migration of the free population from other provinces to La Rioja. Most of the migrants moved to the Llanos, a region experiencing a modest but steady growth in cattle ranching, where much of the land was still vacant.[5]

A census completed by one of the first revolutionary governments in 1814 consistently reinforced the data for 1795. The 1814 census revealed a total population of 14,095, almost the same as in 1795. By this time, the Spaniards constituted 34.2 percent of the inhabitants, the indigenous population had decreased to 22.6 percent, and the population of color, although reduced, continued to be the largest group with 43.2 percent.[6] The population of color consisted primarily of the free population of color, which accounted for 36.6 percent of the total population of the province, and slaves, who comprised 7.6 percent. In 1814, then, the largest bloc within the lower classes was formed by the population of color and, to a lesser degree, indigenous people. This ethnic composition dated at least from 1795.

Due to the lack of adequate sources, it has been impossible to follow the evolution of the ethnic makeup of the province throughout the nineteenth century. As an official report prepared by the surgeon general of the province in 1877 suggests, however, the ethnic groups present in the colonial censuses were still quite visible in La Rioja in the late 1870s. According to the report, Riojan society consisted of three groups: "the white race, that is the wealthiest"; "the mestiza race of indigenous origins, that is the largest"; and "the mestiza race of African origins, that is smaller [than the previous one] in number of people."[7] This impressionistic assessment implies that as late as 1877, race was used as one of the main criterion to think about Riojan society. Yet, it also points to two other factors worth considering: first, it seems that people of Indian descent now formed the majority; and second, it appears that there was an important amount of mestization going on in La Rioja. In this respect, it is essential to clarify the use of terms such as "whites," "people of Spanish origins," "blacks," or "Indians." Following categories established by the colonial administration—or the language and conventions used in Riojan society during the late eighteenth and nineteenth centuries, that is—the terms refer to notional white, black, or Indian people, and not people of purely European, African, or Indian ancestries. As an Englishman who visited the Llanos in the 1820s could observe, a well-to-do estanciero (cattle ranchers) who hosted him "had lost little of his Spanish blood in intermixture with the Indian."[8]

Whites and Blacks

The ethnic makeup of the province had a serious impact on local social relations and culture. Indeed, the large presence of people of African descent shaped some of the religious practices. For example, a copy was made of the statue of the patron saint of La Rioja, San Nicolas de Bari, yet both the old and the new figures were worshiped in the main church. The older statue, dating from the seventeenth century, was still considered the "true" and "miraculous" one, however. This saint's face was "dark" or "bronze," and hence, he was called "the black San Nicolas." The more recent statue was not quite as "miraculous," and since this saint's face was white, he was referred to as "the white San Nicolas."[9]

The denominations of both statues were also related to the practices they had generated. Different groups of parishioners paid homage to each statue of the saint, and the ceremonies in their honor were carried out on different days. The holiday in honor of the white San Nicolas, held on December 6, was celebrated only by "the upper classes with the assistance of the authorities." In contrast, the holiday paying tribute to the black San Nicolas was on December 31, and although the authorities never stopped associating themselves with it, this celebration was considered "genuinely popular" because of the participation of the "common people and the blacks"; as well, the ceremonies surrounding this date had an important indigenous component, which we will analyze further below.[10]

The ethnic composition of the province also shaped the identities of the political parties that contended for power from independence until the consolidation of the national state. This was revealed in the jargon used in everyday political life to refer to the Unitarians and Federalists. At the beginning of 1863, the Unitarian elite of Famatina denounced the followers of Peñaloza in that department because they wanted "to sink their dagger in the heart of a **Unitarian** soldier or of a **white,** as they call us."[11] Similarly, in 1868, a newcomer to the Federalist Party who tried to win the confidence of one of the leaders of the montonera, conceived of the characteristics of the Unitarians and Federalists in La Rioja in the following terms: "They are *whites* . . . but not us, because we are *blacks,* montoneros and bandits."[12]

Ethnicity was present in the interpretations of the history of political violence in the province, too. During the 1860s, when party struggles continued to claim victims from the local elite, one of its members charged that it had been first Facundo, then Tomas Brizuela, and finally Chacho who had perpetuated "hatred and divisions between castes."[13] In other words, the struggle between Unitarians and Federalists in La Rioja lent itself to interpretations that likened the conflict to a caste war. According to this view, the relationship between ethnicity and political identities began to emerge during the time of Facundo, in the early 1820s. One memorialist, who as a child had seen his family succumb to the power of Quiroga, asserted that during the civil wars, Facundo "began to incite the slaves to rebel against their masters," converting them into "prosecutors" of their old owners.[14] This commentary spotlights, in an exaggerated manner, the threat posed to the elite of a caste society by the politicization and mobilization of the popular sectors. The sense of vulnerability becomes clearer if we bear in mind the elites' perception of the nature of the popular classes. A Englishman who visited La Rioja in the 1820s distinguished between "Creoles" and Indians, and his portrayal of the former was particularly negative. In the traveler's opinion, the daily life of "the Creoles" was, above all, associated with "brutality" and their daily disputes, com-

pounded by alcohol, always ended in acts "of blood." This was a consequence, as "was said" in this province, of the "mix" between Indian and
mulatto that produced "a cruel and vengeful character," attributes that the
traveler believed he could confirm with his observations.[15]

One of the most interesting aspects that the visitor associated with
people of color was their supposedly "vengeful" character, which in the
words of the memorialist already cited meant that the slaves, incited by
Facundo, had been transformed into "prosecutors" of their masters. These
comments articulated the change that the elite perceived in traditional social hierarchies: the new social status accorded the gauchos in their role as
clients. In this respect, a story that circulated in the Llanos with Facundo
as its protagonist reveals one of the ways the relation between ethnicity
and politics was represented in the oral culture of the province, and the
role the figure of the caudillo had in the construction of Federalism. The
caudillo, according to the story, had "a servant who was very black and
with dense, curly hair ('motoso')," and who in his daily work, used to pass
in front of "a house of distinguished families." One day, a girl from this
family called him "my little calf" and asked, "Little black one, when will
we marry? And [she also made] some jokes about how the black talked."
This bothered the servant, and as it had happened a number of times, he
decided to tell Facundo. Then,

> Quiroga with his black . . . marched to the house of the girl [and]
> asked her if it was true that she wanted to marry his black, to which
> the girl replied no and that what she said [to the servant] was only a
> joke. . . . [But] the Tiger of Los Llanos . . . [i]mposing his ferocity,
> told her "Choose: you marry my little black or I will cut off your
> head," and the girl in the midst of a flood of tears and desperation,
> had to submit to the caprice of God.[16]

In this story, which has ambiguities that suggest it circulated among the
wealthy as well as the gauchos,[17] Facundo forces and sanctions an inter-
ethnic marriage between blacks and whites, which in La Rioja was exceptional and, apparently, considered anathema by the local elite. In 1877, in
the report cited above, the surgeon general of the province noted that "the
white race . . . is the one with more unions among its members" ("*es la
que más se une entre sí*"), and it is "truly unique to find two white individuals who are not relatives at least two or three times," which was due to
the fact that in most families, "the marriage between relatives is a deeply

rooted tradition."[18] Therefore, in the story, the Federalist caudillo breaks a strong tradition among the local elite of endogamy, subverting one of the fundamental norms for the preservation of ethnic differentiation and racial subordination in a caste society. Besides corrupting ethnic relations, his action, with its clear partisan connotation, once again sanctions patriarchy: it is the father of all Riojans who chooses the girl's mate.

From the point of view of the groups that struggled to maintain their purity of blood, the tale plainly shows the subversive character of the caudillo's relation with his clients and their incorporation into political disputes. And from the point of view of the clients, the story of the "the little calf of Quiroga" commented on some of the forms that Federalism and clientalism (in the form of protection) could take in a caste society. On the one hand, there was a limit to the contempt that those who served could be subjected to by those who displayed racial purity; on the other, the intervention of the Federalist caudillo turns the world upside down and hints at the fall of a barrier, one that was acknowledged in both high and popular culture. In his *Recuerdos de Provincia,* Sarmiento told the story of how he expelled one of his students from the school because "he stubbornly insisted on marrying a beautiful girl, who was white."[19] And one of many songs that referred to the presence of blacks in Riojana society claimed:

> A black must fall in love
> with a girl of his color.
> If he falls in love with a white
> he'll waste time and love.[20]

But the role that the story attributes to the Federalist caudillo may have been more than a simple product of gaucho imagination. It seems to have been fed by the behavior of Facundo, who in his incursions into San Juan, delighted in altering the manners and norms that society considered appropriate for each group. On one occasion, he dressed a black as a priest and made him walk around the city. Another time, Facundo chatted "affectionately" with a black woman seated by his side, "while the priests and nobles of the city were left standing up, since no one said a word to them, or allowed them to leave."[21] Facundo's behavior was actually part of an apparently widespread practice among other Federalist caudillos, who also promoted activities that symbolically turned the social order upside down, and thus, reminded others of the importance of the followers in postindependence Argentina. Rosas, for one, liked to dress two buffoons as a general and bishop, respectively, and parade them through the streets of Buenos Aires.[22]

The Indians

As we have seen, Indians accounted for 26.6 percent of the province of La Rioja's population according to the 1814 census, a fact that certainly shaped various political conflicts. For instance, the inhabitants of the Indian villages in the departments of Famatina and Arauco, as was also previously noted, were a significant force among the Federalist rebels of the 1860s. This contrasted with the ethnic composition of the Unitarians, and consequently, attached a different connotation to that political identity. This phenomenon did not escape the actors' attention, especially the Unitarians. Thus, besides the generic term "gaucho" that the Unitarians applied to those who joined the Federalist rebels, they were often more specific, speaking of "the Indians of Vichigasta," "the Indians of Machigasta," or "the Indians of Arauco."[23] In the same manner, Sarmiento referred to the violence of the montoneros as "Indian revenges"; and more precisely, he considered the rebellions of Chacho to be "peasant Indian movements."[24]

Although there was a significant amount of mestization, reflected in the fact that almost no one in La Rioja in the second half of the nineteenth century spoke Quechua, there were nevertheless institutions, rituals, and oral traditions that suggest the existence of an "Indian" identity in the province. In this respect, the celebrations that began on December 31—and that even today are still the most important religious and public rituals in the province—may be taken as one of the representations of the history of Spanish-Indian relations and the place of the latter in Riojan society. According to oral traditions that continued to circulate in the nineteenth century, during the conquest, San Nicolas de Bari traversed the Riojan region and converted the caciques of the local tribes to Christianity. The saint and caciques, however, confronted a revolt by Indians who opposed conversion. This was forestalled by the appearance of the child Jesus, who with his divine power managed to get the rebels to accept the new religion. In gratitude for such timely help, the saint kissed his feet. After this miraculous encounter between the saint and the child Jesus, the "Mayor of the World," Jesus vanished into thin air.[25]

A ritual "encounter" between the saint and the "Child Mayor" was performed each year on December 31, and the festivities lasted until the third of January. On December 31, the black Saint Nicholas was brought from the main church and carried in procession until he met with the statue of the Child Mayor, who was also led in procession from the house of the family that had been charged with its care. The "meeting" happened in front of the cabildo, when the statue of the saint bowed before the Mayor of the World.

These celebrations were handled by two *cofradías* (religious brotherhoods). The cofradía of "the alfereces," led by the "Main Alferez," was in charge of taking San Nicolas out of the main church and carrying him to the encounter. The cofradía of the *ayllis,* headed by its leader, "the Inca," was responsible for carrying the statue of the Child Mayor and singing religious songs in Quechua. According to some witnesses that attended the celebrations during the second half of the nineteenth century, the ayllis did not understand the songs and repeated them mechanically since, like most of the Indians of the province, by that time they only spoke Spanish.

After the encounter in front of the cabildo, the Inca asked the governor for permission (as their ancestors had done with the mayor in colonial times) to begin the festivities that would end three days later, when San Nicolas and the Child Mayor would take their leave until the following year.

The annual ceremony of December 31 marked the day that the mayors were reconfirmed during the colonial period. The Inca, as leader of the indigenous people, reaffirmed the authority of the Spanish and the Indians' acceptance of their religion, paying homage to the saint and the Mayor of the World, from whom the local mayor, and later the governor, would derive their legitimacy.

These popular celebrations not only legitimated social agreements but also served as a reminder of the differences between the descendants of the conquerors and the indigenous people, thus sustaining the identity of both groups. It is interesting to note that during the celebrations, it was the Inca who represented the chief authority of the Indians of La Rioja.[26] Moreover, at least since the end of the eighteenth century, the Inca was also considered to be an ethnic authority by the Indians of several other provinces, which today form northwestern Argentina.[27] The image of the Inca as leader of the indigenous people and "the lower classes or commoners" was still present in nineteenth century La Rioja not only in the celebration of the encounter but also in oral traditions that, at least in certain respects, emphasized their opposition to and conflict with the descendants of the Spaniards. The image of the ancient kings of Cuzco had been incorporated into the legends "about the hills of Famatina," celebrated by the local people for the supposed mineral riches that they contained. One Riojan notable who was a descendant of the conquerors observed in 1868 that some oral traditions of the first half of the nineteenth century assured that "the souls of the Incas and their first caciques sacrificed by the Spaniards . . . wandered through the hills of Famatina waiting for the hour of *the great emancipation.*"[28] The villagers who circulated these versions in the nineteenth century "in order to confirm these traditions," said that during the insurrection of Tupac Amaru, "the hills of Famatina never stopped thundering and shaking, calling for his vassals," which they interpreted as a call "for the liberty of their race."[29] The Inca was the chief authority, then, of an "indigenous identity" constructed, at least in part, in opposition to the Spaniards and their descendants.

The ethnic dimension of party identities was a relevant aspect of politics in other provinces as well. In Sarmiento's *Recuerdos de Provincia,* the castes tended to be associated with Federalism, an association that was compounded by perceptions of racial tensions and deviance, thus constructing the Federalist masses as "dangerous classes." Sarmiento told the story of a slave, owned by the Mallea family, who "rebelled" against her masters, denounced them "for Unitarians," and informed the Federalists where her owners had hidden their money, which was then taken by political rivals. He also remembered "Piojito," a mulatto who belonged to the Cabrera family, who was "brave" and "tenacious" yet also "sly," and who finally deserted from Facundo's montonera, later to be shot for his crime. But probably, nobody embodied better those Federalists "from the most abject classes of the society" than "the Indian Sayavedra," one of the last descendants of the Huarpes from the barrio of Puyuta, who, drunk, was stabbed to death in a ramble. Years earlier, Sarmiento said, Sayavedra had "almost lanced me in the Plaza of San Juan, calling me savage [Unitarian]."[30]

The very fact that Federalism could so openly identify itself with the castes, as in the case of La Rioja, may explain the capacity of this party to mobilize the lower classes. The ethnic dimension of party identities may also help to clarify the origins of some of the exclusionary practices of the Unitarians or "the whites," among whom colonial values seemed to count more than modern, liberal ideology: in a society so sensitive to race, the background of the lower classes was a sufficient basis for their exclusion. In 1870, as president of the republic, Sarmiento censured the "imprudent" behavior of his Santa Fe party fellows and those from other provinces of the interior:

> The liberal party of Santa Fe . . . had been at the point of being torn apart; but it remained beneath the rancor of the *gaucho plebe,* whom they provoked with *caste* scorn. This also occurred in San Juan and wherever *liberalism* and decency are synonymous with learned, *white* and propertied classes. . . .
>
> We will see if they put one society against the other again and bring us war and assassination.[31]

Federalism and "Christianity"

One night in 1867, when the inhabitants of Tilimuqui, an Indian village in the valley of Famatina, were celebrating a novena in honor of the Virgin of Rosario, they received an unexpected visit from Felipe Varela. The Federalist caudillo, at the time in rebellion against the national government, knelt before the Virgin and handed her his colonel stripes as he made the sign of the cross. Even today, when the Virgin is led in procession, the stripes illuminate her mantle, and so, devotees call her "the Federalist Virgin."[32] The episode and its notable persistence in popular memory highlight the importance of the relationship between Catholicism and Federalism in popular political culture.

The association between Catholicism and Federalism began in the 1820s. Between 1821 and 1824, the government of the province of Buenos Aires, led by Minister Bernardino Rivadavia, implemented political, educational, and clerical reforms. The clerical reforms included a declaration of the freedom of worship, the elimination of church legal immunities, and the expropriation of the property of the regular orders. These reforms were strongly resisted by many members of the church along with the most conservative sectors of the political opposition.[33]

The liberal policies found followers in some provinces of the interior, however. The most notorious example was that of San Juan. The Unitarian Party there decreed the "Carta de Mayo" in 1825, abolishing church legal immunities and declaring freedom of worship.[34] This generated strong resistance in the province. According to Unitarian Governor Salvador María del Carril, who considered himself "a Christian but not as ignorant as the Spaniards wanted us to be," the reforms did not conflict with "the religion that is good for the people and the individuals," but only intended to bring to the province "the lights" and "the knowledge of the rights of each one."[35] In this young liberal's view, only the clergy resisted the reforms because "the naive belief of the people and their ignorance make their fortune." Thus, del Carril believed that the label of "heretics" was being manipulatively applied to him and his party fellows by priests who were fearful of losing their privileges.[36]

During the early stage of the conflict in San Juan, Facundo, who had already emerged as the most powerful man in the interior, remained neutral, despite the requests for support by members of both parties. Yet, from 1826 on, the defense of Catholicism came to be a key motive behind Facundo's intervention in the civil wars. One of his missions was, as Facundo himself proclaimed, to stop the attacks on "the Catholic Apostolic Roman Religion, which our lord Jesus Christ constructed at the cost of much bitterness."[37] To fulfill his goal, he relied on his gaucho followers, whom he called "my valiant defenders of church legal immunities [*fueros*]," and declared that with "divine providence" they would allow him to "mete appropriate punishment to the ministers of impiety."[38]

This defense of Catholicism became part of the resistance of the interior provinces against the new national government, which in 1826, with Rivadavia as president and del Carril as a minister, had sanctioned a Unitarian constitution that limited provincial political autonomy, and as the provincials understood it, also affected their material interests. As one Riojan friar contended, the clerical reforms of the national government brought "impiety" to La Rioja, while the other policies were intended "to bleed our country and leave us to perish as we toil for the happiness of others"—in other words, Buenos Aires wanted to exploit the province for its own benefit.[39] Nevertheless, the friar had no doubt that "God will help us to defend his sacred religion and our beloved province from the ambitions and destructive projects of the president of the republic."[40] By the mid-1820s, then, the struggle in defense of Catholicism was associated with the defense of political autonomy, the interests of the province of La Rioja, and the opposition to Buenos Aires, connections that also became part of popular political culture and persisted into the 1860s.

The language that the Riojan friar and Facundo used to describe the conflict between Unitarians and Federalists was also present in a pamphlet that was dated in San Juan, but reprinted and read throughout the provinces of the interior in January 1827. This pamphlet reproduced a personal letter that Facundo had allegedly sent to a friend from the city of Mendoza in which he explained the reasons for his opposition to the Unitarian government.[41]

The text contained elements confirming certain perceptions that the popular classes had about Facundo (in the letter, the caudillo says, "They fear and love me at the same time"), suggesting that the gauchos were part of the public to which this communication was directed. The pamphlet appealed to the religious culture of the potential readers and their audience. Asterisks at the end of a few paragraphs of the letter referred to footnotes that, as the title of the pamphlet indicated, "were given to the public . . . for their great importance." The footnotes introduced parallels of biblical origin to interpret and comment on what Facundo narrated and explained in his letter. But these parallels also appealed to the political culture of the audience. The religious imagery contained in the pamphlet had been used during independence by priests and lay patriots to condemn the Spanish domination and legitimize the struggle for freedom. Now, the rhetoric of independence was used to legitimize the Federalist cause in the 1820s.[42]

In this letter, Facundo explained that "I saw myself forced to take the sword to sustain the rights of the province [of La Rioja]." The letter then told of an extraordinary feat that many surely found difficult to believe. According to Facundo, at the beginning of his campaign he had only "four" followers, but soon found himself "surrounded by more than one thousand volunteers," which of course "filled him with pride." Lest this unusual occurrence arouse the suspicion of cynics, the letter offered proof: "Don Augustin Lec," a neighbor of Mendoza, had been an "eyewitness" to the event. The way the letter narrated events and offered evidence reproduced the methodology that the church and believers normally used to confirm the occurrence of miracles. The footnote to this paragraph hinted at divine intervention in the events and introduced a significant parallel:

> It appears similar to Moses, when to punish the idolatry of the people said: . . . those who are of God gather around me, and they joined around him the sons of Levi and because of that merit the priesthood was given to his tribe. . . . Also to Matatias, father of the Maccabees, that to defend his religion and homeland against the fierce Antioch exclaimed: "All those that have zeal for the law, follow me.[43]

Facundo defended religion, like Moses and the sons of Levi, and like Matatias had defended his homeland, the caudillo defended his province. But this biblical parallel had a political connotation. A decade earlier, during independence, the patriots had been encouraged to defend "the great cause of América" and die rather than "see the extermination of their homeland, as the religious Maccabees had done."[44] And General Belgrano, one of the founding fathers of the new nation who had defeated the Spaniards in the battlefield, had been depicted as "a hero . . . like the most illustrious of the Maccabees."[45] Thus, the letter also placed Facundo and Federalism in the revolutionary tradition of the new nation.

Furthermore, Facundo continued in his letter, it was because of the justice of their cause that he had no fear "of the power of the so-called Unitarian president," whose "iniquitous project" was *to enslave the provinces* and make them cry tied to the carriage of Rivadavia . . . and also to do away with *the religion of Jesus Christ*." And if it was not just so, the caudillo asked, "*what does this needless freedom of religion and the elimination of the regular [orders] mean?*[46] In this way was the resistance against the Unitarian constitution and clerical reforms extended geographically and politically. It was no longer only La Rioja that rose up to defend its religion and political rights; now, all of the provinces of the interior stood against Buenos Aires. The idea of enslaved territories tied to the carriage of an evil personality referred to an obvious biblical story that had been used during independence. In the 1810s, the 300 years of Spanish domination had been associated with the 400 years of the enslavement of the Israelis under "the heavy-handed domination of the Pharaoh and the Egyptians."[47] As the king of Spain before, it was the Unitarian president who now was associated with the Pharaoh, the biblical archetype of tyrannical power. Thus, the relation between Buenos Aires and the provinces, it was suggested, was of an exploitative, quasi-colonial nature, an idea that in the 1850s would be fully articulated in the language of political economy by intellectuals affiliated with Federalism, like Juan B. Alberdi and Olegario Andrade.[48]

Facundo finally bid farewell to his friend from Mendoza, swearing to him "to submit the tribute of [his] existence before seeing the triumph of *impiety*," which was not going to happen "because even with his weakest arm God can punish the arrogance of those who do not honor him as they should."[49] Here, Facundo included himself in the representations of God and the saints in popular culture. Both exercised justice and "materially" punished mortals with their "arm" or "hand." In this case, it was suggested, Facundo was God's arm.

This type of agitation had concrete effects on the politicization and mobilization of the popular classes, and priests were instrumental in this respect. Pedro Ignacio de Castro Barros, a Riojan priest and prominent political figure in the interior since independence, who in his correspondence with Facundo congratulated the caudillo for both "the defense of our holy religion and our freedom" and confessed that the "letter to the friend of Mendoza had electrified his heart," was particularly active in socializing these ideas with believers.[50] In *Recuerdos de Provincia,* Sarmiento remembered that when Castro Barros passed through San Juan, his preaching "against the impious and heretics . . . inflamed the popular passions against Rivadavia and the reform, . . . and gave credit to bandits like [Facundo] Quiroga and others, whom he called the Maccabees."[51] General José María Paz also remembered that the government of Rivadavia was opposed by "almost all the governments of the interior provinces," which "were supported by the popular masses."[52] According to the Unitarian general, the clerical reforms had served as an excuse "to the followers of the said Federalist Party to fanaticize the multitude and incite it to wage a religious war against us." "This fanaticism," said Paz in language that closely reproduced that used by his rivals, "wanted to portray us as impious, incredulous, and persecutors of the religion of Jesus Christ."[53]

In fact, it was the tangible behavior of the Unitarians that alienated the gauchos from Unitarianism and facilitated their identification with Federalism. This was evident, for example, in an act that occurred while Paz governed the province of Córdoba. During the war against Facundo, Paz had the "sacred vessels and other pieces" of silver that were held in the Córdoban churches appraised in hopes of selling them off to finance part of the conflict.[54] It was communicated to him that he could "collect" 40,000 pesos, and so, he decided to confiscate the silver of the province's churches. But the result was disappointing: apparently, the churches only had 10 percent of what the Unitarian general had been told. The amount that had been collected did not solve his problems. Hence, he had all the silver returned to the churches because, according to Paz, "the hatred of the measure in a province so religious like Córdoba" would be counterproductive. Paz's actions did not go unnoticed, however. In their religious zeal, his rivals later used this episode "in the pamphlets," telling his followers that

Paz had "laid bare and sacked the churches."[55] In another move, Paz made it known that he planned to completely suppress many holy days, which in Córdoba, were "religiously" guarded and "whose observance damaged industry and favored idleness and vice."[56] Such a law would not only attack the practical forms religion took for the popular classes, and the central moments and spaces in their social life, but it would simultaneously increase the number of days they had to work as well.[57] And if the Unitarian government did not manage to implement the law, it was only because of the staunch opposition of the clergy, who, we can infer, did not encounter great difficulties in fomenting resistance among the believers.

The association between Federalism and Catholicism that began in the 1820s had a lasting impact on party struggles and occupied a critical place in the popular political culture of the nineteenth century. In this respect, the figure of Facundo in popular culture is telling. As we have already seen in "the letter to the friend of Mendoza," the caudillo was a hero of Catholicism; likewise, as mentioned earlier as well, the romance and "plot" that lamented Facundo's assassination along with their several oral versions also projected this image of him up to the beginning of the twentieth century. The songs confronted the villain Santos Pérez with Facundo, the hero, under conditions defined in terms of their relation to religion. While Pérez was a "diabolical" criminal that boasted, "I know of no God," Facundo asked the villain to let him confess before dying, but was denied permission, confirming the nature of the villain.[58]

In the decades following the 1820s, the association between Federalism and Catholicism was fed by the Rosista politicization. As we have seen, the gauchos of the interior provinces were familiar with the figure of Rosas, who was considered one of the heroes of Federalism. But in contrast to the Federalist caudillos of the interior, Rosas and his family were integrated into the daily Catholic liturgy of the provinces, as they had been in Buenos Aires.[59] Popular songs also associated the Porteño caudillo with Catholicism and its defense. In one song from the period of the conflict with the coalition of the North, the singer explained that the Unitarians were "treacherous rivals" and "infernal plagues [who] try to devour our precious religion," and suggested, "It is time to die for Rosas."[60] Another song narrated how the "Unitarian traitors" had intended to kill the caudillo, but said that there was nothing to fear since "Rosas was helped by Divine Providence."[61]

Masons and Christians

The final stage of nation-state formation and corresponding outbreak of conflict between the parties, especially during the 1860s, led to a new manifestation of the relation between political identities and religion. This was a consequence of new experiences that were consistent with what had been incorporated into popular political culture since the 1820s. In this respect, an episode that occurred in the department of Arauco in April 1862, during the Chacho's first rebellion against the national government, is revealing. When passing through this department, Colonel José Miguel Arredondo observed, once again, that the villages were almost deserted, barely inhabited by women and children. The men "had left for the mountains" to join the rebels. In response, Arredondo threatened to set fire to the houses if the remaining women did not convince the men to surrender to the national troops. The threat had no effect, and Arredondo burned almost all of Mazan and the Indian village of Aymogasta.[62] Captain Mayer, chief of the Unitarian patrol that set the villages on fire, was particularly ruthless with some of his victims. When he burned the home of Severo Chumbita in Aymogasta, he did not allow the wife of this Federalist caudillo to take out the statue of San José that the family cared for in its adobe hut. This scenario was repeated in other residences.[63]

Barely a week after the fires, Mayer and his soldiers were attacked by a group of gauchos, who killed the Unitarian officer. Some of these gauchos claimed that Mayer had been reached "by the finger of God" and his death was a result of "divine punishment," while other villagers were convinced that his "disastrous end was the visible punishment of San José, who had been burned in the house of Chumbita."[64] In the gauchos' practical notion of religion, God and the saints performed concrete actions, such as extending their "arms," "hands," or "fingers" to reward or punish, even during party struggles.[65]

After this episode, the partisan conflict assumed the character of a religious war. The news of the fire in the villages, where "the most miraculous saints of the area had perished," spread through the entire province. At the end of May 1862, when the rebels surrounded Arredondo and his troops in the city of La Rioja, the gauchos accompanied their attack with the cry, *"Death to the arsonists, death to the heretics.*[66] As Navarro Ocampo remarked, "The religious fanaticism of the masses in La Rioja was more pronounced than in any other province of the interior," so that "to burn a Riojano gaucho, his guardian saint would place in his hands the flag of **Religion or death** with which [Facundo] Quiroga, his God on earth" had conquered the interior.[67] Thus, the Unitarian repression had given the gauchos "a flag, not only of the national government [of the Argentine Confederation] but also that of General Peñaloza defending La Rioja . . . against the enemies of their religious beliefs."[68] As in the 1820s, the defense of the province was linked to the defense of Catholicism, and again, the Federalist caudillo had a prominent role. As a song, composed after the death of Chacho, went:

> Without patria [province] there is no religion,
> without religion there is no patria,
> without Peñaloza, there is no opinion,
> everything will be a disgrace.[69]

The liberal policies of the Unitarians in the interior reactivated, once again, the clergy's mistrust of that party, and the predicament of local priests would provide the gauchos with a language that the Federalist identity and popular experience easily incorporated into the struggle. While governor of San Juan, Sarmiento passed a law in 1862 that allocated ecclesiastical funds to public works and education, and confiscated a chaplaincy to found a school for agriculture. These measures obviously irritated the local clergy. One priest "declared from the pulpit that the governor was a mason" and that "all the masons were disciples of the devil."[70] Sarmiento would say later that those priests, who also fed other rumors that "spread through the common folk," were the "protégés of the old party of Rosas."[71]

Besides discrediting Sarmiento, the language that the cleric used in his attack drew from the Federalist tradition of the Rosas period.[72] At the same time, it also revealed that the sermons of the priests of San Juan responded to the anxiety generated in the church in general by the influence of the Masonic lodges and the attraction they exercised among the political elite, which only intensified during the second half of the nineteenth century.[73] For the gauchos, however, the term "mason" did not necessarily refer to those who belonged to a lodge but was used imprecisely as a synonym for "Protestant," "heretic," or "impious"—all of which were considered to be the enemy of Catholicism or to have a secular attitude toward religion, which ultimately was the same thing.[74] Moreover, the word "mason" was also associated with "foreigner." In the gauchos' ex-

perience, Protestants (or heretics) were foreigners, and the European immigrants who came to Argentina at this time had an important role in the
proliferation of lodges, which the priests did not omit mentioning to their
flock.[75] On the other hand, the fact that the masons were perceived as enemies of religion meant that they were also easily associated with the devil
and witchcraft, accentuating the hostility and distrust of the believers.[76]

The concerns and language of the local clergy would be integrated into
popular political culture and party struggles. At the end of 1862, a montonera from Los Llanos intercepted some San Juan merchants who were
traveling to the city of La Rioja. On detaining them, one of the gauchos
made his disgust known, asserting that during the first rebellion of Chacho
(a few months earlier), the inhabitants of the city of San Juan had supported "the Porteños and the liberals." Then, Juan Gabriel Pueblas, leader
of the rebels and a confidant of Chacho, asked them

> if they were **Christians** or **Masons** . . . [and] immediately told them
> he would reunite his people to come to San Juan **to fight in defense
> of the Christian religion.** . . . And that they should tell the gover-
> nor of San Juan [Sarmiento] and all foreigners . . . that he [Pueblas]
> would come later.[77]

Puebla's affirmation reappeared in other conflicts in the second half of
the nineteenth century, some of which would occur when Unitarianism
and Federalism had already disappeared as parties, and therefore, the religious question would no longer be associated, explicitly at least, with these
identities. It is interesting to review the geographic span, chronology, and
languages of these events, some of which have been ignored up until now
by historians, because they place the conflicts of the 1860s in the interior
provinces within a broader perspective. In 1868, in Santa Fe, the Indians
of the old reducción of Sauce and "the great majority of the city rose up to
the cry of: Down to the masons!" during an attempt to depose liberal Governor Nicasio Oroño. The governor, nicknamed "little Rivadavia," had
established civil marriage and had tried to expropriate the convent of San
Lorenzo to start an agricultural school, measures that were preceded by
the foundation of a Masonic lodge.[78]

This conflict was repeated in the province of Buenos Aires in 1872. In
the village of Tandil, during a rebellion that lasted barely a day, gauchos
exclaimed, "Long live religion! Death to the masons! Kill the gringos and
Basques," and thirty-seven Basques, Italians, and English did indeed fall

victim.[79] The rebels alleged that the foreigners ("gringos") "stole work from Argentines" and "exploited the country." Moreover, the foreigners were "masons [that] are a bad society that has no religion."[80] The gauchos maintained that they had killed the immigrants not on their own initiative but in compliance with the orders of Geronimo de Solané, a healer recently arrived to Tandil who was known by the name "Tata Dios" (literally, "Father God"). According to the gaucho who led the rebellion and was the priest's assistant, Solané "was a man that God had sent to the earth to represent him and punish the bad Christians. . . . [H]e had come to protect and bring happiness to the Argentines."[81] As studies on the event would later indicate, the Tandil massacre had millenarian qualities and was fed by a bitter xenophobia.[82]

One notable aspect of this event was the role that popular political traditions associated with Federalism had in a movement that was supposed to defend religion against masons and foreigners, a question that has been largely ignored by the studies on the massacre. In the first place, one gaucho believed that the rebellion had the objective of "liberating religion," and another was convinced that the massacre would allow the rebels "to be Christians"—contentions that drew these gauchos close to the leader of the Federalist montonera who, ten years earlier in the Llanos of La Rioja, had said they were fighting against the "masons" and "foreigners," and "in defense of Christianity."[83]

The Federalist connotation of such religious statements was even more evident in the distinctive symbol that the gauchos used to identify themselves during the rebellion. The leader had handed out red ribbons to the rebels, the symbol par excellence of Federalism among the popular classes since the 1820s, especially during periods of mobilization. In the words of one gaucho, they used the red ribbon "as a sign that they belonged to the [Christian] religion." And it was probably the sanctity of the cause they defended that gave supernatural powers to this Federalist symbol since, as the rebel leader had told them, "they would fight for that symbol until they win or die, but they would not die because the ribbon would protect them from bullets."[84]

In addition, some of the information contained in the studies on the event suggest that the gauchos also related the defense of Christianity with Federalism on an institutional level. As one rebel described it, during the uprising they shouted, "Long live the Argentine Confederation," the government of the Federalist Party that had disappeared ten years earlier.[85]

This institutional relation was underscored as well by rumors that indicated that the healer Tata Dios had participated in 1870 in the Federalist rebellion led by Ricardo Lopez Jordan in the province of Entre Rios.[86] On the other hand, the attention that the uprising in Tandil merited by certain writers indicates that some contemporaries interpreted the rebellion in partisan terms. A few years after their occurrence, the events in Tandil provided the raw material for a play by Francisco F. Fernandez, titled *Solané*, the real name of Tata Dios, in which he vindicated the healer and denounced the suffering of the gauchos.[87] The author, a young intellectual from Entre Ríos, had been one of the ideologues of the Federalist revolts led by Ricardo Lopez Jordan.[88]

In the 1880s, the northwest of the republic witnessed the violence unleashed by this type of dispute, too. Between 1881 and 1883, the province of Catamarca confronted, in response to the legalization of civil marriage, the "masons" and "the religious ones." Priests from rural areas had an important presence in this struggle, which claimed some lives.[89] Similarly, in 1887, a group of rural settlers in the province of Tucumán rose up "against the gringos and masons," killing three foreigners. According to the rebels, one of whom said that "[he] wouldn't allow any harm to the religion," the foreigners were responsible for a recent cholera epidemic in the province; indeed, argued the rebels, the epidemic was part of a conspiracy "to seize the property of the natives."[90]

The Santa Fe revolt of 1868 was in the Federalist Party's name, and in the Tandil massacre, Federalist traditions had important influence. But in the conflicts in Catamarca in 1881–1883, and in Tucumán in 1887, which both occurred when Unitarianism and Federalism had disappeared as parties, the religious question would only be associated with local political groups. The persistence of the conflict and the language that the actors used suggest that religion's importance transcended partisan struggles, and therefore, that it played a critical role in the construction of the gauchos' Federalist political identity, explaining in part that party's capacity to mobilize people.

As analyzed here, the relationship between Federalism and religion was a phenomenon that displayed notable consistency and permanence only in popular political culture, and owed much to the militancy of the priests at the local level. While this may help in characterizing Federalist mobilizations as a conservative movement, it should be recalled that this association was only one of the several meanings that Federalism took in popular political culture. And, as we have seen, Federalism could also take subversive forms in local and popular political culture.

Still, the religious question does not imply that Federalism was a party that defended the interests of the church or that had any institutional connection to it. Although relations between the most important Federalist caudillos and the church seem to have always been more harmonious than those of the Unitarian leaders, Federalist leaders never unconditionally accepted the suggestions or demands of the church.[91] The attitudes of Federalist caudillos toward religion and liberalism were never homogeneous either. Thus, while some regional Federalist leaders such as Peñaloza and Pueblas proved hostile to the "masons" and defended "Christianity," Urquiza and Santiago Derqui, the two presidents of the Confederation, integrated masonry. In the same vein, in the 1850s and 1860s, the Federalist leaders defended the federal constitution, which was liberal. Perhaps nobody better embodied this ambivalence toward religion and liberalism than Felipe Varela. While the caudillo took a pious stance toward Catholicism, one of his motives in opposing the war against Paraguay was that Brazil, Argentina's main ally, was governed by a monarchy and, not the least, tolerated slavery.

T HE 1860S MARKED a crucial moment in the formation of the
nation-state, a process that the gauchos experienced in several
forms, including war and repression, recruitment and taxation.
Federalism took all this into account, incorporating the gauchos' concerns
into its discourse and mobilizations. As such, the gauchos' experience became part of a national political struggle between Unitarians and Federalists, and in the end, the Federalist identity acquired new meanings.

War and Repression

The military occupation of the interior by the national government's
troops after the battle of Pavón, and the Federalist resistance they encountered up until 1868, entailed both one of the worse wars and harshest crack-
downs that the provinces suffered in the nineteenth century. For some
Federalists, the repression launched by the national government in the
1860s was only comparable to the one unleashed by Rosas in the 1840s.[1]
Indeed, this assessment seemed to be shared by a Unitarian officer when
he condemned some of his comrades because of the "savage character" of
their military operations.[2]

The repression that the state-in-formation applied to politically control
the interior and overcome the massive displays of resistance took several
forms. In some cases, in order to force men to surrender, the Unitarians
implemented large-scale detentions of women and children.[3] In others,
they confiscated the rebels' cattle or harvests, and burned their houses, corrals, and sown fields, which threatened the subsistence of rural families.[4]
Colonel Sandes observed in 1862 that if the war continued, many families
in Los Llanos would die of starvation.[5] The gauchos blamed this aspect

of the war on Porteño repression and, in some instances, Sandes himself. A song, titled precisely "On Came Colonel Sandes," lamented:

> On came Colonel Sandes
> at the head of the Porteños.
>
> .　　.　　.
>
> As the Porteños advanced
> Where could Los Llanos turn?
> How wretched is Rioja!
> Ay, my beloved patria!
>
> At the rate this war is going
> The province will be lost.
> There will be nothing left to saddle
> And nothing left to eat.[6]

The basic existence of many gaucho families was also threatened because the war often meant death for working men, leaving their dependent families bereft. After the first rebellion, Chacho reported that many families were "completely orphaned, having died in the war those persons who provided their subsistence."[7]

Many of these gauchos died in combat, but many others were victims of the widespread and, at times, routine executions that the Unitarians carried out. In February 1862, a Unitarian from San Luis communicated to Sarmiento that the "healthy example of punishment" was necessary to "edify the masses" of the province. With this objective in mind, "executions by bullet" had taken place in the department of Renca, and there was still the need for such a policy.[8] In April of that same year, Colonel Rivas informed General Paunero that he had taken ten followers of the Federalist caudillo Fructuoso Ontiveros prisoner. Although four of them managed to escape, the other six were executed since "when questioned, they testified that they followed Ontiveros because they wanted to do it."[9] The executions did not end there. Only a month later, after further arrests, Rivas communicated to Paunero again that "all prisoners had been executed. . . . [T]his is the only way to moralize this perverse riffraff."[10]

The intensity and scale of the repression was not only a logic consequence of the war but also a product of specific perceptions about Federalism and the gauchos on the part of the state-in-formation. General Paunero, chief of the army in the interior, said that the gauchos "since 1810 have distinguished themselves as our social cancer," an assessment of their

role in the history of the nation that implicitly accepted their physical extermination as one of the ways to eradicate the so-called illness.[11] In addition, it was the criminalization of Federalists, which removed them from
the political domain and delegitimized their resistance, that called down
this type of suppression. When Chacho's second rebellion began in March
1863, President Mitre instructed Sarmiento, chief of the war in the interior,
as follows:

> I want no operation in La Rioja to take on the character of civil war.
> My idea is expressed in two words: *In La Rioja I want a police war.* La
> Rioja is a den of thieves. . . . Declare the montoneros thieves, with-
> out doing them the honor of considering them members of a political
> party, not flattering their pillaging with the name of rebellion.[12]

This conception was not limited to the leadership of the state-in-
formation. It reached down to the officers that concretely conducted the
repression against the Federalists. Colonel Sandes, who as we have seen
was blamed in popular song for the measures in Los Llanos, informed
Rivas that in his military operations, he would treat "the honorable and
hardworking people with great moderation, but not the gauchos, since
it is always necessary to treat them differently, and you know that these
provinces are covered with them."[13] In Sandes's use, "gaucho" was synonymous with "rural bandit." The criminalization of Federalists recommended by Mitre also became part of the jargon used at the local level: the
Unitarians began to routinely apply the epithet "bandit" to all Federalists,
making the two words one and the same.

The Federalists resisted in several ways. They appropriated "bandit" and
used it, in a defiant tone, to define themselves, thereby establishing a war of
meaning against the state in order to neutralize such defamation.[14] Then,
too, they took concrete steps, ranging from participating in acts of collective violence, like the Federalist rebellions, to eluding the authorities. The
case of the Gaitan brothers of Famatina, who combined both strategies,
is illustrative. When captured in 1867, after joining in the rebellion led by
Felipe Varela, one of them said that

> they had always lived in hiding in the mountains, in the last three
> or four years, and that they did not surrender to the authorities be-
> cause they believed that [Unitarian] Commander Linares would send
> them before the firing squad because before [1863] they had served
> [the Federalist leader] Pedro Carrizo as soldiers.[15]

Gauchos also resisted repression by singing songs whose lyrics allow us to reconstruct some of the ways in which they lived this exceptional conjuncture. As one song maintained:

> They say that Iseas has been killed
> Where the pine tree grows.
> Thanks be to God and the Virgin
> That they have killed the assassin!
>
> There they carry off a poor prisoner
> whatever the testimony may be
> his execution ordered
> by the wicked, one-armed Iseas.
>
> Now come his fawning flatterers
> who just to make him happy
> kill another wretch
> because of gossip that they've heard.[16]

The song celebrated a rumor that José Iseas, a Unitarian officer, had been killed. While portrayed as an "assassin" in the song, this seemed a fairly accurate assessment of Iseas in real life when read against the correspondence of some Unitarian officers and Iseas himself. In May 1862, during Chacho's first rebellion, Rivas told Paunero that he had ordered Iseas "to exemplary punish all montoneros he takes prisoner and I know that he is following my orders."[17] And a year later, during Chacho's second rebellion, it was Iseas himself who notified Paunero that after defeating a montonera in Renca, he had "shot several [prisoners] because it was useless to pardon them."[18]

The song also referred to one of the characteristics of the crackdown in the eyes of the Federalists: its arbitrariness. The prisoners were shot "whatever the testimony may be," or because the Unitarian officer heard of some malicious accusation, some "gossip that they've heard." This arbitrariness created a strong sense of insecurity among gauchos, and would have a lasting impact on their perceptions of justice, the state, and its officials. In 1869, Segundo Bazán, a gaucho from Famatina, was accused of cattle rustling by some neighbors in the village of Sañogasta, and in spite of not being guilty of the theft, he offered to pay for the loss. Later on, in a language that echoed the song analyzed above, Bazán would explain that he had accepted responsibility because "[if taken to the authorities,] he was afraid of being shot without any cause, only because of the false accusations made by those individuals."[19] Other criminal trial records from the 1860s and 1870s also show that although innocent, some gauchos would accept charges from the authorities in the belief that it was the only way to avoid further, and worse, consequences.[20]

This sense of juridical insecurity became one of the themes of Federalist discourse in the 1860s. A stanza from a song titled "Long Live General Varela," composed during the rebellion of 1867, proclaimed:

> This reigning patria
> does us no good.
> He who has done no wrong
> is hauled off to the contingent.
> Nothing is gained by prudence
> or cordiality on this occasion.
> Above all for the poor,
> who have no reasons at all.
> Now Varela is good for us
> because he is a man of honor.[21]

Sounding almost like a summary of gauchos' experience in the 1860s, this stanza rejected the Unitarian government ("this reigning patria does us no good") because gauchos were subjected to recruitment (see below), and more important, "the poor . . . have no reasons at all"—that is, they have no rights. Instead, Felipe Varela and a government of the Federalist Party "is good for us." The contrast between the repression and insecurity to which the Unitarian government subjected the gauchos, and the protection that Federalism could offer them, appeared in relation to Chacho and other caudillos as well.

As already mentioned, the 1860s represented an exceptional conjuncture. The war and government repression devastated some provinces of the interior, decimating their populations. The entries in Hilario Lagos's diary allow us to glimpse this misery. In 1867, when the Unitarian officer traversed the Llanos en route from San Juan to La Rioja, he noted that one of the villages they marched by

> seemed inhabited more by ghosts than by people. [There were] only women or some old people or handicapped kids, who inspire mercy because of their poverty and the anguish their faces reflect. The other

inhabitants [the men], some of them are with the montoneros and most of them died in the civil war in the last six years. These wretched people bring from enormous distances the remains of their children, fathers, and brothers [to bury them] in the cemetery of their village.[22]

This trauma was also articulated eloquently in a song:

What a move in these years!
Everything has gone bad!
The wars are so abundant
So many things have been lost!

.   .   .

Now there are no bandits
now everyone's a blue
and their sycophants
go by the scruff of their necks.

In the plazas and in the country
you will see the flowing blood
of the dead Federalists.
The survivors are in flight.

In whom can I trust?

.   .   .

In our General Saá
who will bring us
the tranquillity.[23]

The defeat of the Confederation and the Unitarians' rise to power entailed destruction, violence, and ostracism. Now, Unitarianism was the only legitimate political identity ("now there are no bandits / now everyone's a blue"), and the order reserved for Federalists was death or persecution. Faced with such adverse circumstances, the song invoked another Federalist caudillo, Juan Saá, who it was hoped, would bring "tranquillity" back—that is, protection and peace.

Recruitment

In May 1865, the Argentinean government entered into an alliance with Brazil and Uruguay, declaring war on Paraguay. The war, which lasted until 1870, would mainly affect gauchos, who were forcibly recruited into the National Guard contingents sent to the Paraguayan front. During those years, conscription would encounter heavy opposition in the provinces. It was not the first time that the gauchos of the interior had resisted such efforts.[24] But this draft for the war with Paraguay united new elements at a specific conjuncture, transforming it into an unprecedented social and political conflict of national dimensions.

Many of the government officials and military officers in charge of the recruitment—such as Governor Julio Campos, Colonel Ricardo Vera, and Commander José María Linares—were well-known Unitarians who only a few years earlier had fought against and repressed the Federalist montoneros, which hardly gave the conscription any legitimacy.

The draft was also conducted on an unprecedented scale. The first modern international war that the national state engaged in demanded numbers of men that provinces sparsely populated and decimated by war, like La Rioja, could not provide. According to the instructions of the national government, the authorities of La Rioja were to make available 1,100 National Guard members. Even some Unitarian officers, comparing the conscription quota to the total population of La Rioja, considered the number too high.[25] The recruitment of such a large contingent, moreover, further accentuated the difficulties that many rural families were already facing in 1865. Many men, whose work supported their families, had died in the war of 1862 and 1863. The recruitment was seen as a new, massive attack on the domestic economy of the gauchos, which also explains the resistance it encountered.

Conscription also rested on a high level of violence. The military authorities detained gauchos, stripped them, handcuffed them or tied their hands behind their back, and marched them nude to the distant points where contingents were assembled in each province. Then, the gauchos again marched hundreds of leagues to the city of Rosario, whence they were dispatched to the front. They undertook the whole march as prisoners, under the eye of armed escorts with instructions to execute resisters. When gauchos did manage to escape, the orders were to bring in, "dead or alive, those who resisted."[26] In a sense, the recruitment was a continuation of the war between parties and repression by the same (or very similar) means.

The gauchos responded with various forms of resistance. The most direct was flight into the mountains.[27] This type of evasion was common enough to affect even the haciendas of Unitarian leaders.[28] The gauchos also banded together in small groups that wandered through the country-side, resorting to robbery in order to survive.[29] In other cases, those already drafted incited uprisings within their contingents: when the rebellions were not successful, the instigators paid with their lives.[30]

The Federalist leaders, aware of the magnitude of the problem and the fact that the recruitment was especially targeting their followers—and therefore, that it was also being used to undermine their political base—made the question of conscription part of the discourse of Federalism. The Federalist appropriation of this issue took several forms, including the spread of rumors. Unitarians in San Luis found it difficult to govern and maintain order in the province because of

> the infamous works of our enemies, going to the extreme of telling and inciting the riffraff of both sexes to tell the gauchos and soldiers that they will be soon called to fill the ranks of the army of Paraguay, that they should not comply, that [the Federalist caudillo] Don Juan Saá and others will be here [from his Chilean exile] within three months. These infamies do their work in the countryside and even on the outskirts of the city.[31]

Here, Federalist rumors articulated the resistance within traditional relations of protection and leadership between caudillos and followers. This would also take place in the Federalists' public discourse as well as in more modern contexts, like electoral competitions. In the province of Córdoba, the gauchos and urban lower classes made up the bulk of the electoral shock troops, and so, could play an important role in gubernatorial elections. Thus, "in order to foster the candidature of Luque, the Rusos [Federalists] had led all their country folk and pals in the city to believe that he would send no one to the *slaughterhouse of Paraguay,* not one man.[32]

The gauchos also opposed the recruitment by participating in acts of collective violence—like the montoneras led by Aurelio Zalazar in 1865 and Felipe Varela in 1867—that linked their mobilization in favor of the Federal Party to the conscription problem. In describing Zalazar's rebellion, Lieutenant Colonel Julio Campos, the Unitarian governor of La Rioja and senior officer responsible for recruiting the contingents, said that

> the authors of so scandalous a revolution believed that the disgust that naturally arises among the masses in response to the drafting of

military forces, would better position them in the opinion of the gauchos, whom they hoped to ensnare by convincing them that this government would offer them up without exception to the *Porteños*. This circumstance, together with the name of general Urquiza, which they exploited, and the death of Chacho, for which they claimed revenge, and above all the discontent produced by the contingents on march, gave voice to the revolution.[33]

According to Campos, the intention of the montonera was also to depose him and install as governor of the province Don Manuel Vicente Bustos, a Federalist viewed favorably by national officials, whose administration the national government might eventually tolerate.[34] In the governor's mind, then, the rebels' motivations (what Campos called "the opinion of the gauchos") in joining the montonera of 1865 had been diverse, since the resistance to the contingent was incorporated into other aspects of the Federalist discourse.

It is instructive to see how this was articulated by the gauchos. General Paunero said that "the idea of going to Paraguay is a specter that has these people terrified," which seemed to capture part of the experience of the lower classes who, however, would use a religious language to articulate it.[35] A verse sang in celebration of Zalazar's rebellion said:

> From where Zalazar arose
> like an angel from the heavens
> to free the contingent
> being carried off to hell.[36]

A Llanisto who witnessed the drafting of the contingent by Commander Ricardo Vera (who, among other things, tortured and killed one of the draftees) would say that "at that time the heresy was big."[37] The language provided not only a facile analogy but, in the process, also made it possible to once again add religious connotations to party identities.

As well, the montonera leaders mobilized gauchos by appealing to their perceptions of the very state that drafted them. The national government, which ordered the conscription, was in the gauchos' eyes a Porteño, Unitarian one. The Campos administration in La Rioja was, with good reason, seen as a Porteño occupation in cooperation with the national government, which given the gauchos' experience with the Unitarians in 1862 and 1863, made the conscription inherently illegitimate.

Furthermore, asserted the governor, the rebels wanted to exact revenge for the death of Chacho, and Pascual Jara, a peon from Los Llanos, reported that in the montonera, "everybody cheered General Peñaloza (el Chacho) and Colonel [Felipe] Varela, calling 'death to the government' and especially to Commander [Ricardo] Vera."[38] In this way, the memory of the dead caudillo became part of the Federalist discourse, while one of his lieutenants (at the time in exile in Chile) was recognized as a leader. On the other hand, the threats against Commander Vera were far from mere occasional verbal volleys. In November 1863, as we have seen, Vera captured Chacho and turned him over to Commander Pablo Irrazábal, who assassinated the caudillo. Thus, the gauchos identified Vera as one of the Unitarians responsible for the death of Peñaloza, and ever since then, had made him the target of their bloodiest reprisals.[39] Equally significant, and mentioned earlier as well, Vera had been one of the commanders in charge of collecting the draftees.[40]

In his explanation, Campos also alluded to the use of the name of General Urquiza to mobilize the gauchos. This invocation was typical of the Federalist rebellions in the interior in the 1860s, when the name of the caudillo from Entre Ríos served to legitimate uprisings. In other words, the leaders of the rebellion knew that the Riojan gauchos acknowledged their membership in a political group or community—the Federalist Party—that reached beyond loyalty to regional caudillos and the montoneras that they led. Agustín Barrionuevo, a gaucho from Los Llanos, reported what he had heard from a peon, one of Zalazar's montoneros: "The plan [for the rebellion] had come from Entre Ríos, and thus had been ordered by General Urquiza."[41] Juan Carrizo, a criador from the province of San Juan who was part of the montonera, declared that Zalazar had told him that "he [Zalazar] had orders from General Urquiza to proclaim allegiance to the Federal[ist] Party and incite an uprising in Los Llanos." On hearing this, Carrizo

> took Zalazar aside and insisted that Zalazar show him the order that he had from Urquiza, to which Zalazar replied that there was no need to show it to Carrizo, that the order was among his papers, and although Carrizo repeated his request to see the order, Zalazar refused to do it.[42]

Carrizo's desire to see the written order reveals his knowledge of the montonera and party's hierarchical structure, under which the final authority lay not with Zalazar but the leader of the Federalist Party, General Urquiza. The incident suggests, as well, that there could be limits to regional leaders' capacities to manipulate ("exploit," according to Governor Campos) the name of Urquiza.

The episode also shows how familiar the figure of Urquiza was for the gauchos from La Rioja in the 1860s. Moreover, the figures of the national leaders of both parties were well integrated into popular expressions of politics. In 1862, a Unitarian said that in La Rioja

> reigned the mazorca [the Federalists] with its whole rage, as the militiamen were dressed in red *chiripá* [gaucho trousers], *sabanilla* [kerchief], and hat, all red, and in plain day light, in their parties, shouted "Viva Urquiza! Death to Mitre!" What is more, even their saddle blankets are bordered in red, and they announced that Urquiza was attacking Buenos Aires again, with a large army."[43]

The caudillo from Entre Ríos seemed to have played other roles in the popular culture of the interior provinces not explicitly related to politics.[44] The use of Urquiza's name in Zalazar's rebellion and related incidents also indicates that both the leaders of the montonera and the gauchos inscribed their actions within a political realm that transcended the provincial level and was national in scope.

Still, in a province with no more than 50,000 inhabitants and a minimal state apparatus, political power and authority was perceived in immediate, personalistic terms. Governor Campos, a Porteño and an officer of the national troops, had participated in the suppression of Chacho's rebellions and had personally overseen the recruitment of contingents, which made him the target of gauchos' resentment. It was no surprise, then, that the gauchos joined an attempt to oust him from power.

As Campos' argued earlier, the gauchos' motivations to rebel had been diverse. The governor was not alone in this assessment. In 1865, Dr. Abel Bazán, the national senator for La Rioja, also attempted an explanation that emphasized the complexity of the state-formation process and multiple levels on which the inhabitants of the province experienced the phenomenon. After recognizing "the indomitable warrior nature of the Riojan gaucho," he pointed to

> the sad conditions in this forsaken province after the montoneras of Chacho. Its inhabitants, above all those in the countryside, have seen their houses burned, their fields laid to waste, their livestock de-

stroyed, and the very ground soaked in blood after the barbarous execution of [those who called themselves] their liberators.

It is not surprising, then, that Señor Campos, who rose from those ranks to govern the province while it was under military occupation, should find falling on his shoulders the indignation and hatred of the countryside, which sees in him the representative of that angry past.

If we add to all this that in order to build the provincial treasury, Governor Campos has had to resort to a system of taxation that, however just and legitimate, is applied rigorously and without any consideration of the poverty of the Riojanos, and to which they were not accustomed to paying in earlier times; and if in addition we also consider that some of these Riojanos saw their companions, friends, fathers, and brothers, snatched from their homes and sent naked, bound, and without pay to serve in a war the importance and necessity of which was obscure to them, then we easily come on . . . the clear and simple explanation for that spontaneous commotion that took place in Los Llanos to liberate the contingents, and for that inclination, later demonstrated, to overthrow the governor of the province, who was seen as the author of all these misfortunes.[45]

Zalazar's rebellion was an expression of gaucho opposition to the transformations that the construction of the state imposed on the inhabitants of the countryside: repression, conscription, and taxation (see below) were "the misfortunes" that laid the bases for the montoneros' collective violence.

Resistance to forced recruitment would reappear as a theme in the Federalist discourse of the rebellion led by Felipe Varela in 1867. As we have seen, a song composed during the rebellion denounced the Unitarian government ("this reigning patria does us no good") for several reasons, including the fact that it only reserved the obligation to go to war for the gauchos ("he who has done no wrong / is hauled off to the contingent"). This aspect of Unitarian rule also inspired the violence of the gauchos that joined the montonera. During the rebellion, several gauchos from the departments of Vinchina and Guandacol captured Don Camilo Castellanos, a well-connected hacendado from Vinchina who, in 1865, as a subordinate officer to Unitarian Commander Linares, had helped recruit gauchos.[46] In accordance with the practice of the montonera, he was tried by a "council of war" and sentenced to execution. Castellanos tried to escape as he was led to the execution on his own horse, but the montonero Carlos Farías, an illiterate labrador, toppled him from his mount with a blow from his sword, shouting, "This is how the contingent is drafted!" Immediately, another montonero, a native of the nearby village of Jaguel, slit Castellanos's throat.[47] Farías would later boast that "he had killed a savage."[48] Agustín Molina, another montonero who was an illiterate labrador from Guandacol and who witnessed the death of Castellanos, admitted that "they fought for the Federalist Party," and said

> that the reason they had to assassinate him was that they believed, according to what he had heard [from one of his confederates,] that Castellanos was a spy for Lieutenant Colonel Linares, since he was an officer of the troops of said Colonel, and the *Jaguelista* who killed him did so because it was Castellanos who conscripted the contingent for the army in Paraguay.[49]

Beyond the nature of gaucho resistance to their forced participation in the war, there exists the possibility that the lower classes of the interior perceived of Paraguay as a traditional political ally of Federalism, although the evidence is far from conclusive. The interior's elites, however, clearly saw it this way, so that when Argentina joined the triple alliance, the Unitarians in the interior doubted the Federalists' loyalty to the government of Mitre and believed that they would instead favor Paraguay.[50] And in La Rioja, the identification of Federalism with Paraguay was so strong that the Federalist Party was referred to as the "Paraguayan Club."[51] It is nevertheless difficult to assess how much of this notion formed part of popular political culture. Yet, it is possible that the Federalist leaders broached the idea with their followers. At the end of 1861, Chacho prepared himself to challenge the defeat of Urquiza at Pavón since, as Paunero said, "He believes that Urquiza has 20,000 Paraguayans and however many thousands of *orientales* ready to march on Buenos Aires."[52] And during the rebellion of 1867, Felipe Varela issued proclamations that were distributed in some areas of the interior publicly proposing "peace and friendship with Paraguay."[53]

Taxation

According to Senator Abel Bazán, the tax collection implemented by the government influenced gauchos' decision to join the ranks of Zalazar's rebellion as well. Notwithstanding Bazán's observation, the evidence suggests that these measures did not affect the gauchos in the same way that repression and the draft did—which is not to say that taxation did not generate opposition. In this case, resistance was the product, as Bazán noted, of the particular conjuncture in the province's political development: the decision to actually collect taxes when the province was devastated after several years of war. Taxes, furthermore, had not been imposed before, which also explains the scant legitimacy that they inspired. An episode from Los Llanos serves to illustrate the nature of the conflict.

In March 1865, three months before Zalazar's montonera, the provincial prosecutor initiated a case accusing Don Fermín Bazán, a militia commander from the department of Costa Baja, of sedition. Based on the testimony of Principal Commander of the Department Don Andrés Galo Herrera, the prosecutor reported that Bazán had made the subalterns of the militia under his control sign a "protest." The document was addressed to the national government and called for the resignation of the provincial governor. According to the prosecutor, Bazán promised his militia that "if by this method they would not overthrow [the provincial government], they would do it by means of arms." Bazán, it was alleged, had also

> slandered the conduct of the government in a most ugly fashion, presenting it to the masses and officers of his squadron as a nest of *Thieves of Public Funds*, as an intolerable tyrant, and everybody knows, Your Honor, that the motive of all this invective was to predispose them to an eventual insurrection."[54]

Felipe Corso, a smallholder in Los Llanos, added that Bazán "told them that the government was sacrificing them and only wanted to fill its pockets before abandoning the province."[55] Bazán denied the charges, attributing them to the slander of Don Andrés Galo Herrera, his personal enemy. Later events, however, would refute his assertion.

But let us return to the words of the prosecutor and Corso. On the one hand, they give the impression that taxes were considered illegitimate, and that the sole perceived object of taxation was to enrich members of the government. Other evidence confirms that this was a common view in the countryside, one that would mobilize the people of Los Llanos. In 1874, the Avellanedista militants in La Rioja organized a montonera in Los Llanos with the objective of deposing the governor, who was a favorite of Alsina. Hoping to win the support of a local criador, one of the leaders of the montonera told him, in the tone that Bazán had used nine years earlier, "that they would throw out the thieving government, that there would be no more taxes."[56] In the eyes of the country folk, taxes were a fraud.

This perception had its origin in two phenomena. First, as Senator Abel Bazán stressed, taxes were not traditionally part of the experience of most Riojans. A visitor to the province in 1856 had noted the poverty of state coffers and was surprised at the nonexistence of municipal taxes in the capital. In this observer's opinion, "the poverty of the country" accounted for the dearth of public monies only in part: "The inhabitants of the province are ill-disposed toward the new taxes."[57] Second, the country people's notion of taxes as fraud had concrete roots. Money collected by the departmental branches was sent to the provincial capital, where the greater part of scarce fiscal resources went to pay the salaries and expenses of a rickety provincial administration. Most administration employees, the recipients of those salaries, were city dwellers.

In addition, the words of the prosecutor and Corso speak to other factors that contributed to this perception. Bazán, claimed the prosecutor, called the governor an "intolerable tyrant." In the language of the time, this referred to the repression and violence with which the government had taken, and still maintained, military control of the province. According to Corso, Bazán had also accused the government of wanting to "fill its pockets before abandoning the province," which indicated that the government of Campos was seen as a foreign element; more precisely, a Porteño government. Given the experience of the Riojans with the Porteño representatives of the national government, it is not surprising that tax collection lacked legitimacy.

As we saw above, Commander Bazán denied the charges against him, saying, among other things, that they were the slanderous work of Don Galo Herrera, the principal commander of the department. Yet, as the prosecutor observed, one of the goals of Bazán's exhortation was to "predispose" the militia to an eventual insurrection. The anticipated insurrection would indeed take place three months later, in the rebellion led by Aurelio Zalazar, and as mentioned earlier, taxes seemed to be one of the gauchos' motivations to join this rebellion.

These tensions lingered even after November 1865, when Zalazar's montonera was put down. A year later, on November 27, 1866, the official newspaper reported the conflict in the Llanos. According to the newspaper, Tránsito Tello, a former commander of the militia of the department of Costa Baja, "was inciting the masses," explaining to them that when the departmental judge, Galo Herrera, "decreed a fine, he did it without legal authority."[58] Twenty days later, *La Regeneración* stated that rebellion had broken out in Los Llanos, and that the first victim had been the Principal Commander and Departmental Judge Don Andrés Galo Herrera. A band of gauchos attacked Galo Herrera in his home, and in the presence of his wife, slit his throat and then decapitated him.[59]

"What is behind the assassination of Commander Herrera?" asked the title in the official newspaper, as it attempted an explanation. Those responsible, the newspaper contended, were the militia commanders, Fermín Bazán and Tránsito Tello. Both were "the most bloodthirsty enemies" of Herrera. The roots of Bazán's resentment lay in Herrera's removal of him as head of the militia, while the disagreement with Tello began when "Herrera ordered Tello to pay the fine prescribed by law for selling a steer without the proper license [sales tax]."[60] The need to "build a provincial treasury," which Senator Abel Bazán had remarked, had inspired the violence against tax collectors.

But was Herrera's death related to the conflict between Unitarians and Federalists? With the exception of the presence of Commander Bazán, who introduced personal motivations devoid of political considerations into the occurrence, the evidence seems to imply that the assassination of Herrera was part of the struggle between these political parties. Bazán was a Unitarian, and just months after the death of Herrera, Felipe Varela would order that Bazán's own throat should be slit.[61] Bazán's personal rancor, and his opposition to Campos's government and its fiscal policies, led him to participate in the assassination of Herrera.

Unlike Bazán, the other protagonists in the conflict (Tello, Herrera, and the gauchos who assassinated him) did have clear and consistent histories of political activity. Commander Tránsito Tello was the son of a Rosista governor, and he himself had fought alongside Chacho in the rebellions of 1862 and 1863.[62] Herrera had already been the target of the small Federalist montoneras wandering about Los Llanos in 1865, and members of those montoneras had tried to assassinate him.[63] As well, Herrera had been one of the leading Unitarian commanders in the struggle against Zalazar's montonera: after subduing it, he took numerous gauchos prisoner and forcibly incorporated them into the contingents marching to the Paraguayan war. In addition to his position as tax collector, Herrera could add recruiter and repressor of Federalist gauchos to the list.[64]

As portrayed by the criminal procedures against them, the gauchos who assassinated Herrera had political histories as steady as their victim's. Tello and Bazán gave the order to murder Herrera to Indalecio Nieto, an illiterate labrador and mule driver from Costa Baja, who led the band that slit the principal commander's throat. Nieto was a middle-ranking Federalist leader among those who mobilized montoneras in the 1860s. In his criminal trial, Nieto admitted that in 1865, one year before Herrera's assassination, "he had been present [in the uprising of Zalazar] and was also present in the raid on a contingent in La Edionda."[65] He also testified that he had participated in various rebellions with Santos Guayama and had collaborated with Sebastián Elizondo in the rebellion that deposed Unitarian Governor Nicolás Barros in 1868. Similarly, Rosa Quintero, a peasant from Los Llanos who took part in the assassination of Herrera, declared that "he had always gone with Indalecio Nieto," just as he followed Guayama and Elizondo.[66]

Thus, the violence against Herrera was a product of more than his role as tax collector and conscription agent; it was deeply rooted in the political affiliations of the victim and his enemies, too. Herrera's political fellows attached this same interpretation to a list of victims of the Federalist montonera published in the official newspaper in 1867, in which Herrera's name appeared.[67]

Popular memory preserved Herrera's assassination as an episode symbolic of Los Llanos's resistance against taxes and tax collectors. In the 1890s, a popular minstrel from Tama, a village in Los Llanos, composed lyrics denouncing the then–tax collector, Segundo Valdés. In language that echoed that used by Bazán three decades earlier, the singer remembered that a previous tax collector had been assassinated "for his extremes of tyranny," threatening Valdés with hints of the same fate:

> There goes Don Segundo Valdés
> leaving clouds of dust behind.
> Let him not suffer the fate of
> Galo Herrera![68]

FEDERALISM DOMINATED LA RIOJA starting in the 1820s, and still showed a notable capacity to shape politics in the 1860s. Yet, a decade later, by the late 1870s, Federalism had disappeared as a political force. How to explain its demise? What happened with the loyalties it aroused up until the late 1860s? In reality, not only Federalism but Unitarianism as a political identity also disappeared; and their fate was a consequence of the formation of the national state that, in the 1860s and 1870s, crucially reconfigured the political landscape of the interior and, indeed, the nation as a whole.

It is necessary to explore some of the concrete effects this process had on La Rioja and other areas of the interior. To begin with, the wars of the 1860s decimated the Riojan Federalist leadership. In addition to Chacho and Felipe Varela (who died in his Chilean exile in 1870), seven of the thirty-three middle-rank Federalist leaders also died in the conflicts; another three were arrested, and by 1872, were serving sentences; three more received amnesties; others, unheard of again, probably escaped to Chile; and Guayama never completely surrendered, remaining an outlaw until he was finally killed in 1878. Thus, seven years of almost uninterrupted civil war undermined the Federalists' capacity to resist and their political will. This was acknowledged by the Federalist leaders when, led by Elizondo in August 1868, they revolted with the purpose of negotiating an amnesty for themselves and their followers. The weakness of the Federalists was even more evident several months later, in January 1869, when a few middle-rank leaders tried to organize a new montonera to allegedly protect themselves from the persecutions of Unitarian Commander Ricardo Vera. Some of the caudillos refused to participate and it was difficult to mobilize gauchos "because they could not find men."[1] Without consensus, the leaders and some followers disbanded. The authorities observed with some relief that "the masses resisted the mobilization" since they were "demoralized" and "discontent."[2] The assassination of Urquiza in 1870 was also a decisive blow to the Federalist cause, robbing the regional caudillos of a figure that had been a permanent point of reference since 1852.

The defection of some of its leaders undermined the Federalist Party as well. Although these decisions involved a good deal of opportunism, they should also be seen as part of the changes that the national state brought to politics in the interior. Some Federalists were convinced that the new order was inevitable, and that the provinces had neither the military nor economic capacity to resist. The alternative was to seek accommodation, and in this respect, the history of the Catamarqueño caudillo Octaviano Navarro, who in 1867 switched to Unitarianism, is telling. Navarro belonged to a Federalist family that had controlled Catamarca (in close association with the Molina family) since 1846, when his father, Manuel, became governor of the province.

In late 1861, Navarro and the Molinas were "convinced that the question would be decided not in the interior but in the littoral, where the true contending powers are."[3] When Peñaloza invited them to revolt and negotiate by force, therefore, Navarro and the Molinas rejected the strategy. Not only was it useless to confront Buenos Aires but armed resistance would bring war and destruction to Catamarca. Later, aware that the new national government "wanted to leave nothing Constitutional [Federalist] in the provinces," Navarro and the Molinas left office, and the Federalist-controlled provincial legislature appointed as governor a low-profile Federalist in liberal guise.[4] Yet, Buenos Aires did not accept the compromise, and early in 1862, forced Navarro to go to Chile in exile.[5] Navarro was allowed to return in 1863 to Catamarca, where he avoided political involvement for the next four years. During this time, he witnessed one of the most unstable and violent periods in the history of Catamarca ("The Night of the Seven Years," as local historians called it), in which the province was devastated, as he and the Molinas had anticipated in 1861. In 1867, when the rebellion of Felipe Varela was unfolding, Navarro was again approached by some of his allies, who asked for his political and material support. Once again, he refused to participate in armed resistance. In retaliation, the Federalists began to butcher the cattle of his hacienda and, apparently, also threatened him ("*comenzaron a hostilizarlo*"). Thus, "hurt in his interests," in mid-1867, Navarro offered to cooperate with the Taboadas to fight against Felipe Varela and impose order in Catamarca.[6] Now, after six years of chaos and violence in the Andean interior, Mitre and the Taboadas welcomed the caudillo's assistance, hoping that Navarro would bring stability and consensus to the region. But what did this change of allegiance actually mean?

Navarro's accommodation did not include all Catamarca Federalists. To begin with, most of the militias that he had headed in his campaign against Varela were not from Catamarca; rather, they had been mobilized in Salta by Salteña authorities, who received orders from the national government and the Taboadas to put them under Octaviano's command.[7] Neither did Navarro's about-face include the Molinas, who as Octaviano himself said, became "his most bloodthirsty enemies," and left a mark on Catamarca's collective memory.[8] Yet, this change of allegiance would also disappoint some Unitarians. When Navarro was ordered to fight against Felipe Varela, who in defeat was marching northward to Bolivia, he closely followed the montonera but avoided combat. Octaviano's ambivalence in the campaign was underscored time and again by Felipe Varela himself in his documents, and aroused the criticism of some Unitarians who said that Navarro was accompanying Felipe Varela rather than "persecuting" him.[9] Symptomatically, too, after the rebellion had been completely defeated, several middle-rank leaders negotiated their amnesties with Navarro, and later, if in trouble, would seek his protection. That is, some of their former comrades would continue to trust him.[10]

Thus, after trying for six years to accommodate as a Federalist to the post-Pavón order in the interior, Navarro switched allegiances. To some extent, Navarro's story paralleled Urquiza's. But while his political and military power, and that of Entre Ríos, allowed Urquiza to maneuver as a Federalist for almost a decade, the civil war in the interior, as well as Catamarca and Navarro's own limitations, narrowed Navarro's options and finally forced him to switch (and yet, Urquiza's assassination also showed that even for him, accommodation was not easy).[11]

But the new political landscape being carved out by the national state in the interior also forced some displacement of allegiances in the Unitarian Party. Navarro negotiated his incorporation into Unitarianism with the Taboadas, who had their own reasons to welcome Octaviano. The Taboadas, of long Unitarian tradition, had been in control of Santiago del Estero for fifteen years and had been crucial to Mitre's success in the North. Yet, by mid-1867, when they opposed Sarmiento's presidential candidacy, they began to realize that the new order they had done so much to create was beyond their control and could easily turn against them (especially the national army). Soon, they began to emphasize that their understanding with Navarro allowed them to develop "a politics purely of the provinces" ("*una política puramente de las provincias*"), which would limit the influence of the national state in the interior.[12] From then on, the Taboadas fell out with the national government (particularly with Sarmiento), suffering several blows that culminated with their defeat at the hands of the national army in 1875.

The decisive presence of the national army, however, was not the only change that the formation of the national state brought to the interior. There were other institutional transformations as well that worked in the political reconfiguration. For instance, the federal justice system began to be organized in the interior, and judges were appointed. Although sanctioned by the constitution of 1853, the government of the Confederation had not had the resources to implement such a judiciary. But the conflicts of the 1860s made clear the necessity of accelerating its organization to the point that, it can be argued, the pace and geography of its development followed closely that of the montoneras: in the case of La Rioja, the federal court was established in early December 1863 (a few weeks after Chacho had been assassinated and the Federalist rebellion contained) and set to work immediately, trying and sentencing some of the rebels. The work of the federal courts soon had an impact on the local political jargon: Riojans began to distinguish between *presos provinciales* (convicted by the provincial courts for "sedition" or revolt against provincial authorities) and *presos nacionales,* (convicted by the federal courts for the crime of "rebellion"— that is, revolt against the national government).[13]

In addition, for the first time since independence, the Porteño political elite was willing to subsidize the provincial administration. Although the sums allocated to the provinces were small in absolute terms, they represented a large portion of provincial resources. For example, in 1870 in La Rioja, the national subsidy covered 50 percent of the budget and represented almost double the amount that the Riojan government expected to collect in the province.[14] In this way, the national state pumped money into the local economies and the expanded provincial administrations provided more employment for the local elites, which robbed Federalism of at least some of its old themes and helped dissuade future conflicts. On the other hand, since these subsidies were completely discretionary, they were also used to punish and reward provinces—that is, they were a powerful means of political discipline and centralization.[15]

Several measures were also taken to control the Riojan countryside and diminish the influence of Federalism. Between 1866 and 1869, the rural departments were divided into several smaller ones and more government officials were appointed, thus facilitating the surveillance of the countryside. Moreover, National Guard detachments were permanently deployed throughout the province, a measure of particular interest to the national government. Although the National Guards were supposed to be provincial militias made up of mobilized citizens, in 1869, almost half of those guards stationed in the Llanos under the command of Colonel Ricardo Vera were from other provinces, revealing the authorities' distrust of the Llanistos.[16] In addition, these National Guards were not on the payroll of the poor Riojan provincial administration but that of the national government, which wanted to make sure there were always resources for these troops.[17]

Yet, as the governor recognized in his message to the legislature in 1869, the presence of the National Guards in the countryside was only "a transitory remedy." To deal with the "ignorance that is the primordial cause [of caudillismo]," the national government set up elementary schools.[18] With a notable zeal, Sarmiento's administration decreed that in the rebellious Llanos, each department should have two schools, while for the other departments one would be enough. Attendance was mandatory, and the enthusiasm of the national government was only matched by local authorities in the Llanos, who sometimes violently enforced the law, dragging children from their homes.[19] In 1869, the governor reported, 967 children were attending the new schools. Still, as he pointed out, education was "slow in its results," and so, in the meantime, National Guards would maintain "peace and order."[20] Schooling was not the only method used by Sarmiento's administration in this long-term cultural struggle. The old department of Costa Baja was divided up, and the new departments were renamed Independencia, San Martin, and Belgrano, reflecting the growing influence of the liberal conception of the history of the new nation. But it was in the old department of Costa Alta, the home of Facundo and Chacho, that the authorities put special emphasis: it was renamed Rivadavia, after the political enemy of Facundo and his antithesis in liberal discourse. After half a century of struggle, "civilization" had finally conquered the heartland of "barbarism."

The success of the national state was accompanied by some limitations as well, as the folklore collection of 1921 suggests. The surnames of the 189 elementary school teachers (working in almost as many schools in a very sparsely populated province) who gathered the information in 1921 reveal that the vast majority were descendants of the families that had lived in the region since colonial times (including people of Indian background) and had participated on both sides of the political conflict during the nineteenth century. That is, the school system set up in the late 1860s had successfully incorporated (through education and public employment) the people from rural La Rioja into the state and nation.[21]

Yet, the repertoire they collected showed that Federalism died hard, especially in the countryside. For some of the informants, the songs and stories they provided were part of a meaningful, albeit distant, past. One teacher who herself told some stories, for example, said she was the great-grandniece of Peñaloza and had heard these stories from her grandfather, a nephew of Chacho. But she also recorded other stories told by her husband, the child of a Unitarian captain, who "had persecuted the montoneros."[22] For some, then, old political differences seemed irrelevant. But for others, the nineteenth-century conflicts and parties did not appear so distant and foreign. Some of the informants, who clearly wanted to speak, still preferred (with the obvious complicity of the locally born and raised teachers) to hide their identities. A story collected in Famatina that justified the 1867 execution of Unitarian Commander Linares, who had terrorized that department and whom even his comrades considered "bloodthirsty," was told by "a lady" who heard it from "her father, who as a soldier acted in the montoneras." Yet, although the teacher recorded that the lady was seventy years old, she was unable to provide her name because the informant was "unknown" ("*desconocida*") in that department.[23] Actually, the resilience of Federalism in rural popular culture had been already acknowledged in 1879 by the commentators who explained the success of

El Gaucho Martín Fierro and *La Vuelta de Martín Fierro,* resorting to the political inclinations of their readership and audience. "In the country-side," they said, "the Federal[ist] idea had been the creed pronounced even in martyrdom and the program of frank struggle during long years," and they concluded that "traditions cannot be erased from one day to another, much less if they come soaked in blood."[24]

CONCLUSIONS

THIS BOOK EXPLORED the institutional context of caudillismo and its influence on party conflicts. The limitations of the provincial state selectively impacted different sectors of the local elite, and hence, affected their political affiliations. A federal system of government that assured the political autonomy of the province was the best alternative for the caudillos, who thanks to their ability to mobilize clients, had the capacity to practice politics at the local level. But other sectors of the elite without cliental—and so, little opportunity to compete for political power at the local level—were in favor of a centralized system with a strong state presence at the local level. When seen from the interior of the country, the centralization of power was not only a consequence of the policies implemented by the national state;[1] it was also actively sought by certain sectors of the provincial elites. In the conflict between Unitarians and Federalists, then, two political projects were contested, with important ramifications for different sectors of the provincial elites. And it was the weakness of the provincial state apparatus (and initially, the national one as well) that gave the lower classes a decisive role in the political struggle, forcing the elites to cultivate a cliental. In this respect, the agrarian conditions and historical development of social relations in the Llanos and Famatina differently impacted (although they did not determine) the capacity of respective elites to establish vertical ties of solidarity and mobilize people.

Contrary to what has been argued,[2] the process of state formation generated a great deal of resistance among the rural lower classes, which also affected the pace and form that the process took. The time and money spent, the military effort exerted, and the strategic alliances created by the national government in order to impose its political and military power over the national territory cannot be understood without taking into account the mobilization of the lower classes on behalf of Federalism and its leaders. In addition, the survival of the federal system of government, in spite of the strong centralization process (from 1862 to 1880), cannot be completely explained without considering the capacity exhibited by the provinces to resist that process, a resistance made possible, again, by the identification of the rural lower classes with the Federalist cause.

The social background of the rebels reveals that they were neither criminals nor military professionals, and the montoneras were neither an expression of rural banditry nor a way of life.[3] The montoneras were one of the forms that partisan struggles took and one of the ways that gauchos were involved in politics. Furthermore, the heterogeneous social background of the rebels in general and the leaders in particular suggests that politics in the rural areas was not a realm monopolized by local elites. That is, as seen from the countryside of La Rioja, the struggle between Unitarians and Federalists was not an intraelite conflict but one that involved the most diverse sectors of society.

This inquiry into the nature of the political participation of the gauchos showed that the montoneras had a militialike organization. As such, portrayals of caudillo mobilizations as "barbarian democracy" or "inorganic democracy" should be understood as popular involvement in politics but not as signs of democratic practices.[4] And while at times mobilizations resembled the world turned upside down (which gave them egalitarian overtones), it did not mean that the montonera was an organization without hierarchies or well-defined responsibilities.[5]

Immediate material motivations, such as monetary rewards or access to different types of goods, played a crucial role in political mobilizations. Long-term patron-client relations were also one of the dimensions of the connection between caudillos and gauchos. These bonds were constructed in everyday life, and their forms corresponded to the necessities that the agrarian conditions and social relations imposed on the gauchos. Benefits of the relationship ranged from material aid for gauchos' subsistence to the protection that caudillos could provide to their clients. But the immediate motivations or the material exchange involved in patron-client relationships did not work in a sociocultural and politico-ideological vacuum.[6] The gauchos' personal and partisan identification (or lack of) with the leaders also counted in the decision to join (or resist) a mobilization.

Caudillista leadership included emotional and cultural dimensions, too. The caudillo's social life at the local level was a key component of the relation between leaders and led; indeed, it was one of the ways in which a personal attachment developed between them. At the same time, the charisma of the caudillos was not so much a consequence of the leaders' personal qualities but rather the qualities attributed to them by the regional culture—that is, the gauchos' perceptions of the caudillos. Thus, caudillista charismatic leadership was the followers' construction.[7] In this respect, the analysis of folklore also revealed the foundational role of Facundo's leadership: as the first caudillo of postindependence La Rioja, he was fundamental within regional culture in defining how a caudillo should behave.

There was a political dimension to the ties between leaders and led as well. Years of mobilization meant that the caudillo-follower relationship developed in the context of political struggles in which party identities emerged, and party allegiances were explicitly and publicly acknowledged. The caudillo-follower relationship created space for the political awareness of the followers, and eventually, for the political identification between leaders and led. Moreover, caudillista leadership (Chachismo) could be one of the meanings that party identity (Federalism) could take at the local level.

Party identity has been an important concern in this study. Several phenomena—from agrarian social relations, to ethnic and religious identities, to the experience of gauchos during the process of state formation—shaped Federalism at the local level. Some of them, like the conflictive agrarian relations and the ethnic differentiation in the province, had been at work since colonial times. Others, like the parties' positions on religion and the recruitment for the Paraguayan war, reflected certain aspects of the political struggle in different moments of the nineteenth century, involving both national and international arenas of conflict. Thus, party identities in the 1860s involved experiences that had developed over several time periods, and reflected processes at the local, national, and international levels.

Facundo's leadership was fundamental to the development of this party identity. The oral repertoire featured him as a religious, agrarian, and ethnic hero, embodying several of the meanings of Federalism in La Rioja. In other words, Facundo's figure both represented and constructed the Federalist Party identity at the local level, another way in which caudillista leadership was articulated with meaningful party politics.

The evidence also shows that, at the local level and especially among the lower classes, the enemies of the Federalists were referred to as "savages [Unitarians]" instead of liberals (sometimes, liberals would refer to themselves as Unitarians). This language stressed the actors' perceptions of the continuity over decades of the nature of the conflict, which was also reflected in other staples of the local political jargon (whites vs. blacks, masons vs. Christians), party symbols (Unitarianism continued to be identified with the color blue), and the victims of Federalism (some of the families that lost members to the 1860s' montoneras had suffered losses during the Federalist mobilizations of the 1820s and 1830s as well.

Party identities, then, were crucial in orienting people politically, and it was the quality of those identities that probably accounted for the consistency that rebels displayed in their political affiliations. And the fact that many leaders lost their lives fighting on behalf of Federalism suggests that consistency also implied a certain level of commitment. Therefore, the concept of factional politics is insufficient to explain the conflict between Unitarians and Federalists during the state-formation process in La Rioja.[8] Political identities were socially and ideologically differentiated, and more important, weak party loyalty (the alleged tendency of actors to switch sides), a major element in the "factional politics" argument, does not seem to have been a dominant feature in the Riojan countryside. Party inconsistency seemed to have been more common among urban and professional politicians without their own following and power base, than among rural caudillos and their cliental, who exhibited a good deal of continuity in their affiliations.

Finally, a few words about nation formation, myths, and oral culture. As we have seen, gauchos had a view of politics that was national in scope. Although party identities could have specific connotations at the local level, gauchos were aware that the conflict between Unitarians and Federalists encompassed all fourteen provinces, a political space that they identified as the Argentine Confederation or Argentine republic. This national perception of politics was a result, in part, of the workings of oral culture that defined a national political space among the gauchos. This finding takes the process of nation formation out of the exclusive dominion of literacy and printed manifestations of nineteenth-century high culture, like novels and newspapers, and places it as well in the realm of popular culture and the unlettered.[9] Facundo's mythic image, a significant presence in the oral repertoire, was thus part of this process of nation formation. At the same time, through Sarmiento's writing, this myth was smuggled into high culture and appropriated by the Unitarian liberal elite to design a project for modern Argentina in which the countryside, caudillos, and Federalist gauchos that had fueled Facundo's legend would occupy a distinctly inferior place. Thus, in both popular and high cultures, and in contradictory partisan terms, Facundo's myth worked toward the formation of the nation.

Reflections on Peasants and Politics in Latin America

As I said at the beginning, this book is part of a recent and larger trend in Latin American history that called for the necessity of studying the larger political processes, particularly those of state and nation formation, "without leaving the people out."[10] As research on other areas, especially Mexico and the Andes, has shown, in Argentina the rural lower classes also affected the pace and outcome of the nineteenth-century historical process. On the one hand, the results presented here seek to restore the relevance of rural life and politics in the history of Argentina up to at least the 1870s, a past largely obliterated by the predominantly urban experience of the twentieth century. On the other hand, and as it has been suggested by other authors, the incorporation of "politics from below" into the account of the historical process should modify our understanding of what is "above" as well.[11] Hence, the study of caudillismo in La Rioja reveals that, as in Mexico and the Andes, nineteenth-century political movements were not class based, and caudillos were not completely autonomous political actors: as in the rest of Spanish America, the struggle for nationhood in Argentina cut across classes, and the rural lower classes and caudillos were both terms of the same political equation. Similarly, the study of Riojan rebellions indicates that, as in other areas of the continent, knowledge of the historical process requires an analysis that integrates politics at the local, regional, national, and international levels.[12]

As the literature on other regions of the continent has shown, this work also argues that the historical importance of caudillismo extended far beyond personal or factional quarrels. Actually, the analysis of caudillista struggles sheds light on the process of state and nation formation, and is a privileged window into the history of Spanish American nations.[13]

Nevertheless, it is the methodological challenge implicit in this approach to politics in Latin America that offers the richest possibilities to establish a dialogue across regions and nations. As in the case of other studies, an adequate explanation of caudillismo confronts the problem of understanding what motivated "the people," especially the rural lower classes, to participate in politics or rebel. What was the role of, say, "material interests" versus "ideological motivations" (to present a certainly simplistic dichotomy) in the mobilizations?[14] The study of such questions in La Rioja suggests the "overdetermination" of rural collective action—that is, that numerous aspects of both a "material-social" and "ideological-cultural" nature shaped the political action of the gauchos.

But to understand the overdetermination of rural collective action implies the methodological challenge of getting to the "crucial but intangible dimensions of campesino mentality."[15] Here, as some authors have maintained, it is necessary to integrate culture and politics, and to seek for the relationships between political practices, ideologies, and other aspects of the actors' experiences (such as religion, ethnicity, superstitions and beliefs, or perceptions of agricultural cycles, to name only a few), and see the meanings they generated and the way they impacted on the political conflict.

It is in the reconstruction of this "soft tissue"[16] that historians of popular and rural politics confront the greatest problem: the high rate of illiteracy throughout most of the history of Latin America, as well as the instability and weakness of state and private institutions, have limited the availability of written records. Yet, there are ways of overcoming, at least partially, this barrier. In the case of La Rioja, folklore and the records from criminal trials brought against the gauchos after the rebellion proved productive in the reconstruction of at least some aspects of the voice of the illiterate and their practices. It is also clear, however, that almost any type of document—when critically used, when cross-examined and triangulated with other sources—may prove crucial in this reconstruction as well. In this respect, even "traditional" and elite-generated sources, like correspondence or tax records, may shed light on unsuspected aspects of the popular experience. Finally, the diversity of the popular experience, and necessity of understanding the relationship between phenomena as disparate as political practices, religion, ethnicity, and so on, create interpretative and research challenges that, for the time being, seem to be beyond the reach of national-scale studies. Instead, local or regional accounts have proved to be more useful in understanding on-the-ground politics.[17]

NOTES

All abbreviations and full citations can be found in the bibliography.

Introduction

1   Francisco Sarmiento to Domingo F. Sarmiento, Caucete, 5 June 1862, AS, 7975 *armario* (cabinet) 1. Emphasis in the original.

2   The word *gaucho* is used throughout in a denotative sense: Argentine gauchos were the rural lower classes, regardless of their position in the economy. They could be peasants, artisans, peons, or even miners. For a treatment of the use of this word in the voice of the protagonists, see chapter 4.

3   Terán, *Alberdi Póstumo,* 237–49; and Hernández, *Vida del Chacho.*

4   Gutiérrez, *El Chacho, Los Montoneros,* and *La Muerte de un Heroe;* and Borges, "El General Quiroga va en Coche al Muere," in *Obras Completas,* 1: 61, "Los Llanos," in *Textos Recobrados, 1919–1929,* 182, and prologue to Sarmiento's *Facundo,* in *Obras Completas,* 4: 125–29.

5   Sarmiento, *Facundo.*

6   See Wolf and Hansen, "Caudillo Politics."

7   Halperín Donghi, *Revolución y Guerra,* and *Hispanoamérica Después de la Independencia.*

8   Lynch, *Argentine Dictator,* and *Caudillos in Spanish America.*

9   See Burns, *The Poverty of Progress.*

10 Chasteen, *Heroes on Horseback.* See also some of the contributions (including my own) in Goldman and Salvatore, *Caudillismos Rioplatenses.*

11 See Stevens, *Origins of Political Instability in Early Republican Mexico;* Gootenberg, *Between Silver and Guano;* and Graham, *Patronage and Politics in Nineteenth-Century Brazil.*

12 Sarmiento, *Facundo.*

13 This *revisionismo* view depicts the Federalist caudillos from the provinces as the em-

bodiment of national values in opposition to the pro-European Unitarian elites from Buenos Aires. See Chávez, *Vida del Chacho;* Ortega Peña and Duhalde, *Felipe Varela Contra el Imperio Británico;* De Paoli and Mercado, *Proceso a los Montoneros;* and Pomer, *Cinco Años de Guerra Civil (1865–1870).* More recently, Shumway, *The Invention of Argentina,* has brought some of the *revisionista* themes and approaches back to the discussion of nineteenth-century Argentina.

14 See Burgin, *Aspectos Económicos del Federalismo Argentino;* and Chiaramonte, *Mercaderes del Litoral,* and *Ciudades, Provincias, Estados.*

15 See Myers, *Orden y Virtud;* and Sábato, *La Política en las Calles.*

16 For several exceptions, see Oszlak, *La Formación del Estado Argentino;* and Botana, *El Orden Conservador,* and *La Tradición Republicana.*

17 See Adelman, *Republic of Capital.*

18 For Argentine politics, see Halperín Donghi, *Revolución y Guerra, Proyecto y Construcción,* and *José Hernández.* For the rest of Latin America, see Halperín Donghi, *Hispanoamérica Después de la Independencia,* and *The Contemporary History of Latin America.*

19 Recent exceptions that take this perspective in the city and province of Buenos Aires are Sábato, *La Política en las Calles;* and some of the contributions in Goldman and Salvatore, *Caudillismos Rioplatenses.*

20 My work has been influenced by a diverse body of literature, from which I benefited in formulating the questions and strategy of my research. Some of the works are Levine, *Black Culture and Black Consciousness;* Agulhon, *La Republique Au Village;* Burke, *Popular Culture in Early Modern Europe;* Genovese, *Roll, Jordan, Roll;* Darnton, *The Great Cat Massacre;* and Geertz, *Local Knowledge.*

21 There is now a growing body of literature on peasant politics in Latin America that has concentrated in areas like Mexico or the Andes. Some of the most inspiring works are Wells and Joseph, *Summer of Discontent, Seasons of Upheaval;* Joseph and Nugent, *Everyday Forms of State Formation;* Mallon, *Peasant and Nation;* Knight, "The Mexican Revolution," and "Weapons and Arches in the Mexican Revolutionary Landscape"; Stern, *Resistance, Rebellion, and Consciousness in the Andean Peasant World;* Van Young, "The Raw and the Cooked," and "To See Someone Not Seeing"; Guardino, *Peasants, Politics, and the Formation of Mexico's National State;* Thurner, *From Two Republics to One Divided;* and Walker, *Smoldering Ashes.* See also *Hispanic American Historical Review* 79, no. 2 (May 1999) for a special issue on Mexico's new cultural history. For a fascinating and solid study of collective action among urban slaves, see Reis, *Slave Rebellion in Brazil.* Scott's studies of peasant politics in Southeast Asia and his theoretical reflections on peasant resistance were also essential to my work. See Scott, *Weapons of the Weak,* and *Domination and the Arts of Resistance.*

22 The most populated province in the interior was Córdoba, with 132,000 people. Many provinces were in the range of La Rioja: Jujuy, 35,000; San Juan, 42,000; San Luis, 37,000; and Mendoza, 47,000 (see Maeder, *Evolución Demográfica*).

23 For a general history of La Rioja, see Reyes, *Bosquejo Histórico.*

24 Cited in Perez Fuentes, "El Chacho," 235, 239.

25 For narratives of some of the 1860s' rebellions, see Reyes, *Bosquejo Histórico;* De la

Vega Díaz, *Mitre y el Chacho;* Ortega Peña and Duhalde, *Felipe Varela Contra el Imperio Británico;* and De Paoli and Mercado, *Proceso a los Montoneros.*

26 The attitude of the Chilean government was a response to two aspects of the international policy of Mitre that were considered hostile and menacing to Chile. On the one hand, Mitre had not only rejected the invitation to form part of the alliance of Chile, Peru, and Bolivia that, at the time, was carrying on a war against the Spanish Crown in the Pacific, but because the Argentine government maintained a neutral stance, Mitre had also allowed Spanish ships to renew their supplies in Buenos Aires before heading off to fight along the coast of Chile. On the other hand, the alliance of the Argentine government with Brazil, a monarchy that practiced slavery, was viewed with resentment and suspicion by the Chilean liberals, who feared for the weakness of the republican governments in South America.

1 Caudillos, Provincial Elites, and the Formation of the National State

1 On provincial states, see Chiaramonte, "Legalidad Constitucional," and *Mercaderes del Litoral.*

2 The budgets were utilized for lack of a better source. I examined the account books of the provincial treasury, available only since 1858, and found that until 1865, they contained incomplete information for some months of each year. The budgets do not say anything about how much was *actually* collected and spent. In spite of these limitations, I think the budgets provide a fair representation of the scale of public finances in the province. Other evidence seems to confirm their reliability as well: while the livestock taxes for 1858 were estimated as 3,000 pesos in 1860, the government of La Rioja actually collected 3,007 pesos. See *Registro Oficial de la Provincia de La Rioja,* 3: 81–82.

3 "Actas de la Legislatura de La Rioja," AGN, VII–21–5–6: 134–38, 159–62, and following unnumbered pages.

4 Ibid. The revenues estimated for 1858 included: commercial licenses, 1,657 pesos; sales taxes (*alcabala*), 266 pesos; public slaughterhouses, 1,144 pesos; official seals for documents, 476 pesos; real estate taxes, 4,448 pesos; livestock taxes, 3,000 pesos; and "from the state," 84 pesos.

5 Mensaje del Gobierno Provisorio del Estado de Buenos Aires a la Honorable Asamblea Legislativa (1860); the author thanks Alejandra Irigoin for the communication of these figures.

6 Romano, "Finanzas Públicas de la Provincia de Córdoba."

7 See Burgin, *Aspectos Económicos del Federalismo Argentino;* and Chiaramonte, Cussiánovich, and Tedeschi, "Finanzas Públicas." The only exception was the province of Corrientes; see Chiaramonte, "Finanzas Públicas de las Provincias del Litoral," and *Mercaderes del Litoral.*

8 Santa Fe, among the poorest of the fourteen provinces, included on its payroll no less than 218 people and as many as 440; see Chiaramonte, Cussiánovich, and Tedeschi, "Finanzas Públicas," 95.

9 On this aspect of Federalism, which has been amply noted in the historiography, see Burgin, *Aspectos Económicos del Federalismo Argentino,* chapters 4 and 5; and Halperín Donghi, *Proyecto y Construcción,* 62–66.

10 On the articulation of the economies of the interior with the Andean and Pacific markets, see Langer, "Espacios Coloniales." For a comparative analysis of the articulation of the littoral and interior provinces with the Atlantic market, see Schmit and Rosal, "Las Exportaciones del Litoral Argentino"; and Rosal, "El Interior Frente a Buenos Aires."

11 Régulo Martínez to Bartolomé Mitre, Villa de Famatina, 30 December 1862, AGM, 12: 261–62.

12 José Frías to Marcos Paz, Tucumán, 1 October 1862, AMP, 3: 87; and Emilio Salvigni to Wenceslao Paunero, Tucumán, 13 September 1863, AP, 7–5–14–1152.

13 José Posse to Domingo F. Sarmiento, Tucumán, 12 May 1862, in Castro, *Epistolario Sarmiento-Posse,* 102.

14 Ibid.

15 In 1864, a San Juan notable diagnosed a similar situation as one of the main problems of his province. According to this Unitarian, only the police in the city and two rural villages were paid. In the rest of the province, the appointed commissaries were poor citizens, whose conditions either led them to abuse their offices or prevented them from discharging their duties well. This explained, he concluded, why "authorities are impotent" and "robbery is very frequent" (Domingo de Oro to Bartolomé Mitre, 3 January 1865, AGM, 26: 164–66).

16 Domingo F. Sarmiento to Bartolomé Mitre, San Juan, 31 July 1862, *Mitre-Sarmiento,* 151–52. Emphasis added.

17 See Pérez Fuentes, "El Chacho y el Pronunciamiento," 223–28; Mercado, *La Degollación,* 109–57; and Chávez, *Vida del Chacho,* 44–49.

18 Wenceslao Paunero to Ignacio Rivas, Córdoba, 1 July 1862, AGN, 10–2–2–3. Emphasis added.

19 Emilio Salvigni to Wenceslao Paunero, Tucumán, 13 September 1863, AP, 7–5–14–1152.

20 Lucas Llanos to Paulino Orihuela, Costa Baja de los Llanos, 15 February 1862, AGM, 11: 45–46.

21 Cited in Navarro Ocampo, *Actor,* 245–46.

22 Ibid.

23 José Frías to Marcos Paz, Tucumán, 18 January 1862, AMP, 2: 196; and Navarro Ocampo, *Actor,* 312.

24 Cited in Navarro Ocampo, *Actor,* 243.

25 Cited in Halperín Donghi, *Proyecto y Construcción,* 369. The extension and intensity of this experience may be inferred from the fact that even the provincial Unitarians would sometimes refer to "the selfish character of the Porteños," or would say that "the chiefs of the national troops believe that all that belongs to the provinces is trash and as such they treat it" (Natal Luna to Manuel Taboada, La Rioja, 22 August 1863, in Taboada, *Los Taboada,* 3: 430; and Gregorio Brihuega to Domingo F. Sarmiento, La Rioja, 22 August 1863, AS, 3604, carpeta 33).

26 Pastor del Moral to Wenceslao Paunero, Rioja, 20 February 1863, AP, 7–3–7–616.

27 José Uriburu to Wenceslao Paunero, Salta, 10 May 1862, AP, 7–4–12–872.

28 Emilio Salvigni to Marcos Paz, Tucumán, 29 January 1862, AP, 7–1–1–76.

29 Wenceslao Paunero to Ignacio Rivas, Córdoba, 10 May 1862, AGN, X–2–2–2.

30 See Halperín Donghi, *Proyecto y Construcción*. My preference for Unitarian does not mean excluding the use of terms such as liberal or Mitrista, which I consider clear enough anyway.

31 Emilio Salvigni to Wenceslao Paunero, Tucumán, 13 September 1863, AP–7–5–14–1152; José Frías to Marcos Paz, Tucumán, 18 January 1862, AMP, 2: 195; José Frías to Marcos Paz, Tucumán, 1 September 1862, AMP, 3: 78; and José Frías to Marcos Paz, Tucumán, 1 October 1862, AMP, 3: 85–86. Emphasis added.

32 Domingo F. Sarmiento to José Posse, San Juan, 22 January 1862, AS, 433, carpeta 5.

33 Bartolomé Mitre to Régulo Martínez, Buenos Aires, 11 March 1864, AS, 7494, arm. 1. Martínez, Mitre's personal envoy to the interior, had relayed the concerns of provincial Unitarians to Mitre.

34 José Posse to Marcos Paz, Tucumán, 1862, AMP, 3: 64.

35 See José Frías to Marcos Paz, Tucumán, 5 January 1862, AMP, 2: 167; José Frías to Marcos Paz, Tucumán, 28 June 1863, AMP, 3: 168; Emilio Salvigni to Wenceslao Paunero, Tucumán, 13 September 1863, AP–7–5–14–1152; and Régulo Martínez to Bartolomé Mitre, Tucumán, 22 February 1864, AGM, 26: 88–89.

36 Navarro Ocampo, *Actor,* 61, 157.

37 Francisco del Prado to Wenceslao Paunero, Melincué, 12 July 1863, AP, 7–7–22–1945.

38 See "Causa criminal contra los autores y complices del conato de Revolución contra las autoridades legales de la provincia," 1869, AJP (LR), criminal, B–#34, 37.

39 Sarmiento, "Contestación del Gobierno de San Juan a la circular del ministerio del Interior Sobre el Estado de Sitio," San Juan, 26 June 1863, in *Memoria del Ministerio del Interior,* 1864, 127–41. Emphasis added.

40 Ibid.

41 "Patricio Fernández–Vicente Peñaloza–La Hediondita," 1854, AJP (LR), civil, F–5, 14.

42 Ibid.

43 De la Vega Díaz, *Cuestiones de Historia Menuda,* 19–20. The author used the civil case V–#14 in AJP (LR).

44 "Don Cruz Sosa contra la testamentaría de Don Domingo Bazán reclamando lo que le corresponde como hijo natural," 1859, AJP (LR), civil, S–#1.

45 "Causa criminal contra Francisco González por rebelión y otros delitos," 1864, AJP (LR), criminal, G–#8.

46 Fermín de la Colina, cited in Chávez, *Vida del Chacho,* 212.

47 Domingo de Oro to Bartolomé Mitre, San Juan, 3 January 1865, AGM, 26: 164–66.

48 "Censo General que Demuestra el Número de Habitantes de la Provincia de La Rioja," 1855, *Registro Oficial de la Provincia de La Rioja,* 1: 124–25.

49 *Primer Censo Nacional,* 430.

50 Luis Molina to Domingo F. Sarmiento, Mendoza, 31 January 1862, AS, 7506, arm. 1.

51 In the province of Santa Fe, "in 1860 the tribunal of Alzada, or appeals, was com-

posed of three legos judges. When a legally complicated case came before the tribunal, the body consulted a lawyer in Buenos Aires and, according to his dictate, the final verdict would be passed down. There were no lawyers, only this and that legal impostor" (Aldao, "Prólogo del Traductor," 14).

52 Domingo de Oro to Wenceslao Paunero, Buenos Aires, 9 June 1867, AP, 7–3–8–750.

53 José Frías to Marcos Paz, Tucumán, 22 June 1862, AMP, 3: 27. See also José Frías to Marcos Paz, Tucumán, 18 August 1862, AMP, 3: 66.

54 "Actas de la Legislatura de La Rioja," session of 23 July 1857, AGN, 7–21–5–6: unnumbered.

55 Ibid., session of 14 July 1857, AGN, and Gobierno to the Sala de Representantes, AHLR, Correspondencia Recibida, box 1, 14.

56 "[I have met] all the decent men that this town has, and most of them are public employees" (Régulo Martínez to Bartolomé Mitre, La Rioja, 14 January 1863, AGM, 12: 267–69).

57 Told by Pedro Sánchez, eighty-five years old in 1921, Manantial de Obanta, Tucumán, in Fernández Latour, *Cantares,* 165. Another version was recited in Yacú Hurmana, Santiago del Estero, by an eighty-nine year old in 1921; ibid., 90. For the Riojan version, see Carrizo, *Cancionero Popular de La Rioja,* 3: 9.

58 CFED, Provincia de La Rioja, Punta de los Llanos, dossier 81, informant: Manuel Antonio Díaz, seventy years old in 1921.

59 The argument developed in the remaining pages of this chapter roughly follows Alan Knight's insights on the nature of "agrarian revolutions" and "serrano movements" during the Mexican Revolution; see Knight, "Peasant and Caudillo." I owe this comparative perspective to the comments of one of my anonymous readers.

60 "Correspondencia del Eco [de Córdoba]," *La Regeneración,* 14 January 1866.

2 *Unitarians and Federalists in Famatina*

1 Domingo Villafañe to Ignacio Rivas, Rioja, 12 June 1862, AGN, X–2–2–2; and Domingo B. Dávila, "Orígenes Nacionales," 77–79.

2 Domingo B. Dávila to Francisco S. Gómez, Villa de Famatina (Chilecito), 25 October 1862, cited in *El Famatina Reformado,* 14 November 1862; and Régulo Martínez to Domingo F. Sarmiento, Chilecito, 23 December 1862, in *Mitre-Sarmiento,* 164–66.

3 "Nuevas Montoneras en La Rioja," *El Eco de Córdoba,* 8 January 1863; Francisco S. Gómez to Wenceslao Paunero, Rioja, 20 January 1863, in *El Famatina,* 2 February 1863; Francisco S. Gómez to Chacho Peñaloza, Rioja, 29 December 1862, cited in *El Famatina,* 14 February 1863; "Correspondencia," *El Eco de Córdoba,* 10 February 1863; and "Correspondencia," *El Eco de Córdoba,* 12 February 1863.

4 Tomás Santa Ana to Marcos Paz, Catamarca, 10 March 1863, AMP, 3: 157–58.

5 Domingo B. Dávila, "Orígenes Nacionales," 3: 567.

6 Reyes, *Bosquejo Histórico,* 30–52.

7 The 1,878 pesos in real estate taxes corresponded to 466,959 pesos in landed property

registered in 1855; see *Registro de la Contribución Directa del Departamento Famatina,* 1855, AJP (LR).

8   The valley produced 1,200,000 bottles annually, the value of which was estimated at 25,000 pounds sterling; see Rickard, *The Mineral,* 153–60, 182.

9   Ibid. Annual production was estimated at 59,000 ounces of silver, which had an approximate value of 16,000 pounds sterling.

10 Ibid. The total value of wheat (500 tons annually) and corn (9,000 *fanegas* [3.89 bushels] annually) was estimated at 7,000 pounds sterling.

11 Ibid.

12 "Censo General que Manifiesta el Número de Habitantes de la Provincia de La Rioja, levantado el 26 de febrero de 1855," *Registro Oficial de la Provincia de La Rioja,* 1: 124–25; and "Informe de Josef Nicolás Ocampo," Anguinán, 16 May 1806, adjoined to Padrón del Curato de Anguinán (Famatina), Archivo del Arzobispado de Córdoba, legajo 19, 2:unnumbered pages.

13 See Sarmiento, *El Chacho,* 81–84.

14 "Don Crisólogo Chaves y compartes pidiendo posesión y uso de los terrenos comprendidos en la merced de Tilimuqui," 1873, AJP (LR), civil, C–#104, 1–16.

15 The outline is only approximate because the sources do not provide equally consistent and broad information about, for example, the distribution of mining property, the volume of capital dedicated to commerce, or the value of cattle held by rural property owners, aspects necessary for a more complete panorama of the distribution of wealth in the valley. Nevertheless, the *Registro* does detail real estate taxes, and in a predominantly rural society, the distribution of property in land represents the distribution of wealth fairly accurately. The *Registro* recorded as well the names of the proprietors, the tax that was paid, and the value of the property. The document also specified where the properties were located, and whether they were rural, urban, or mining possessions. Finally, it indicated whether the property was obtained by purchase, inheritance, or through rights to communal lands of the town in which they were located. The *Registro,* however, did not specify the activities undertaken on a property, or the amount of land or volume of water each property had.

16 *Registro de la Contribución Directa del Departamento Famatina,* 1855, AJP (LR). The criteria followed by the assessors who conducted the *Registro* was to note each of the existing properties in the department, which numbered 905. Since the *Registro* also records the name of each of the proprietors, I was able to organize the information according to name. Thus, I could confirm that some proprietors had two or three properties, and conclude that the 905 properties were in the hands of 842 proprietors. The register included only proprietors, and made no suggestion of what proportion of the valley's inhabitants were without land. The provincial census of 1855, however, registered 1,378 families in the department of Famatina. Assuming, by a conservative estimate, that each of the 842 proprietors noted in the *Registro* represented one family, the number of families without property would be 536. I say that the supposition that each proprietor corresponds to one family is conservative because the alternative would be to consider that some families included more than

one proprietor, which would make the proportion of families without property even higher.

17 "Informe de Josef Nicolás Ocampo."

18 French, "On the Province," 381–406.

19 In the village of Cuchiyaco, on the border of the departments of Arauco and Famatina, where the proprietors were *labradores* (peasants) and *comuneros* (owners of communal lands), a property valued at 98 pesos had six hours of water (48 pesos) and two plots for cultivation (50 pesos) ("Causa de Celestino Brizuela contra los vecinos de Paslimpato sobre turno de agua," 1870, AHLR, unclassified, 4, 18–27).

20 For the poverty and scarcity in Vichigasta, see French, "On the Province," 394; and "Diario de Marcha de Hilario Lagos," Nonogasta, 23 June 1867, AFL–PCHL. Of the sixty-three proprietors in Vichigasta, all but one had properties valued at 31 pesos.

21 Law 124, art. 3, approved 12 December 1865, in *Registro Oficial de la Provincia de La Rioja* 3: 547.

22 The labradores whose properties were worth 125 pesos or less represented 22.9 percent of the population of the valley. The landless, as mentioned earlier, represented 38.5 percent.

23 I consider smallholders those whose properties were valued at up to 500 pesos. This categorization is certainly approximate. In 1861, a large landowner of Famatina who visited the neighboring department of Guandacol (whose economy was similar to Famatina's) maintained that properties of 500 pesos did not even reach the category of "middling fortune" because they produced a "miserable sale" (Maximiliano Dávila to Carmelo Valdez, Hornillos, 12 November 1861, AHLR–CDV, carpeta 7, 72).

In Cuchiyaco, a property of " 'more than 300 ps.' had 14 hours of water (116 pesos 2 reales), an orchard of more than 70 fig trees, with an adobe hut and two more fields with alfalfa; and a property of 'more than 400 ps.' had 12 hours of water (99 pesos), more than 100 fig trees, . . . two plots for cultivation which have alfalfa as well," and an adobe hut (Causa de Celestino Brizuela contra los vecinos de Paslimpato sobre turno de agua," 1870, AHLR, unclassified, 4, 18–27).

24 "Testamento ortogado por Pascual Gonzalez el año 1845," AJP (LR), Copia judicial de 1855, civil, G–#78, 1.

25 More than two-thirds (72 percent) of the ninety-eight landowners in Pitui had properties valued at 250 pesos.

26 Carrizo, *Cancionero de La Rioja,* 2: 360.

27 I roughly include in this group those landowners whose properties were valued at between 500 and 1,250 pesos. Again, this is only an approximate categorization.

28 The legislation that regulated the payment of the *contribución territorial* stipulated that "undivided properties" would be considered for the payment of the *contribución directa* as "belonging to one owner," who would be responsible for the tax. The law gave the individual "the full right to demand of the other *comuneros* [owners of communal lands] their corresponding share" (Law 124, art. 6, approved 12 December 1865, in *Registro Oficial de la Provincia de La Rioja,* 3: 547).

29 "Don Fernando Olivera contra Lorenzo Casiba sobre un contrato por un derecho de

agua," 1844, AJP (LR), civil, O–#3; and "Convenio entre Hipólito Segovia y Patricio Montesino sobre un terreno en Vichigasta," 1856, AJP (LR), civil, S–#8.

30 "Testamento otorgado por Pascual Gonzalez el año 1845," AJP (LR), Copia judicial de 1855, civil, G–#78, 2.

31 My category of larger landowners includes those with properties valued at 1,250 pesos or more. To arrive at the percentage, from the entire capital belonging to the notables, 244,944 pesos, I subtracted the 14,500 pesos that they had in urban properties and mining, so that the rural wealth of the elite was 230,444 pesos.

32 The Dávilas and Ocampos, for example, had resolved a legendary rivalry with a marriage that united the daughter of the most prominent landowner of the department, Don Ramón Doria (who belonged to the Dávila family and had changed his name to take possession of Sañogasta's *mayorazgo*, an estate inherited by primogeniture), with one of the Ocampos.

33 The 1801 assessment of the Hacienda de Nonogasta, which in 1855 belonged to the García family, allows us insight into the structure and value of the various components of the hacienda, particularly the importance of wine: land for foodstuffs (twenty-four square leagues), 800 pesos; water (four *marcos* [a measure of water]), 2,000 pesos; grape vines, 4,106 pesos; and unirrigated and unimproved land, 1,331 pesos. The total value of the hacienda was 8,237 pesos ("Don Crisólogo Chaves," ff. 25–35; and "Inventario de los bienes entregados a Doña Concepción del Moral con arreglo a la minuta de entrega que hizo Doña María Cedano a Don Santiago Gordillo," Nonogasta, 2 September 1835, AFZ–PFI, carpeta 1).

34 Such was the case with the Soaje brothers and Don Manuel Iribarren, who had ranches in Vinchina valued at 10,017 and 9,300 pesos respectively ("Lista de contribuyentes del derecho territorial de los departamentos de Vinchina y Guandacol, en el presente año de 1864," *El Riojano,* 11 November 1864.

35 Felix Antonio Izaguirre to Tristán Dávilla, Campanas, 2 February 1863, in AFZ–CTD.

36 French, "On the Province," 395–402.

37 Rickard, *The Mineral,* 164–76; and *Registro Oficial de la Provincia de La Rioja.*

38 Maximiliano Dávila to Carmelo Valdez, Hornillos, 12 November 1861, AHLR–CDV, carpeta 7, 72. This practice was also common in other departments of the province.

39 "Informe de Josef Nicolás Ocampo." Miners' wages were paid primarily in-kind (grain, wine, etc.) with products from the landlords' haciendas or goods from small stores, which were also owned by the landlords (AFZ–PFI, carpeta 1, 1828, 68–87).

40 "Causa criminal contra Solano Andrada por muerte a Don José Manuel Pazos," 1861, AJP (LR), criminal, A–#4.

41 Ibid., 5–6.

42 Ibid.

43 Ibid., 19–20.

44 "Pedro Gordillo solicita protocolización de una escritura original en que intervienen como partes Pedro Antonio Gordillo y varios indios de Malligasta," 1874, AJP (LR), juzgado de paz, G–#102, 1, 2; "Convenio ante el Superior Tribunal de Justicia sobre agua entre comuneros de Anguinán," 1833, AJP (LR), civil, C–#508; and "Con-

venio de compra entre Tristán Dávila y Mamerto Carrizo," 15 October 1864, in AFZ–CTD.

45 In the valley haciendas, the value of water was more than double that of the land itself ("Don Crisólogo Chaves," 25–35).

46 "Convenio ante el Superior Tribunal de Justicia," 1; and "Don Fernando Olivera," 2.

47 According to the *Registro* of 1855, Gómez was proprietor of a hacienda valued at 3,000 pesos and Moreta had property valued at 31 pesos; "José Luis Moreta contra Vicente Gómez por despojo de agua," 1864, AJP (LR), civil, M–#20. For other cases in Chañarmuyo, Pituil, and Campanas, see AFZ–PFI, carpeta 1, 175–76, 187.

48 "José Luis Moreta contra Vicente Gómez," 2.

49 With the development of mining centers in the Chilean Norte Chico in the 1830s, the labor market widened. The poorest peasants began to migrate seasonally to Copiapó and Huasco, which lay only a week's journey from the valley. By midcentury, Chilean mines had become a major employer of valley peasants, so that a census taken in Copiapó in 1855 would reveal 10,000 Argentineans living in that mining city, of which "a major part was Riojanos" (Sarmiento, *El Chacho,* 85).

50 Rickard, *The Mineral,* 177–78.

51 G. Dávila, "El Mineral," 104.

52 "Causa criminal contra Segundo Bazán por abigeato," 1870, APJ (LR), criminal, B–#10, 25.

53 The total was worth 16,000 pounds sterling annually; see Rickard, *The Mineral,* 177–78.

54 Jacinto Rincón to Ordoñez, Rioja, 30 December 1862; and *El Famatina,* 14 February 1863.

55 Joaquín González to Tristán Dávila, Nonogasta, 13 November 1855, AFZ–CTD.

56 "Vecinos de la Villa de Famatina (Chilecito) a D. F. Sarmiento," Famatina, 23 October 1862, in *Mitre-Sarmiento,* 167–68.

57 Régulo Martínez to Domingo F. Sarmiento, Chilecito, 23 December 1862, in *Mitre-Sarmiento,* 164–66; and Domingo F. Sarmiento to Bartolomé Mitre, San Juan, 28 December 1862, in *Mitre-Sarmiento,* 164–69.

58 Régulo Martínez to Domingo F. Sarmiento, Chilecito, 23 December 1862, in *Mitre-Sarmiento,* 164–66.

59 While the 1855 register shows him in possession of land and water rights worth only 750 pesos, in the 1860s, Angel was a partner in a mine valued at 2,000 pounds sterling; see Rickard, *The Mineral,* 166–76.

60 "Causa por cobro de pesos: Clásico Galíndez contra Justo Gordillo," 1857, AJP (LR), juzgado de paz, G–#63.

61 According to Vicente Almandoz Almonacid, a Unitarian notable in Famatina, in *Felipe Varela y sus Hordas en la Provincia de la Rioja* (Córdoba: Imprenta del Eco de Córdoba, 1869), cited in Reyes, *Bosquejo Histórico,* 250.

62 French, "On the Province," 399.

63 In the case of the labradores, whose occupation supposed the cultivation of land, it is possible that they did not appear in the *Registro* of 1855 because, at the time, they had not yet come of age.

64 I found information on the marital status of only eleven of the fifteen rebels.

65 "El 2ndo Jefe del ejército del Interior contra Eusebio Arguello, Casto Olivera y Bonifacio Carrizo por delito de rebelión," 1867, AJF (LR), penal, legajo 2, 3.

66 Reyes, *Bosquejo Histórico,* 267.

67 Samuel García to Ordoñez, Villa Argentina, 8 December 1862, cited in *El Famatina,* 23 January 1863.

68 Ibid.

69 "Don Felisísimo de la Colina contra Cansio Olmedo por indemnización de daños y perjuicios causados en el año 67 en la montonera que asoló la provincia," 1869, AJP (LR), criminal, O–#39, 1–8.

70 De Paoli and Mercado, *Proceso a los Montoneros,* 162.

71 Sarmiento, *Facundo,* 47.

72 De Paoli and Mercado, *Proceso a los Montoneros,* 159.

73 "Don Felisísimo," 10.

74 Reyes, *Bosquejo Histórico,* 262; and "Las Víctimas de la Montonera del '67," *La Regeneración,* 18 July 1867.

75 Reyes, *Bosquejo Histórico,* 267; and "Las Víctimas de la Montonera."

76 "Diferentes Notas y actuaciones sueltas," 1867, AJF (LR), penal, legajo 2, 20–21; "Las Víctimas de la Montonera"; and Zalazar, *Montonereando.*

77 D. Dávila, "Orígenes Nacionales," 69–72.

78 "El Coronel Tristán Dávila," *La Regeneración,* 16 August 1867. This obituary was originally published in *El Nacional* (Buenos Aires).

79 Although the *Registro* of 1855 records Dávila's properties and water rights at a worth of 750 pesos, we know that in 1857 he possessed a ranch in the neighboring department of Vinchina assessed, with improvements and livestock, at 1,666 pesos. The *Registro* also showed that in Campanas, where Dávila lived, his wife's family owned land and water worth 6,000 pesos. Commerce and transport, too, figured largely in his interests: these lucrative activities were possible thanks to the mule teams he raised and maintained on his ranch in Vinchina. Moreover, he owned a mill, which allowed him to grind the wheat and grain he bought from labradores to later sell as flour in the neighboring provinces. See "Inventario de la Estancia Monte de Tigre, Vinchina, enero de 1857," and various documents about land transactions in Vinchina, AFZ–PFI, carpeta 2, 12, 21–23, 25–28, 29–31, 44; and Félix Antonio Izaguirre to Tristán Dávila, Campanas, 2 February 1863, AFZ–CTD.

80 Restituta I. de Dávila to Tristán Dávila, Campanas, 5 November 1865, AFZ–CTD. Emphasis added.

81 Boman, "Pueblos de Indios del Antiguo Curato," 281.

82 For instance, Don Juan Gregorio Villafañe and his son-in-law Don Diego Catalán, wealthy hacendados and merchants, bought the lands of thirteen comuneros, small proprietors from the Indian village of San Blas de los Sauces, between 1830 and 1847; see ibid., 265–66, 279–81.

83 In 1829, after the battle of La Tablada, Facundo shot three Del Morals (a father and two sons) along with other Unitarians, an episode that was incorporated into local folklore (see chapter 6). Another Del Moral and two more Unitarians were executed

(they had their throats cut) by General Tomás Brizuela in 1836. And, as we have seen, the montonera of 1867 killed another member of the family in Famatina. See Reyes, *Bosquejo Histórico,* 73–75; and Luna, *De Comicios,* 74.

84 Boman, "Pueblos de Indios del Antiguo Curato," 247–48.

85 Ibid.; and Pérez Fuentes, "El Chacho y el Pronunciamiento," 236–37.

86 Rosario Hererra de Rincón to Abel Bazán, Rioja, 29 April 1868, cited in Luna, *De Comicios,* 57–58.

87 Don Severo's property, which he claimed he had inherited from his mother, was assessed at 1,990 pesos ("Causa de Don Nicolás Barros contra Don Severo Chumbita por cobro de pesos," 1873, AHLR, 26–28).

88 Boman, "Pueblos de Indios del Antiguo Curato," 248–49. In 1807, out of a total of twenty-two families in Aymogasta, the heads of seven had the last name Chumbita. The surname Chumbita was also widely used in the neighboring village of Machigasta.

89 Daniel Del Moral to Domingo Villafañe, San Antonio, 2 January 1862, AHLR–CDV, carpeta 8, 1.

90 Ibid.

91 Ibid.

92 Frutos Barros to Domingo Villafañe, Anjullón, 9 May 1862, AHLR–CDV, carpeta 8, 38.

93 Frutos Barros to Domingo Villafañe, Aymogasta, 3 August 1862, AHLR–CDV, carpeta 8, 67; and Angel Vicente Vera to Domingo Villafañe, Tinogasta, 30 August 1862, AHLR–CDV, carpeta 8, 74.

94 "Causa criminal contra Gaspar Vargas, Rosario Aibar, Carmelo Ontivero, Solano Quintero y Julián Díaz por suponerselos reos del delito de falso testimonio," 1872, AJF (LR), penal, legajo 5, 1–3. The documents from this trial include a transcript of Severo Chumbita's trial for his rebellion against the national government and his responsibility in the death of the Del Morals. Severo's testimony, almost a decade later, basically confirmed Daniel Del Moral's version of the fight at the party. The original record of Severo's trial has apparently been lost. As far as I know, Pedro De Paoli and Manuel Mercado were the last historians to have worked with the document, and they reproduced it only partially in *Proceso a los Montoneros* without mentioning the information related to the Del Morals' execution.

95 See Reyes, *Bosquejo Histórico,* 196; and De la Colina, *Crónicas,* 25.

96 "Interrogatorio de Melitón Córdoba a José Mercedes Chumbita (preso)," Machigasta, 6 December 1863, *Revista,* 51. Another version, circulated widely in La Rioja and believed by many, asserted that the decision to kill the Del Morals was made by Mercedes, who disobeyed Severo's orders to take the prisoners to the city of La Rioja. Reyes (*Bosquejo Histórico*) and De la Colina (*Crónicas*), however, both concur that it was Severo who ordered the executions.

97 Sarmiento, *El Chacho,* 83–84. Emphasis added.

98 A rich correspondence tells of the conflict in las Lagunas: see Régulo Martínez to Gelón, Mendoza, 18 May 1862, AS, 5016, armario 1; Luis Molina to Domingo F. Sarmiento, Mendoza, 23 May 1862, AS, 7509, armario 1; Domingo F. Sarmiento to Luis

Molina, San Juan, 16 May 1862, AS, 3805, carpeta 35; and Coronel Lino Almandoz to Bartolomé Mitre, Rosario, 30 November 1862, *AGM,* 12: 177–80.

99   CFED, Provincia de La Rioja, Talacán, dossier 69, "Anecdotas Históricas: Las tres cruces," informant: Arturo Herrera, thirty years old in 1921; and CFED, Provincia de La Rioja, Arauco, dossier 130, "Tradiciones populares," informant: Rosario Fuentes, seventy-one years old in 1921.

100   CFED, Provincia de La Rioja, Los Sarmientos, dossier 10, "Anécdota," informant: Benjamina Dávila, fifty-nine years old in 1921.

101   "Men of all countries and stations delight in the successful accomplishment of a swindle . . . , if the terms of a transaction are clearly understood, a story of clever cheating receives universal response. . . . Especially if the cheater is naturally weaker or poorer than his adversary, the interest in the swindle is heightened" (Thompson, *The Folktale,* 165, 198). On trickster tales as a form of resistance, see Scott, *Domination and the Art of Resistance,* 162; and Levine, *Black Culture and Black Consciousness,* 103–33.

102   Maximiliano Dávila to Carmelo Valdez, Hornillos, 12 November 1861, AHLR–CDV, carpeta 7, 72.

103   CFED, Provincia de Catamarca, Huillapima, dossier 228, "Anécdota," no informant.

104   D. Dávila, "Orígenes Nacionales," 291. See also Villafañe, *Reminiscencias,* 61–62.

105   CFED, Provincia de Catamarca, Coneta, dossier 6, "Anécdota," informant: no name, forty-eight years old in 1921.

106   Cited in Carrizo, *Antiguos,* 90–91. In this song, the gauchos want to banish Cachilico because the harvest has proved abundant and they do not need the stew any longer. The singer, though, considers the gauchos to be ungrateful.

3   *The Society of the Llanos*

1   Report in "Matrícula del curato de Los Llanos de La Rioja echo por su cura y vicario," 16 November 1806, Archivo del Arzobispado de Córdoba, legajo 20, vol. 2, unnumbered pages.

2   "Censo general que Manifiesta el Número de Habitantes de la Provincia de La Rioja, levantado el 26 de febrero de 1855," *Registro Oficial de la Provincia de La Rioja,* 1: 124–25; and De Moussy, *Description Geographique,* 3: 401.

3   Report in "Matrícula del curato de Los Llanos"; and French, "On the Province," 390.

4   Report in "Matrícula del curato de Los Llanos"; and Denis, *Valorización,* 99–106. The reservoirs were large depressions created to collect and store water from the summer rains. A "bucket" was a deep cavity dug into the ground until it revealed water from underground springs. From there, criadores drew water in leather buckets for their livestock.

5   Report in "Matrícula del curato de Los Llanos."

6   On various aspects of this migration, see Guzmán, "Los mulatos-mestizos," 71–107. Other evidence for this migration during the 1820s can be found in AQ, 4: 134–35.

7   According to a report from the parish of Los Llanos in 1806, an optimistic estimate

of all its livestock would not be more than 30,000 head ("Matrícula del curato de Los Llanos"). The Englishman O. J. French, who lived in the province from 1826 to 1828, claimed that there were only 16,000 head of cattle in Los Llanos at that time ("On the Province," 390). Tax paid in cattle for 1841 and 1842 was estimated at "more than 1,000 head" each year, indicating that the number of animals would be about 20,000 given that the proportion paid in taxes—the *diezmo*—was actually 5 percent ("Juan Llanos por sí y sus hermanos contra la testamentaría de Hipólito Tello por cobro de pesos," 1872, AJP (LR), civil, LL–#4, 30, 64).

8   The total for the province in 1888 was 160,000 head of cattle (Latzina, *L'Agriculture*, 303–6). This census was conducted when the expansion of cattle production from around the foot of the sierra into the surrounding plain was about to reach its maximum point.

9   De Moussy, *Description*, 1: 248, 2: 117–18.

10   For Corrientes, see Chiaramonte, *Mercaderes del Litoral*; for Buenos Aires, see Lynch, *Argentine Dictator*, 78.

11   The provincial census of 1855 registered 686 families in Costa Alta: thus, if we assume that each of the 409 proprietors included in the *Libro de Registro de las Propiedades Territoriales del Departamento Costa Alta y del Medio de Los Llanos* (1855, AJP [LR]) was a head of household, then the number of families without property would reach 277—that is, 40.37 percent of the department's population. This assumption is conservative because the alternative would be to consider that some families contained more than one proprietor, making the proportion of families without land higher. The figures on families are from "Censo general que Manifiesta el Número de Habitantes."

12   In the department of Costa Alta, there were 345 criadores and 129 inhabitants working primarily in agriculture. This proportion was inverted in Costa Baja, where there were only 276 criadores and 641 labradores.

13   Denis, *Valorización*, 104.

14   "Causa criminal contra Bernabé, José Angel, Mateo y Facundo Quintero por delito de cuatropea," 1870, AJP (LR), criminal, Q–#4.

15   Ibid.

16   A recent (still partial) study of the 1795 census of Los Llanos indicates that 25 percent of the heads of families included in the document were agregados; see Guzmán, "Los Mulatos-Mestizos," 84. In the varied documentation consulted here for the nineteenth century, however, there is practically no reference to or information about this institution. In the only two references that pointed to the institution's existence, it appears that the authorities tried to encourage settlers in Los Llanos to become agregados of a criador (patrón), who would then be responsible for the conduct of the agregado and his family. Even so, one of these references suggests that this was not always easily achieved. See AQ, 4: 134–35; and the papers of Elías Quintero (justice of the peace of Solca), 1830–1840, Archivo de Miguel Bravo Tedín, unnumbered pages.

17   Between 1778 and 1795, the mestizo-mulatto population grew throughout the province of La Rioja, from 1,906 to 6,633 individuals, so that this group went from 20

to 47 percent of the province's total population. In Los Llanos, the proportional growth appeared to be even greater. The available information indicates that there were 353 mestizo-mulatto inhabitants in 1778; by 1795, that number had risen to 1,658. See Guzmán, "Los Mulatos-Mestizos," 81.

18 Report in "Matrícula del curato de Los Llanos."

19 "Causa contra Domingo Montibero por hurto de animales vacunos," 1877, AJP (LR), criminal, M–#34, 1–3.

20 See ibid.; "Causa contra Procopio Flores y Vicente Galván por abigeato," 1876, AJP (LR), criminal, G–#20, 14; and "Causa contra Román Argañaraz y Pedro Vicente Barrios por delito de abigeato," 1870, AJP (LR), criminal, A–#17, 12.

21 See "Causa criminal contra Florencio Molina por robo de unos caballos y prendas de la ciudad de San Juan," 1869, AJP (LR), criminal, M–#12, 2–3.

22 "Declaraciones que declara Ramón Flores de todos los robos que ha visto robar," Saladillo, 23 January 1835, papers of Elías Quintero (justice of the peace of Solca), 1830–1840, Archivo de Miguel Bravo Tedín.

23 "Causa criminal contra Juan Aguero y José Molina por robo," 1875, AJP (LR), criminal, A–#2, 11.

24 "Causa criminal contra Bernabé, José Angel," 1.

25 "Juan Llanos por sí y sus hermanos contra la testamentaría de Hipólito Tello," 75–76.

26 See Denis, *Valorización,* 102; Boman, "Pueblos de Indios del Antiguo Curato," 235; and "Don Fermín de la Colina promueve juicio de testamentaría sobre la sucesión de Don Paulino Orihuela," 1888, AJP (LR), Registro Juicios Sucesorios, O–#230, 21–23.

27 *Libro de Registro.*

28 Olivera, *Transformaciones,* 22–25.

29 *Libro de Registro.*

30 See, for example, notarial documents in "Legajo de Tierras Fiscales #1," 1813–1878, AHLR, 84, 148, 218.

31 "Don José González pide autorización para vender un derecho en la estancia de 'Ampatá,' perteneciente a su hija," 1875, AJP (LR), civil, G–#27, 7–8.

32 Legajo #1 de Tierras Fiscales, 1813–1878, AHLR, 63, 67; and "Sucesión de Lucas Llanos y Desposoria Arias," 1911, AJP (LR), Registro de Juicios Sucesorios, LL–#24.

33 Ley 124, art. 6, passed 12 December 1865, in *Registro Oficial de la Provincia de La Rioja,* 3: 547.

34 Olivera, *Transformaciones,* 25.

35 *Libro de Registro.*

36 Ibid.

37 Ibid.

38 *Libro de Registro;* and "Causa criminal contra Santiago Montaña por cuatrero," 1871, AJP (LR), M–#16, 19.

39 *Libro de Registro;* and Legajo #1 de Tierras Fiscales, 1813–1878, AHLR, 168–69.

40 In this group, I include those landowners with property values between 1 and 149 pesos; they represented 56.73 percent of all proprietors.

41 Report in "Matrícula del curato de Los Llanos." Francisco Antonio Quintero, for

example, who owned a ranch and an orchard valued at 116 pesos in 1855, also owned seventeen head of cattle, twenty-eight horses, and other livestock such as goats, all worth an additional total of 178 pesos; see *Libro de Registro;* and "Protocolización solicitada por el Coronel Ricardo Vera en representación de Francisco Antonio Quintero," 1889, AJP (LR), civil, Q–#47.

42 "Causa criminal contra Santiago Montaña," 11–13.

43 De la Vega Díaz, *Cuestiones de Historia Menuda,* 27–30; and "Causa contra Román Argañaraz y Pedro Vicente Barrios," 7.

44 "Causa criminal contra Santiago Montaña," 3–5, 13–15; and "Causa criminal seguida contra José Víctor Herrera por complicidad en la Rebelión armada contra las autoridades nacionales promovida por el General Peñaloza," 1864, AJF (LR), penal, legajo 1, 20.

45 "Causa criminal contra Juan Aguero y José Molina," 1875, AJP (LR), criminal, A–#2, 3–5.

46 "Bonifacia Villacorta pide desembargo de hacienda," 1850, AJP (LR), civil, V–#3, 30, 37.

47 Ibid., 37, 38, 52. This legal dispute involved Bonifacia Villacorta and her granddaughters Brígida and Francisca Bargas. According to the *Libro de Registro,* in 1855, Villacorta had facilities and land for ranching in Patquía worth fifty-three pesos, and twenty-one head of cattle worth seventy-four pesos. The Bargas each owned a house (worth forty-six and sixty-two pesos), and had a herd of twenty head.

48 *Primer Censo Nacional,* 415.

49 I place those landowners whose properties were valued at between 150 and 699 pesos within this group, which represented 24.7 percent (101 out of 409 individuals) of the total number of proprietors.

50 The parish report from 1806 recounted that below the small group of large proprietors, and above those with just a few head of cattle, there was a group of "very few" residents who had "100, 200, 300, and 400 head of cattle" (report in "Matrícula del curato de Los Llanos").

51 "Documentos de Don Juan B. Manzano y litis con Don Juan Manuel Arias sobre deslinde del Medanito," 1859, AJP (LR), civil, M–#11; and "Patricio Fernández–Vicente Peñaloza–La Hedionita," 1854, AJP (LR), civil, F–#5.

52 *Libro de Registro.*

53 "Don Abraham Mendoza contra los intereses de Don Bernardo Carrizo," 1864, AJP (LR), civil, M–#23; and "Don Baltasar Torres contra Juan Bernardo Carrizo por cobro de animales," 1866, AJP (LR), civil, T–#9.

54 I have included in this group those landowners whose properties were valued at 699 pesos or more. This translates into only nineteen criadores, or 4.64 percent of the total number of proprietors.

55 Three of the caudillos' siblings were owners of the "Mascasi ranch," worth 1,000 pesos, and other small properties in Noqueves, San Antonio, and Malazán valued at 161 pesos. The widow and children of Facundo inherited a "right to the water and communal fields of Tuanín," worth 1,000 pesos (*Libro de Registro*).

56 "Patricio Fernández–Vicente Peñaloza–La Hedionita"; and de Paoli, *Facundo,* 25–26.

57 Report in "Matrícula del curato de Los Llanos."

58 The review of relevant judicial documents for this study proved unfruitful, and the few discoveries were not reliable. For example, the inventory of the estate of Paulino Orihuela corresponds to the *Libro de Registro*'s description of his land, but refers to only thirty-four head of cattle, which obviously cannot be accepted. ("Don Fermín Colina promueve juicio de testamentaría sobre la sucesión de Don Paulino Orihuela," 1888, AJP (LR), Registro de Juicios Sucesorios, O–#230). The same discrepancy arises in a judicial case that specifies properties. While the real estate corresponds to estimates in the registry, the count of cattle is too low ("Eusebio Bargas contra Don Paulino Ahumada sobre jactancia," 1866, AJP (LR), V–#16).

59 De Moussy, *Description,* 1: 248, 2: 117–18.

60 In 1874, a herd of 530 cattle—including tamberas (dairy cows), calves, yearlings, and so on—was taxed at a value of 6,043 pesos, averaging 11.40 pesos a head; see "María Concepción Sanchez de Garay solicita se le nombre tutora y curadora de sus hijos," 1874, AJP (LR), civil, G–#26.

61 "Patricio Fernández–Vicente Peñaloza–La Hedionita."

62 Chávez, *Vida del Chacho.*

63 Angel Vicente Peñaloza (750 pesos), Cesario Ocampo (750 pesos), Carmen Peñaloza (550 pesos), Francisco Javier Fernández (337 pesos), Pedro A. Peñaloza (125 pesos), José María Peñaloza (93 pesos), Candela Peñaloza (62 pesos), and Mercedes Peñaloza (31 pesos) (*Libro de Registro*).

64 The total value of the family's properties, according to the 1855 registry, was 2,161 pesos, principally in a ranch and a right in a merced. The latter, valued at 1,000 pesos, was part of Facundo's estate, having been bought with the respectable wealth that Facundo accumulated thanks to his political career. But the evolution of the rest of the family was quite different. In 1855, the other three offspring of Don Prudencio Quiroga were proprietors of a commonly held ranch worth 1,000 pesos, which it is safe to assume they inherited from their father. Thus, their individual shares and holdings would place them among the medium-sized proprietors.

65 Sábato, *Agrarian Capitalism,* 177.

66 Lynch, *Argentine Dictator,* 73–76.

67 Fitte, *Bienes Sucesorios.*

68 These figures are all in pesos fuertes (silver coins). Most of the original figures in the will were in pesos moneda corriente (paper pesos of the province of Buenos Aires). The original total of 1,443,057 pesos moneda corriente has been converted at the exchange rate of seven to one (used in the will) to arrive at the 200,000 pesos fuertes total noted here.

69 Facundo was responsible for collecting the tax imposed on cattle in the province, facilitating the building up of his herds and his active participation in the cattle market. In addition, he appeared to hold a monopoly on the sale of beef in the province. Still, even taking these privileges into account, it is improbable that his cattle inter-

ests would have accounted for his fortune. Indeed, after his death, his "successors" in La Rioja (Brizuela, Tello, Llanos, and Chacho) "inherited" his position as cattle tax collector without rising above their "modest" conditions as Los Llanos ranchers. See AQ, vols. 3 and 4; and "Juan Llanos por sí y sus hermanos contra la testamentaría de Hipólito Tello, por cobro de pesos," 1872, AJP (LR), civil, LL–#4.

70 Sarmiento, *Facundo,* 191.

4   Gauchos, Montoneros, and Montoneras

1   Regulo Martínez to Bartolomé Mitre, La Rioja, 14 January 1863, AGM, 12: 265–67.

2   Navarro Ocampo, *Actor,* 80, 168–69. Interestingly, while Mitre's personal envoy categorized Severo Chumbita, a caudillo from Arauco, as Indian, a Unitarian from the Riojan elite perceived him as a gaucho (see Regulo Martínez to Bartolomé Mitre, La Rioja, 14 January 1863, AGM, 12: 265–67; and De Paoli and Mercado, *Proceso a los Montoneros,* 196–97.

3   See chapter 7.

4   Peñaloza to José Olegario Gordillo, Tama, 28 February 1857, cited in Mercado, *La Degollación,* 140–44; and Chacho Peñaloza to Justo José Urquiza, 6 December 1854, cited in Bosch, "Urquiza y el Ultimo Levantamiento," 151.

5   Navarro Ocampo, *Actor,* 80–81, 308.

6   "Causa Criminal contra Fermín Bazán por sedición en los Llanos," 1865, AJP (LR), B–#595, 1.

7   "Sumaria tomada a los individuos que la policía tomó presos la noche del 17 de enero, 1874, en la imprenta de Bravo," 1874, AJP (LR), criminal, A–#18.

8   Cited in De Paoli and Mercado, *Proceso a los Montoneros,* 196–97.

9   For the use of these terms, see some of the stories in chapter 6.

10 "Causa criminal contra Eugenio Sosa y Rosa Quintero," 1872, AJP (LR), criminal, Q–#5, 5–6.

11 Ibid.

12 "Contra Feliciano Martínez por robo de un buei," 1875, AJP (LR), criminal, M–#28.

13 Ambrosio Sandes to Ignacio Rivas, Villanueva, 2 October 1862, AGN, X–2–2–2.

14 "Causa seguida al Capitán de Montoneros Juan Darío Balboa," 1830, Archivo Judicial de Catamarca, in Rodríguez, *Historia Judicial de Catamarca,* 37–39; and "De la causa criminal seguida de oficio contra los reos presentes Don Manuel V. Bustos [y otros]," 1865, Segundo cuaderno, AJF (LR), penal, leg. 1, 9.

15 José Manuel de la Fuente to Hilario Lagos, Don Diego, 16 August 1868, AIM, 6937; and Santos Guayama to Marceliro Quiroga, 13 June 1868, AHLR–CNB, carpeta 12, 196.

16 "Sumario instruído por el juez de paz de Belgrano y por orden del señor Gobernador en campaña, sobre los sucesos que se desarrollan desde el 29 de enero pasado, perturbando con la sedición y las montoneras el orden público de la pcia," 1874, *Revista,* 90, 93.

17 De Paoli and Mercado, *Proceso a los Montoneros,* 110.

18 Poem by Vicente Almonacid, in *El Riojano,* no. 6, 31 July 1863.

19 Benarós, "Estudio Preliminar," 32–33.

20 Absalón Ibarra to Antonino Taboada, in Taboada, *Los Taboada,* 3: 411; "Causa criminal sin carátula," 1865, AJP (LR), B–without number, 1–2; and "Causa criminal contra José de los Santos Echegaray Carrizo por participación con la rebelión encabezada por Felipe Varela," 1867, AJF (LR), penal, legajo 2.

21 "Sucesión de Lucas Llanos and Desposoria Arias," 1911, AJP (LR), Registro de Juicios Sucesorios, LL–#24; and "Juan Llanos por sí y sus hermanos contra la testamentaría de Hipólito Tello por cobro de pesos," 1872, AJP (LR), civil, LL–#4.

22 While I know for a fact that Nieto and Guevara were illiterate, I have no information either way concerning Zalazar.

23 "Causa criminal seguida de oficio contra los reos presentes Don Manuel Vicente Bustos [y otros]," 1865, Segundo Cuaderno, AJF (LR), penal, leg. 1, 113–14.

24 Navarro Ocampo, *Actor,* 253.

25 "[Captain Mercedes Chumbita] moved the troops that time . . . [by saying] publicly to the soldiers that [Commander] Don Sebero [Chumbita] had orders from General Peñaloza to move his forces and was not doing it, but that he [Mercedes] was going to do it, as the General had ordered." ("Causa criminal contra Gaspar Vargas, Rosario Aibar, Carmelo Ontiveros, Solano Quintero y Julián Días por suponérseles reos del delito de falso testimonio," 1872, AJF [LR], penal, legajo 5, 10–11).

26 "[Lucas Llanos, Juan Gabriel Pueblas, Gerónimo Aguero, and others got together with Chacho and] have asked that the General, although he is not marching with the forces to San Juan, declare his support, given the moral significance that his declaration would have for the masses" (Sixto Fonsalida to Domingo F. Sarmiento, Valle Fértil, 27 March 1863, AS, 2023, carpeta 16).

27 It is important to remark that I do not have homogeneous information for these rebels. While in some cases I know their occupations, I do not know their marital status, and vice versa. This explains the discrepancies in the totals for tables 7 through 12.

28 This comparison is only an estimate because the group of montoneros considered here includes non–La Riojans as well; see "Censo General que Manifiesta el Número de Habitantes de la Provincia de La Rioja, Levantado el 26 de Febrero de 1855," *Registro Oficial de la Provincia de La Rioja,* 1: 124–25.

29 Sarmiento, *El Chacho,* 75.

30 Fernández Latour, *Cantares,* 240.

31 "Causa contra Adrián Guzmán por suponérsele cómplice en un asesinato perpetrado en la sierra de Catamarca y haber andado con Guayama en la última montonera," 1870, AJP (LR), criminal, G–#66, 2–3.

32 "Causa contra Elías Butierrez por atribuírsele el crímen de rebelión," 1868, AJF (LR), legajo 3, 20–28; and "Contra Don Carlos Traverza por complicidad con los rebeldes encabezados por Felipe Varela," 1867, AJF (LR), penal, legajo 2, 37–39.

33 "José C. Rodríguez contestando cargos que se le hacen sobre cargo militar conferido por Felipe Varela," 1871, AJP (LR), civil, R–#50, 1; and Juan Francisco Orihuela to Ricardo Vera, Jachal, 14 September 1862, AGM, 12: 257–58.

34 "Sumario instruído por el juez de paz de Belgrano," 102–05.

35 "Contra Elías Butierrez por atribuírsele el crimen de rebelión," 1868, AJF (LR), penal, legajo 3, 42–49.

36 "De la causa criminal seguida de oficio contra los reos presentes, Dn. Manuel Vicente Bustos [y otros]," 1866, Segundo cuaderno, AJF (LR), penal, leg. 1, 70–73.

37 "Causa criminal contra Eugenio Sosa y Rosa Quintero," 1872, AJP (LR), criminal, #5, 3, 7–8; and Severo Chumbita to Argel Vicente Peñaloza, Aymogasta, 27 March 1863, in "Causa contra Gaspar Vargas, Rosario Aibar, Carmelo Ontivero, Solano Quintero y Julián Díaz por suponerselos reos del delito de falso testimonio," 1872, AJF (LR), penal, legajo 5, 3–5.

38 Written version in Carrizo, see also oral version in Maipú, province of Buenos Aires. Both in Fernández Latour, *Cantares,* 54, 64.

39 "Causa criminal contra José Antonio Manrique, José Desiderio Fernández, José Naranjo, Juan de las Rosas Paredes, José Antonio Reinoso y David Ibañez por delito de sedición," 1865, AJP (LR), criminal, M–#8; 9–10; and "Causa contra Ramón Nieto por habersele atribuído ser cabecilla de una montonera en Arauco y haber desobedecido el llamado que le hacía el gobierno," 1874, AJP (LR), criminal, N–#17.

40 "Contra los autores de la destrucción de los marcos puestos por el juez de paz de la Costa de Arauco," 1874, AJP (LR), criminal, O–#52.

41 Carrizo, *Cancionero Popular de Tucumán,* 2: 323. See also other similar songs in the same volume, 2: 317, 2: 350; and in Carrizo, *Antiguos,* 90–91.

42 Paz, *Memorias,* 1: 250–51, 2: 104–7.

43 Ignacio Rivas to Wenceslao Paunero, Mendoza, 7 January 1862, AP, 7–1–2–144; Ignacio Rivas to Wenceslao Paunero, los Llanos, 4 May 1862, AP, 7–6–16–1254; Ignacio Rivas to Wenceslao Paunero, Catuna, 22 May 1862, AP, 7–6–16–1252; and José M. Arredondo to Wenceslao Paunero, Rioja, 3 April 1862, AP, 7–1–2–181.

44 Ignacio Rivas to Wenceslao Paunero, Olta, 31 March 1862, AP, 7–5–15–1203.

45 Ignacio Rivas to Wenceslao Paunero, Olta, 31 March 1862, AP, 5–15–1206.

46 Ibid.; and Ignacio Rivas to Wenceslao Paunero, Llanos, 19 April 1862, AP, 7–5–15–1227.

47 Navarro Ocampo, *Actor,* 164.

48 Ignacio Rivas to Wenceslao Paunero, Mendoza, 7 January 1862, AP, 7–1–2–144.

49 CFED, Provincia de Catamarca, Chumbicha, dossier 210, informant: Ponciano Roldán, eighty-seven years old in 1921.

50 "In that battle of Manantial was where Peñaloza's wife, who is considered as valiant as he is, fighting at his side protected the life of her husband, receiving a large wound in her forehead and stopping another blow against the General" (Navarro Ocampo, *Actor,* 294).

51 Cited in Chávez, *Vida del Chacho,* 32.

52 Régulo Martínez to Bartolomé Mitre, Catamarca, 24 January 1863, AGM, 12: 271.

53 Ponciano Roldán, interview in CFED, Provincia de Catamarca, Chumbicha, dossier 210.

54 "De la causa criminal seguida de oficio contra los reos presentes Don Manuel V. Bustos [y otros]," 64–65.

55 "Reclamo de Juliana Díaz en favor de su madre Dolores Díaz destinada a la frontera de Santiago del Estero," 1868, AJF (LR), penal, legajo 1, 5; and Antonino Taboada to Natael Morcillo, Catamarca, 7 February 1868, in Reyes, *Bosquejo Histórico,* 270–71.

56 Navarro Ocampo, *Actor,* 201–2.

57 "Contra Don Carlos Traverza por complicidad con los rebeldes encabezados por Felipe Varela," 1867, AJF (LR), penal, legajo 2, 11.

58 "Destrucción y Ruina!!! Páginas de Sangre," *La Regeneración,* 14 July 1867.

59 "Contra Don Carlos Traverza," 13.

60 Restituta Izaguirre de Dávila to Tristán Dávila, Campanas, 26 February 1852, AFZ.

61 Reyes, *Bosquejo Histórico,* 260.

62 Olmos, *Historia de Catamarca,* 198–200.

5   Caudillos and Followers

1 Ignacio Rivas to Wenceslao Paunero, Llanos of La Rioja, 21 April 1862, AP, 7–5–15–1119.

2 Ignacio Rivas to Wenceslao Paunero, Llanos of La Rioja, 19 April 1862, AP, 7–5–15–1227.

3 Ignacio Rivas to Wenceslao Paunero, Tama, 9 April 1862, AP, 7–5–15–1200.

4 When a militia commander asked one of his officers if the soldiers were ready to fight the montoneras, the officer responded positively, saying that the goal of the militia was "to combat the enemy and not to eat beef without reason" ("Causa criminal contra Exipión Dávila por complicidad con la rebelión que ha tenido lugar en esta provincia encabezada por Felipe Varela," 1867, AJP (LR), penal, legajo 2, 17–19).

5 While traveling through the Llanos of La Rioja, an Englishman noticed that the peasants from that region "seldom taste other animal food than what they obtain in the chase—the flesh of the vicuña or the guanaco." And on one of his stops, when he requested meat for dinner, one of the Llanisto hosts responded that "we can hardly procure meat for ourselves here" (French, "On the Province," 384).

6 Cited in Di Lullo, *Cancionero Popular de Santiago del Estero,* 67.

7 Fernández Latour, *Cantares,* 306; collected in El Quimil, Provincia de Tucumán.

8 Hipólito Pastoriza to Sarmiento, Rioja, 25 June 1863, AS, 5118, armario 1; José M. de la Fuente to Hilario Lagos, Tinogasta, 28 October 1867, in AFL–PCHL, 201; Gaspar Taboada to Absalón Ibarra, Santiago del Estero, 28 May 1863, in Taboada, *Los Taboada,* 3: 407–8; and Gaspar Taboada to Absalón Ibarra, Santiago, 10 June 1863, in Taboada, *Los Taboada,* 3: 421.

9 "Causa criminal contra Agustín Molina por rebelión," 1872, AJF (LR), penal, legajo 5, 6.

10 "Causa criminal contra Florentino Vega, Vicente Contreras y Manuel Escalante por atribuírseles participación en la rebelión encabezada por Felipe Varela en esta provincia," 1868, AJF (LR), penal, legajo 3, 6; and De Paoli and Mercado, *Proceso a los Montoneros,* 84.

11 CFED, Provincia de La Rioja, dossier 69, Talacán, "Anecdota Trágica," informant:

Arturo Herrera, thirty years old in 1921. Note in the dossier: "This story was told by people that passed away (it refers to Juan de Dios Aranda, one of the protagonists of the episode)."

12 CFED, Provincia de La Rioja, Ciudad de La Rioja, dossier 59, "Montoneros," 44, informant: Serafina Reyes.

13 Octaviano Navarro to Bartolomé Mitre, Catamarca, 20 January 1868, AIM, 6520.

14 Angel Reyna, eighty-five years old in 1921, cited in Fernández Latour, *Cantares,* 302.

15 See the case of the troops of Facundo in "Batallón de Infantería: Lista de pago de tropa," Rioja, 17 December 1827, AQ, 4: 452–58.

16 Taboada, *Los Taboada,* 2: 387–92.

17 José Arredondo to Domingo F. Sarmiento, Rioja, 17 February, AS, 1899, carpeta 14; and "Causa criminal contra el Juez de Paz del Departamento Independencia Jesús Vera, por coacción ejercida contra la libertad del sufragio de los ciudadanos," 1874, AJF (LR), penal, legajo 6, 1.

18 "Sumario levantado en la villa de Dolores," Córdoba, 13 October 1862, AP, 7–26–8–2359, unnumbered pages.

19 *Registro Oficial de la Provincia de La Rioja,* 2: 395, 440–42.

20 Navarro Ocampo, *Actor,* 247. Carlos Angel wanted to reward his followers for their participation in the second rebellion of Chacho and the siege of the city of La Rioja in June 1862.

21 Cornelio Loyola to Juan Barbeito, San Francisco, 17 November 1863, in Taboada, *Los Taboada,* 3: 436.

22 Gregorio Vera to Tristán Dávila, Tama, 22 April 1862, AHLR–CDV, carpeta 8, 28.

23 Francisco Sarmiento to Domingo F. Sarmiento, Caucete, 5 June 1862, AS, 7975, armario 1. Emphasis in the original.

24 On this language, see chapter 6.

25 CFED, Provincia de La Rioja, dossier 65, 46, no informant. The Unitarians were also referred to as "patriots," and therefore, Unitarianism was called "the patria." Apparently, this was the result of two factors. On the one hand, the Unitarians were identified with (equated to) the "patriot army" of the first revolutionary decade, that is, the armies sent by Buenos Aires to the interior during the wars of independence. Describing the Unitarians of the interior as patriots was a way of associating them with Porteño. On the other hand, patria in rural slang meant "the government" or "the national or provincial state" (the horses owned by the government were known as *caballos patrios*). In the 1860s, then, because of the Unitarian hegemony, patria could also mean Unitarianism. For the use of *patriotas* as a synonym for Unitarian, see CFED, Provincia de San Juan, Pampa Vieja, dossier 161, "Cuento Histórico," informant: Santiago Villafañe, 110 [*sic*] years old in 1921; and CFED, Provincia de San Juan, Valle Fertil, dossier 50, "Tradiciones Populares." On the use of patria as a synonym for the government, see Mansilla, *Excursión,* 2: 380–82.

26 Domingo F. Sarmiento to Wenceslao Paunero, San Juan, 23 September 1863, AS, 2099, carpeta 16. See also "Causa criminal contra Martín Corbalán por haber intentado seducir para una rebelión a un soldado del regimiento de caballería #1 de línea," 1865, AJF (LR), penal, legajo 1.

27 "Causa criminal contra José Antonio Manrique, José Desiderio Fernández, José Naranjo, Juan de las Rosas Paredes, José Antonio Reinoso y David Ibañez por delito de sedición," 1865, AJP (LR), M–#8, 13–14.

28 Domingo B. Dávila, "Orígenes Nacionales," 75.

29 "Causa criminal contra Bernabé, José Angel, Matco and Facundo Quintero por delito de cuatropea," 1869, AJP (LR), criminal, Q–#4, 7–8.

30 Argel Vicente Peñaloza to Wenceslao Paunero, Guaja, 31 July 1862, AP, 7–7–22–1978.

31 Don Cruz Sosa, contra la testamentaria de Don Domingo Bazán reclamando lo que le corresponde como hijo natural," 1859, AJP (LR), civil, S–#1, 23, 27, 28, 50.

32 Ibid., 13.

33 Ibid., 24, 27–28.

34 Ibid., 20–21.

35 Ibid., 14. Unfortunately, the court record left off one year after the case began, so the outcome is unknown.

36 "Causa criminal contra Francisco González por rebelión y otros delitos," 1864, AJP (LR), G–#8, 4–5.

37 Ibid.

38 Roldán and Coppari, "La Personalidad del Chacho," 118.

39 Sixto Fonsalida to Domingo F. Sarmiento, Valle Fértil, 27 March 1863, AS, 2023, carpeta 16.

40 Mercado, *Las Quince Muertes,* 96 97; and Sarmiento, *El Chucho,* 72.

41 Villafañe, *Reminiscencias,* 60–61.

42 CFED, Catamarca Province, Chumbicha, dossier 210, informant: Ponciano Roldán, eighty-seven years old in 1921.

43 Navarro Ocampo, *Actor,* 75.

44 Villafañe, *Reminiscencias,* 57; and Sarmiento, *El Chacho,* 77.

45 On Brizuela's style of dress, see Villafañe, *Reminiscencias,* 57; on Chacho's, see the descriptions of various contemporaries in Luna, "El Chacho en la Literatura Nacional," 78–79.

46 Navarro Ocampo, *Actor,* 276. According to this sympathizer of Peñaloza, the caudillo could barely "put his signature." On the fact that a poor education was common among the richest criadores of Los Llanos, see Reyes, *Bosquejo Histórico,* 274.

47 Domingo B. Dávila, "Orígenes Nacionales," 292.

48 Argel Vicente Peñaloza to Justo José Urquiza, 6 December 1854, in Bosch, "Urquiza y el Ultimo Levantamiento," 151.

49 Ignacio Rivas to Bartolomé Mitre, Catuna, 15 June 1862, AGM, 11: 261–63; and José Arredondo to Bartolomé Mitre, La Rioja, 22 November 1863, AGM, 26: 195.

50 "Declaraciones remitidas por el General Taboada referentes a los individuos Dn. Jacinto Rincón [y otros]," AJF (LR), penal, legajo 2, unnumbered pages. Emphasis added.

51 "Causa criminal contra Santiago Montaña por cuatrero," 1871, AJP (LR), M–#16, 19.

52 Peñaloza died on November 12, 1863, and Zalazar first appeared on the regional political scene in June 1865.

53 Ambrosio Sandes to Ignacio Rivas, Nonogasta, 7 March 1862, AGN, X–2–2–2.

54 Ignacio Rivas to Wenceslao Paunero, Valde de Ventanita, 8 April 1862, AP, 7–5–15–1196.

55 Wenceslao Paunero to Bartolomé Mitre, Córdoba, 24 June 1862, AGM, 11: 118.

56 "Causa criminal contra Exipión Dávila por complicidad con la rebelión que ha tenido lugar en esta provincia encabezada por Felipe Varela," 1867, AJF (LR), penal, legajo 2, 21–22.

57 Ramón Gil Navarro Ocampo to Justo José Urquiza, Córdoba, 11 February 1867, AFSB–CRGNO.

58 Ibid.; and "Causa criminal contra Exipión," 22–23.

59 "Causa criminal contra Exipión," 17.

60 Ibid., 64–65.

61 Exipión Dávila to San Román, letter in *La Regeneración,* 10 October 1867, in "Causa criminal contra Exipión," 33.

62 "Causa criminal contra Exipión," 20–21.

63 Ibid.

64 Ibid., 64–65.

65 Ibid.

66 Ibid., 33.

67 See chapter 2.

68 The 1868 conflict arose over the presidential elections of that same year. The army supported the candidacy of Sarmiento, while the Dávilas and their regional allies, the Taboada family of Santiago del Estero, backed the candidacy of Elizalde. This conflict also accounts for the indictment of Exipión, whose actions would have otherwise been overlooked. On these events in La Rioja's political struggles, see Luna, *De Comicios,* 13–67.

69 Fray Laurencio Torres to Abel Bazán, 22 April 1868, in Luna, *De Comicios,* 55.

70 "Governor Dávila has pardoned the montoneros Chumbas (father and son), Elizondo, Gutiérrez, [and] Zalazar, and ordered them to mobilize their troops" (Ricardo Vera to José Manuel de la Fuente, Rioja, 13 May 1868, AIM, 6928).

71 Rosario Herrera de Rincón to Abel Bazán, La Rioja, 29 April 1868, in Luna, *De Comicios,* 57–58. The cheers referred to the rumored but never implemented electoral alliance of Urquiza with the Taboada family for the presidential election of 1868. Felipe Varela's name was also shouted together with Urquiza's.

72 Luna, *De Comicios,* 55.

73 Collected in Milagro, La Rioja, informant: Romualdo Flores, sixty-five years old in 1921, in Fernández Latour, *Cantares,* 267.

74 CFED, Provincia de La Rioja, Plaza Vieja, dossier 25, "Relato de la campaña contra los montoneros en la parte norte de la Provincia de La Rioja y Este y Norte de Catamarca," informant: Santiago Salcedo, eighty years old in 1921.

6 Facundo and Chacho in Songs and Stories

1. Sarmiento, *El Chacho*, 172.
2. Scott, *Domination and the Arts of Resistance*, 221.
3. Ibid., 222.
4. Chasteen, *Heroes on Horseback*, 5, 119.
5. Scott, *Domination and the Arts of Resistance*, 222.
6. Geertz, *Local Knowledge*, 143.
7. Ibid., 129.
8. Ibid.
9. Chasteen, *Heroes on Horseback*, 4.
10. Facundo and Chacho were not the objects of rituals or festivals as was the case with Rosas in Buenos Aires. As far as I know, no homage was paid to them through architecture or the visual arts either. In the case of Facundo, his portrait appeared in Federalist almanacs published in Buenos Aires, but there is no evidence to suggest that these books circulated widely in the interior of the country. The inclusion of Facundo, whose political career and rule is not at the center of this book, requires an explanation. On the one hand, the rich body of popular representations of Facundo affords us an exceptional opportunity to explore the issues raised in this chapter. On the other, Facundo's was the first caudillista experience in postindependence La Rioja, and hence, a foundational one that helped to define in the Riojan rural culture the qualities that a caudillo should have.
11. In 1921, the National Education Council ordered elementary schoolteachers throughout the country to interview older people in their communities. The teachers wrote down the oral repertoire provided by the informants and sent it to Buenos Aires, where the collection was eventually housed at the Instituto Nacional de Antropología y Pensamiento Latinoamericano. The only systematic work on this collection is the excellent compilation of songs with a strictly political content by Fernández Latour, *Cantares*. Several works inspired me to use folklore as one of the ways to uncover popular representations of caudillos. In addition to Scott, *Domination and the Arts of Resistance*, see Levine, *Black Culture and Black Consciousness;* Burke, *Popular Culture in Early Modern Europe;* Robert Darnton, *The Great Cat Massacre;* and Vovelle, "La Representation Populaire de la Monarchie." On the methodological questions related to the use of folklore, oral traditions, and testimonies, I benefited from insights on the use of the WPA in the United States; Blassingame, *Slave Testimony;* Vann Woodward, "History from Slave Sources"; and Perdue, introduction to *Weevils in the Wheat*. On the rich possibilities of oral testimonies to illuminate the culture of the informants, see Portelli, *The Death of Luigi Trastulli*.
12. These figures do not include the different versions of each song. In some cases, up to sixteen variations of the same song have been uncovered. See Carrizo, *Cancionero Popular de Salta,* and *Cancionero Popular de La Rioja;* and Fernández Latour, *Cantares.*
13. Navarro Ocampo, *Actor*, 308.
14. Paz, *Memorias*, 2: 254.

15 Private Diary of Ramón Gil Navarro Ocampo, Uspayata, Mendoza, 18 March 1846.

16 Navarro Ocampo, *Actor*, 61.

17 Fernández Latour, *Cantares*, 236. Collected in La Dorada, Catamarca, informant: Enriqueta Romero, seventy-five years old in 1921.

18 This figure includes different versions of the same song. Here, we only count the songs collected in 1921 and not those gathered by folklorists in other collections.

19 The Federalist leaders were positively mentioned on 107 occasions and the Unitarians 23 times. It is especially interesting to make comparisons between contemporary figures. While Facundo was evoked 20 times, General Paz was only mentioned twice. Urquiza was referred to 25 times, yet Mitre and Sarmiento were mentioned only twice and once, respectively.

20 Rosas "ordered the liberation" of a prisoner condemned to death who had composed the famous and popular (and clearly anonymous) ballad of the Bien-te-veo bird; see Hudson, *Far Away*, 128–29. The other version concerns Felipe Varela's arrest of several citizens in Belén, Catamarca, during his 1867 rebellion against the national government. Among the victims was Abraham Aguilar, a famous popular composer. Felipe Varela had imposed in-kind and cash fines in exchange for the prisoners' freedom, and since Aguilar was poor, he made use of his creativity, composing a *decima* (ten-line stanza composition) in favor of the rebellion. This piece "opened for him the doors of the jail" (the 1921 collection gathered one version of Aguilar's alleged decima, which is illustrative of some of the motivations and goals of the rebels). See Fernández Latour, *Cantares*, 264–65.

21 Private Diary of Ramón Gil Navarro Ocampo, Asequiones, San Juan, 16 March 1846.

22 In the somewhat deteriorated version collected in Catamarca in 1921, only Rosas is mentioned. Juan Alfonso Carrizo collected another version, better preserved, in Salta at the end of the 1920s, in which the presence of Ibarra is clear. See Fernández Latour, *Cantares*, 88–89.

23 Ibid., 89–92.

24 Private Diary of Ramón Gil Navarro Ocampo, Asequiones, San Juan, 16 March 1846.

25 For such sermons and patriotic speeches, see Carranza, *Clero Argentino*, esp. 1, 92–93, 109, 126, 166. Atahualpa was the other often-invoked legitimate monarch of the Americas, while the Spanish kings were tyrants associated with the pharaoh. The use of the rhetoric of independence in the civil wars that followed has been pointed out by various studies on Rosismo. In this case, it was used on behalf of Unitarianism.

26 Lavaysse's nickname, Almanac, referred to his creativity and unique personality, which is confirmed by other entries in Navarro Ocampo's diary and the nice portrait of the Santiago Unitarian left by Lucio V. Mansilla in *Entre-Nos*, 512–17.

27 Private Diary of Ramón Gil Navarro Ocampo, Stockton, 31 December 1850.

28 Fernández Latour, *Cantares*, 38–39. Collected in Los Herrera, Tucumán, n.d. In other versions (from the provinces of Santiago del Estero, San Luis, and Buenos Aires), Ibarra is replaced with Estanislao López or Juan Manuel Rosas.

29 Fernández Latour, *Cantares*, 33.

30 Garavaglia and Gelman, "Rural History of the Río de la Plata, 1600–1850," 92–93.

31 Pérez Fuentes, "El Chacho y el Pronunciamiento," 239.

32 Bazán, A. R. *Historia de La Rioja,* 357.

33 Ibid., 373–75.

34 Navarro Ocampo's diary as well as travel accounts and memoirs from the nineteenth century are full of references to the ubiquity of storytelling and singing among the gauchos. It was quite common for them to tell tales around a fire at night or to hum songs while working. The literally thousands of songs and stories gathered in 1921 and in other collections are a testimony to the importance of these activities. In La Rioja, even today, singing and composing are long-lived phenomena.

In terms of the spoken word, there were few regions where the majority of the rural lower classes spoke Indian languages as first languages. In the province of Corrientes, most of the lower classes spoke Guaraní, and Quechua predominated in the province of Santiago de Estero and some areas of the province of Jujuy. Yet, it is possible that many people were bilingual to some degree. In the case of Santiago de Estero, the vast majority of the songs that referred to nineteenth-century political events were sung in Spanish. See Di Lullo, *Cancionero Popular de Santiago del Estero.*

35 For a view that emphasizes the exclusive role of literacy and printed materials in the process of nation formation, see Anderson, *Imagined Communities.*

36 CFED, Provincia de Catamarca, Chumbicha, dossier 210, "Narración: Vicente Peñaloza (El Chacho)," informant: Ponciano Roldán, eighty-seven years old in 1921.

37 Thompson, *The Folktale,* 3–6, 14.

38 Thus, the songs and stories about Felipe Varela are clearly informative and lack any hint of mythologizing. With one exception, in none of the stories does he appear as the lone protagonist, nor in events that are not directly related to politics. Present only in stories after 1860, Varela appears as a leader in tales that refer to the rebellion rather than to him specifically. Perhaps this was due to the facts that Varela was out of the region for many years and his sociability in rural areas was, apparently, limited. Varela was essentially a military man and professional politician, not a rural proprietor and country dweller.

39 The word *mythogenic,* the concept, and a discussion on how this process takes place, are taken from Burke, *Popular Culture in Early Modern Europe,* 149–77, esp. 169–70.

40 Although it is obvious that certain songs and stories were composed after the death of the caudillos, the archetypes and motifs that they expressed shaped not only the cultural perception of what a caudillo should be but also influenced the political loyalties that the gauchos showed toward Federalism, the party in which the caudillos had contended.

41 On the necessity of subjecting folklore (and for that matter, any other source used to study popular political culture) to cross-examination, see Wells and Joseph, *Summer of Discontent, Seasons of Upheaval,* 9–17.

42 CFED, Provincia de La Rioja, Vargas, dossier 78, "Anécdota: El Tigre de Los Llanos," informant: Gavina Romero, ninety-five years old in 1921.

43 CFED, Provincia de San Juan, Dos Puentes, dossier 78, "Pérdida de una Piña de Plata," no informant.

44　CFED, Provincia de La Rioja, Punta de Los Llanos, dossier 81, "Las Montoneras," informant: Manuel Antonio Díaz, seventy years old in 1921.

45　CFED, Provincia de La Rioja, Chamical, dossier 175, "Guerrillas del General Peñaloza con Linares," informant: Felipe Paz, ninety-one years old in 1921.

46　See Burke, *Popular Culture in Early Modern Europe*, 150–55; and Scott, "Patron-Client Politics and Political Change in Southeast Asia," 126.

47　It is interesting to note that some of the qualities attributed to the caudillos were similar to those attributed to King Ferdinand VII in Mexican popular culture during independence. The Spanish King could be seen in two distant places at the same time, traveling in disguise in a veiled coach or wearing a silver mask, and was considered a fatherly figure. Moreover, independence leaders, especially Ignacio Allende, were conflated with the figure of the King, and some of the qualities of the latter were attributed to the former. See Van Young, "The Raw and the Cooked," 79–81, 83.

48　Carrizo, *Cancionero Popular de La Rioja*, 2: 51–54. For a story organized around the same motif but referring to different circumstances, see CFED, Provincia de La Rioja, Los Sarmientos, dossier 10, informant: Isabel B. de Luna, ninety years old in 1921.

49　Carrizo, *Cancionero Popular de La Rioja*, 2: 51–54. On the "king in disguise" motif, see Burke, *Popular Culture in Early Modern Europe*, 152.

50　Hudson, *Far Away*, 127. These stories made their way to literature. For instance, Hudson endowed his fictional caudillo General Santa Coloma with this quality in his classic novel of 1885, *The Purple Land*. And Ricardo Guiraldes, in a collection of short stories that he claimed were anecdotes he had heard, used the same motif to tell a story about Rosas; see his "Juan Manuel," in *Cuentos de y de Sangre*, 19–23.

51　CFED, Provincia de San Juan, Dos Puentes, dossier 78, "Pérdida de una Piña de Plata." In this story, Facundo, thanks to his astuteness, discovers who stole a piece of silver and restitutes it to the owner. The story is obviously modeled on motif J1141.4 in which "a false message is sent to the thief's wife to induce her to send the stolen jewel as a bribe to the judge"; "almost any legend dealing with a wise king may enter into the Solomon cycle" (Thompson, *The Folktale*, 189, 266).

52　Cited in Bazán, "Las Bases Sociales de la Montonera," 57–58.

53　One of the caudillo's assassins, "Roque Junco told them, / What a mistake I've made / we've killed Quiroga, / and he was such a dear father" (Carrizo, *Cancionero Popular de La Rioja*, 2: 58; collected in Guandacol, La Rioja, informant: Javier Ahumada, seventy-six years old in 1940). Facundo also referred to the people of La Rioja as "my children" (G. Dávila, "El Mineral," 78).

54　CFED, Provincia de Catamarca, Capital, dossier 45, "Campañas del General Navarro," informant: Corina T. de Amador, sixty-five years old in 1921. In 1862, Navarro Ocampo also defined General Navarro as the "Caudillo and Father" of Catamarca (*Actor,* 44). Note the similarity with the language defining the king-subject relation in France: the popular culture of the ancien régime "conforte l'image du roi pere, 'ses sujets son ses enfants' . . . 'un bon pere et des bons enfants, se cheriront et seront contents'" ["reinforces the image of the king-father, his subjects are his children, a good father and his good children will love each other and will be happy"] (Vovelle, "La Representation Populaire de la Monarchie").

55 CFED, Provincia de La Rioja, Siempre Verde, dossier 112, "Anécdotas," no informant.

56 CFED, Provincia de La Rioja, San Antonio, dossier 139, "Narración hecha por el Señor Balbino Garay."

57 CFED, Provincia de San Juan, no location, dossier 1, "Anecdotas: El Chacho," no informant.

58 CFED, Provincia de la Rioja, Siempre Verde, dossier 112, "Algunos datos sobre la muerte de Peñaloza," no informant. The story contains information and themes that reappear in songs about the event.

59 CFED, Provincia de La Rioja, El Zapallar, dossier 58, "Tradiciones Populares," informant: Dorotea Altamirano, ninety-four years old in 1921.

60 Luna, *Los Caudillos,* 148.

61 "In pious legends everywhere a popular theme is the incognito wanderings of the saints or other holy men . . . in the world of mortals. . . . Christ and Peter are not always received honorably. . . . [T]he greedy peasant woman (type 751), although her cake is made to grow magically larger, she gives the holy visitors only a morsel. As a result, she is punished" (Thompson, *The Folktale,* 150).

62 Roldán and Coppari, "La Personalidad del Chacho," 115–16.

63 Poem by Vicente Almonacid, in *El Riojano,* no. 6, 31 July 1863.

64 Natal Luna to Wenceslao Paunero, Rioja, 16 May 1862, in AP, 7–1–3–226.

65 The most complete folkloric analysis of all the versions is in Fernández Latour, *Cantares,* 40–66.

66 Fernández Latour, *Cantares,* 41. Collected in Moisés Ville, Santa Fé, informant: Dionisia de Zummer, sixty-six years old in 1921.

67 Ibid.

68 CFED, Provincia de La Rioja, Siempre Verde, dossier 112, "Algunos datos sobre la muerte de Peñaloza," no informant; and Fernández Latour, *Cantares,* 232.

69 Fernández Latour, *Cantares,* 43. Collected in Guayascate, Córdoba, informant: Jacinto Díaz, eighty years old in 1921.

70 Ibid.

71 Fernández Latour, *Cantares,* 50. Original version of the "plot," written in 1835.

72 Fernández Latour, *Cantares,* 42–43. Collected in Provincia de Córdoba, Guayascate, informant: Jacinto Díaz, eighty years old in 1921.

73 Fernández Latour, *Cantares,* 44. Collected in Las Peñas, Catamarca, informant: Venancio Ramírez, eighty years old in 1921.

74 Fernández Latour, *Cantares,* 42. Collected in Cobos, Salta, informant: Francisco Nogales, seventy years old in 1921.

75 For reflections on this method of punishing political enemies, see Navarro Ocampo, *Actor,* 170–71.

76 Fernández Latour, *Cantares,* 63. Collected by Guillermo Terrera in Córdoba, no informant indicated, n.d.

77 Carrizo, *Cancionero Popular de La Rioja,* 2: 57. Collected in Guandacol, informant: Javier Ahumada, seventy-six years old in 1940. Other versions collected in 1921 also make reference to the "herones"; see Fernández Latour, *Cantares,* 42–43.

78 Carrizo, *Cancionero Popular de La Rioja,* 67. Collected in Atiles, informant: Luis Agapito Roldán, eighty years old in 1940.

79 See the versions collected in Provincia de Salta, Cobo, informant: Francisco Nogales, seventy years old in 1921; Provincia de Córdoba, Guayascate, informant: Jacinto Díaz, eighty years old in 1921; Provincia de Catamarca, Guayamba, informant: Andrónico Cisneros, seventy-one years old in 1921; and Provincia de Catamarca, Las Peñas, informant: Venancio Ramírez, eighty years old in 1921. All in Fernández Latour, *Cantares,* 42–44.

80 Carrizo, *Cancionero Popular de La Rioja,* 2: 60.

81 When the Federalist rebellion of February 1867 broke out in La Rioja, the rebels "marched against Yrrazábal. . . . [H]e was persecuted for a league losing three men dead and leaving prisoners [behind]. . . . [T]he revolutionaries did not forgive Commander Vera either . . . for he is who took Peñaloza and handed him over to Yrrazábal who, as you know, killed him with his lance" (Ramón Gil Navarro Ocampo to Urquiza, Córdoba, 14 February 1867, AFSB–CRGNO). Vera was also the target of Federalist violence in a small plot in the Llanos, in February 1865, and during Zalazar's rebellion in June of that year.

82 "La Muerte del Zorro," *El Imparcial,* 20 November 1863.

83 CFED, Provincia de Catamarca, Chumbicha, dossier 210, informant: Ponciano Roldán, eighty-seven years old in 1921.

84 CFED, Provincia de La Rioja, Punta de Los Llanos, dossier 81, "Las Montoneras," informant: Manuel Antonio Díaz, seventy years old in 1921.

85 Fernández Latour, *Cantares,* 233. La Rioja, El Horno, dossier 106, informant: Estanislao Díaz, sixty-nine years old in 1921.

86 Ibid.

87 CFED, Provincia de La Rioja, Punta de Los Llanos, dossier 81, "Las Montoneras," informant: Manuel Antonio Díaz, seventy years old in 1921.

88 José Arredondo to Wenceslao Paunero, Malanzán, 4 December 1863, AP, 7–2–5–473.

89 CFED, Provincia de La Rioja, Punta de Los Llanos, dossier 81, "Las Montoneras," informant: Manuel Antonio Díaz, seventy years old in 1921.

90 Fernández Latour, *Cantares,* 232. This song, collected in 1921, was reconstructed from verses relaid by four informants, all from the province of Catamarca: Ramón Pío Fernández, eighty-four years old (La Merced); Ponciano Roldán, eighty-seven years old (Chumbicha); Octaviano Ramos, seventy-eight years old (Icaño); and Ramón Rodríguez, seventy years old (La Merced).

91 CFED, Provincia de La Rioja, Chamical, dossier 175, "Guerrillas de General Peñaloza con Linares," informant: Felipe Paz, ninety years old in 1921.

92 The testimonies of Estanislao Díaz and Manuel Antonio Díaz were quite informative, yet they did not mention Vera's role in the event. It was Irrazábal, guided by Francisco, who captured Chacho and then assassinated him. I believe this silence was

intentional. Both informants were from the Llanos, a region where the Vera family maintained an important presence for many years, and where Ricardo Vera was a strongman. These silences, when adequately compared to other sources, highlight the value of folklore and oral testimonies, especially how hot certain issues still were in 1921.

93 CFED, Provincia de La Rioja, Siempre Verde, dossier 112, "Algunos dato sobre la muerte de Peñaloza," no informant.

94 Fernández Latour, *Cantares,* 234. Collected in Ojo del Río, San Luis, informant: Fortunata de Funes, sixty-two years old in 1921.

95 Fernández Latour, *Cantares,* 232.

96 Ibid., 233. The extraordinary ability to triumph over death is associated with heroes in many different societies. The best known of all stories about rulers as popular heroes is the one in which a ruler is not really dead; see Burke, *Popular Culture in Early Modern Europe,* 152.

97 Fernández Latour, *Cantares,* 235. Collected in Nogoli, San Luis, informant: Nicolás Jofré, eighty years old in 1921.

98 Paz, *Memorias,* 256. One notable example, which repeated a common motif, was his famous dark horse, a wise animal that allegedly advised Facundo on military and political decisions ("in Homer Achilles's horse speaks and advises him" [Thompson, *The Folktale,* 278–79]).

99 Paz, *Memorias,* 254.

100 Fernández Latour, *Cantares,* 56. Original version of the romance, collected in Salta by Juan Alfonso Carrizo.

101 CFED, Provincia de San Juan, Desamparados (Valle Fertil), dossier 117, no informant. This story seems to be a partial combination of many types and motifs: "A general pattern is found in nearly all stories of magic objects. There is the extraordinary manner in which the objects are acquired, the use of objects by the hero, the loss (usually by theft), and the final recovery" (Thompson, *The Folktale,* 70). In another section, Thompson clarifies that these stories function thanks to the belief that "the world is filled with objects that defy all the laws of nature and which obtain miraculous results without ordinary labor" (ibid., 253).

102 Fernández Latour, *Cantares,* 42. Collected in Provincia de Salta, Cobo, informant: Francisco Nogales, seventy years old in 1921.

103 Fernández Latour, *Cantares,* 32–33. The first evidence linking Facundo with the figure of the tiger is in *El Repetidor* (San Juan), 23 October 1826: "Ya el tigre feroz, el azote de los riojanos, el immoral Facundo Quiroga" (cited in Salomón, "Manifiesto de la preburguesía argentina," 55).

104 French, "On the Province," 386.

105 Ibid., 387.

106 CFED, Provincia de Catamarca, Villa Cubas, dossier 73 (first dispatch), "Cuento: el tigre uturunco," informant: Nicco Bustos, seventy-four years old in 1921.

107 Ibid.

108 Paz, *Memorias,* 2: 255.

109 CFED, Provincia de Catamarca, Huillapima, dossier 228, "Anecdota," no informant; and CFED, Provincia de La Rioja, Los Sarmientos, dossier 10, "Anecdota," informant: Benjamina Dávila, fifty-nine years old in 1921.

110 CFED, Provincia de Los Llanos, Vargas, dossier 78, "Anécdota: el Tigre de los Llanos," informant: Gavina Romero, ninety-five years old in 1921.

111 CFED, Provincia de La Rioja, Punta de los Llanos, dossier 81, "Las Montoneras," informant: Manuel Antonio Díaz, seventy years old in 1921. A "memoir" written by Ramón Gil Navarro Ocampo in 1862 (one year before the death of Peñaloza), unpublished until 1984, records the same event and details that Díaz gave in 1921, using the same apologetic tone to describe the caudillo. But, Navarro Ocampo places the occurrence at the battle of Rincón, in 1827, and not the battle of Ciudadela in 1831. The evidence from Facundo's archive, however, indicates that the event happened neither at Rincón nor Ciudadela but rather at a third battle site, El Tala, which like the other two is in Tucumán, late in 1826. See Navarro Ocampo, *Actor,* 279–80; and AQ, 4: 248–49.

112 CFED, Provincia de San Juan, Villa Mercedes, "Anécdota," informant: Ramón Hernández, eighty years old in 1921.

113 See the analysis of the stories that form the cycles of heroes in a "primitive culture" in Thompson, *The Folktale,* 329–44.

114 On the importance of the study of tests in this type of story, see "Test-Theme Motifs," in Thompson, *The Folktale,* esp. 339, 341–42.

115 See Villafañe, *Reminiscencias,* 60; D. Dávila, "Orígenes Nacionales," 292.

116 CFED, Provincia de La Rioja, Capital, dossier 59, "Relación de Quiroga con el Chacho," informant: Inocencio Peñaloza (grandson of Chacho), no age.

117 For instance, "Basilisco" was believed to have a powerful gaze, and according to Ramón Gil Navarro Ocampo's diary entry of 10 January 1848, its fame was widespread in the mid–nineteenth century.

118 CFED, Provincia de La Rioja, Vargas, dossier 78, "Anécdota: El Tigre de los Llanos," informant: Gavina Romero, ninety-five years of age in 1921.

7 Whites and Blacks, Masons and Christians

1 Domingo B. Dávila, "Orígenes Nacionales," 3: 289.

2 Guzmán, "Los Mulatos-Mestizos," chart 3. Today's Argentinean northwest is comprised of the provinces of La Rioja, Catamarca, Santiago del Estero, Tucumán, Salta, and Jujuy.

3 Ibid. Jujuy was the only province with a majority of Indians.

4 These changes raise questions about the reliability of sources; nevertheless, we can make certain speculations. With respect to the decrease in the indigenous population, it is possible that a good part of the decline, in absolute as well as relative terms, owed to the passing of some natives into the "Spanish" category, a widespread phenomenon during the eighteenth century throughout the entire region. Moreover, the absolute increase in the Spanish population closely approximates the

decrease in the indigenous population. See Guzmán, "Los Mulatos-Mestizos," 76–77, chart 3.

5   Guzmán, "Los Mulatos-Mestizos," 81, 84–85.

6   *Primer Censo Nacional,* 415.

7   *Provincia de La Rioja: Memoria del Ex-Medico Titular,* 50–51.

8   French, "On the Province," 384.

9   A. Bázan, *Vida de San Nicolás,* 129ff.

10 Ibid.

11 "Correspondencia," *El Eco de Córdoba,* 10 February 1863; emphasis in original.

12 Ramón Bravo to Sebastián Elizondo, in "Causa criminal contra los autores y complices del conato de revolución contra las autoridades legales de la provincia," 1869, AJP (LR), criminal, B–#34, 26–28; emphasis added. Seeking to be accepted by the Federalists, this new ally also defiantly used the labels that the national government applied to those who fought in this party ("montoneros and bandits").

13 "El Coronel Tristán Dávila" (obituary), *La Regeneración* (La Rioja), 16 August 1867.

14 Domingo B. Dávila, "Orígenes Nacionales," 3: 72.

15 French, "On the Province," 398. French lived in La Rioja from 1826 to 1828.

16 CFED, Provincia de La Rioja, Siempre Verde, dossier 112, "El Becerrito de Quiroga," no informant.

17 Referring to Quiroga as "God" was one way the Riojan elite commented negatively on the caudillo's omnipotence.

18 *Provincia de La Rioja: Memoria del Ex-Medico Titular,* 34, 50, 51.

19 Sarmiento, *Recuerdos de Provincia,* 76. The episode occurred in rural San Luis.

20 Carrizo, *Selección del Cancionero Popular,* 242.

21 Sarmiento, *Facundo,* 126, 128.

22 During the War of Independence, future Federalist caudillo Manuel Dorrego was also partial to this type of display. See Hudson, *Far Away,* 105–6; and Martínez Estrada, *Muerte y Transfiguración,* 2: 241–42.

23 Pedro Gordillo to Carmelo Valdés, Villa de Famatina, 7 September 1867, *La Regeneracion* (Rioja), 10 October 1867; and Domingo B. Dávila, "Orígenes Nacionales," 3: 532, 4: 78.

24 Sarmiento, *El Chacho,* 81–84.

25 A. Bázan, *Vida de San Nicolás,* 145ff.

26 According to those who recorded the oral traditions of the historical origins of the encounter, the ceremony was a Jesuit creation to communicate to the Indians the divine origins, and therefore legitimacy, of the conquerors' power and the Indians' conversion. As such, it was the Jesuits who proposed the Inca to represent the chief authority of the Indians of La Rioja. This version was initially formulated in 1893 by Joaquín V. González in *Mis Montañas,* and is accepted by A. Bázan in *La Vida de San Nicolás.*

27 This was the case during the rebellion led by Tupac Amaru in 1780, which generated acts of resistance in various provinces of the interior. In La Rioja, for example, the militia rebelled and refused to repress other uprisings in neighboring provinces,

which according to the authorities, were related to the great rebellion of Peru. In Jujuy and Salta, where there were also uprisings, it was said that "the poor want to defend themselves from the tyranny of the Spaniard and that killing all of them . . . only would govern the Indians through the disposition of their Inca-King" (Lewin, *La Insurreción*, 75–76). The incitement to rebel was well received not only by the Indians but also had "been accepted . . . by many plebeians," among whom it was rumored that "they had their Inca-King, who had been crowned in Peru and he was against the Spaniards and on behalf of the lower classes" (ibid., 79, 80).

28 G. Dávila, "El Mineral," 85; emphasis in original.

29 Ibid., 86.

30 Sarmiento, *Recuerdos de Provincia*, 42, 45–46, 231, 276–77.

31 Castro, *Epistolario entre Sarmiento y Posse*, 291. Emphasis added.

32 Zalazar, *Montonereando*, 59.

33 Shumway, *The Invention of Argentina*, 101–6.

34 Halperín Donghi, *De la Revolución*, 242–47.

35 Salvador Maria del Carril to Juan Facundo Quiroga, San Juan, 6 July 1825, AQ, 3: 233–34.

36 Ibid.

37 Juan Facundo Quiroga to José Ramón Alvarez, Tucumán, 4 July 1827, AQ, 4: 382.

38 Ibid.

39 Friar Manuel Cernadas to Juan Facundo Quiroga, Rioja, 8 July 1826, AQ, 4: 148–49.

40 Ibid.

41 "Carta Misiva del Sr. General Don Juan Facundo Quiroga a un amigo suyo de Mendoza, que se da al público con notas por su mucha importancia," San Juan, 28 January 1827, AQ, 4: 310–12.

42 Jorge Myers has recently studied the resignification of the rhetoric of independence by the Rosista regime. In this case, we see that Federalism had appropriated this rhetoric before Rosas took power. In addition, here the religious language was used not only as a vehicle for a liberal ideology, as it has been argued, but also to react against some of the consequences of liberalism, like the clerical reforms. See Myers, *Orden y Virtud*.

43 "Carta Misiva."

44 "Oración Patriótica que en el solemne día aniversario del 25 de Mayo de 1815, celebrado en la ciudad de Tucumán dijo el Doctor Pedro Ignacio de Castro Barros," in Carranza, *El Clero Argentino*, 1: 112.

45 "Acción de Gracias por la victoria ganada en Tucumán el 24 de septiembre de 1812, pronunciada el 27 de Octubre del mismo año en la iglesia de la Merced," in Carranza, *El Clero Argentino*, 1: 32.

46 "Carta Misiva." Emphasis in the original.

47 "Oración Patriótica," 1: 108.

48 Halperín Donghi, *Proyecto y Construcción*, 63–65, 362–67, 370–84.

49 "Carta Misiva." Emphasis in the original.

50 Pedro Ignacio de Castro Barros to Facundo Quiroga, Córdoba, 21 February 1827, AQ, 4: 330–31. See also his "Oración Patriotica" cited above.

51 Sarmiento, *Recuerdos de Provincia*, 240.

52 Paz, *Memorias*, 2: 244.

53 Ibid.

54 Ibid., 248–49.

55 Ibid.

56 Ibid., 244–45.

57 In some regions of Rio de la Plata, the religious celebrations when work was prohibited accounted for a quarter of the year. For more on this question, and the social importance of these celebrations, see the stimulating work by José Pedro Barrán, *Historia de la Sensibilidad en el Uruguay*, 130–45.

58 This preoccupation with confession is a recurrent theme in popular songs that refer to the deaths of Federalist caudillos. For example, a song about the death of Juan Felipe Ibarra, which called him "the most Federalist" and rejoiced that his death was not caused by "any barbarous Unitarian traitor," also made it clear that the caudillo of Santiago del Estero had confessed before "he was called by the justice of the Creator" (Fernández Latour, *Cantares*, 145–46). The confession helped define the caudillo as a good Christian and confirmed that he would be received by God. And as we have seen, according to the songs, Chacho also had the opportunity to confess before he was assassinated.

59 Santiago Villafañe, who had been a soldier of Governor Benavídez, remembered that in Rosas's time in San Juan, people had to wear a "red sash that said 'Long Live the General of the Federal Nation,'" and that those who attended mass "had to make the sign of the cross, reciting, 'In the name of the Holy Confederation / Long live Don Manuel Rosas / and Doña Encarnación [Ezcurra-Rosas's wife]'" (CFED, Provincia de San Juan, Pampa Vieja, dossier 161, "Epoca: La Tiranía," informant: Santiago Villafañe, 110 [*sic*] years old in 1921.

60 Fernández Latour, *Cantares*, 95. The only version of this song was collected in Tucumán, no informant.

61 Fernández Latour, *Cantares*, 112–13. Collected in La Merced, Catamarca, informant: José C. Rodríguez, ninety years old in 1921. The three other versions of this song are from the provinces of San Luis and Santiago del Estero.

62 Navarro Ocampo, *Actor*, 78–79.

63 Ibid.

64 Ibid., 81–82, 169.

65 This image of God appears in many popular songs. For example, "God wants to punish them / With his divine justice / . . . God will raise his hand / They will be punished" (cited in Goldman, "El Levantamiento de Montoneras contra Gringos y Masones," 64).

66 Navarro Ocampo, *Actor*, 168. Emphasis in the original.

67 Ibid., 80; emphasis in original.

68 Ibid., 168.

69 Fernández Latour, *Cantares*, 228. Collected in Salana, La Rioja, informant: Evaristo Gómez, ninety-five years old in 1921.

70 Bunkley, *Vida de Sarmiento*, 349–50.

71 Sarmiento, *El Chacho,* 108.

72 The Rosista regime called its political rivals "viles masones" and "unitarios logistas" (see Salvatore, "Fiestas Federales," 50).

73 In the case of Brazil, for example, these sermons would have an important influence on millenarian movements; see Levine, *Vale of Tears.*

74 CFED, Provincia de Catamarca, El Recreo, dossier 104, informant: Natividad de Barrionuevo, eighty years old in 1921.

75 On the presence of English Protestants in La Rioja, and the locally held perception of them as "heretics," see G. Dávila, *El Mineral,* 75.

76 Bunkley, *Vida de Sarmiento,* 350; and Régulo Martínez to Mitre, San Juan, 25 October 1862, AGM, 12: 254.

77 "Los Bandidos Pueblas, Aguero and C.," *El Famatima Reformado* (Rioja), 3 December 1862. Emphasis added.

78 Aldao, "Prólogo del Traductor," 16–17.

79 Nario, *Tata Dios,* and *Los Crímenes;* for a more recent and comprehensive approach, see Lynch, *Massacre in the Pampas.*

80 Nario, *Tata Dios,* 82–83.

81 Ibid., 91.

82 See Nario, *Tata Dios;* and Slatta, *Los Gauchos.* According to these studies, this millenarianism on the gauchos' part was a reaction to the accelerated integration of the Porteño countryside to the world economy. In Lynch, *Massacre in the Pampas,* it was not millenarianism but xenophobia and popular Catholicism.

83 Nario, *Tata Dios,* 91, 124.

84 Ibid., 91, 93.

85 Nario, *Los Crímenes,* 23.

86 Ibid., 14.

87 Fernandez, *Solané.*

88 Chàvez, *El Revisionismo,* 25–28.

89 CFED, Provincia de Catamarca, Icaño, dossier 131, informant: Lola C. De Figueroa, thirty-seven years old in 1921.

90 Goldman, "El Levantamiento de Montoneras contra Gringos y Masones," 59.

91 Jorge Myers showed than even Rosismo subordinated religious matters to the very secular business of government; see his *Orden y Virtud,* 85–92.

8   State Formation and Party Identity

1 See Felipe Varela to Justo José Urquiza, Copiapó, 23 January 1864, in Chávez, *Vida del Chacho,* 186; and Navarro Ocampo, *Actor,* 126–27.

2 See Hilario Lagos to Roberto Barquint, Rioja, 26 October 1867, AFL–PCHL.

3 See Jose B. Aguilar to Ignacio Rivas, Ilisca, 24 February 1862, AGN, X–2–2–2.

4 See Ignacio Rivas to Wenceslao Paunero, Los Llanos, 8 May 1862, AP, 7–6–16–1253; Navarro Ocampo, *Actor,* 78–79; and Reyes, *Bosquejo Histórico,* 185.

5 Ambrosio Sandes to Wenceslao Paunero, Represa de Tello, 22 May 1862, AP, 7–1–3–230.

6   Fernández Latour, *Cantares,* 230. Collected in La Chimenea, La Rioja, informant: Cristano Brizuela, sixty years old in 1921.

7   Angel Vicente Peñaloza to Wenceslao Paunero, Guaja, 31 July 1862, AP, 7–7–22–1978.

8   Buenaventura Sarmiento to Domingo F. Sarmiento, San Luis, 3 February 1862, AS, 7907, armario 1.

9   Ignacio Rivas to Wenceslao Paunero, Las Liebres, 22 April 1862, AP, 7–6–16–1253.

10 Ignacio Rivas to Wenceslao Paunero, Los Llanos, 4 May 1862, AP, 7–6–16–1254.

11 Wenceslao Paunero to C. Bousquet, Río IV, 16 February 1867, AIM, 7275.

12 Bartolomé Mitre to Domingo F. Sarmiento, Buenos Aires, 29 March 1863, AS, 1820, carpeta 14; emphasis in original.

13 Ambrosio Sandes to Ignacio Rivas, Villanueva, 2 October 1862, AGN, 2–2–2.

14 See, for instance, the song on page 169 of this chapter.

15 "Contra Toribio, Ramón y Blas Gaitán (hermanos), Carmen Alvarez y Eliceo Zalazar por partícipes en la última rebellion en esta provincia," 1867, AJF (LR), penal, legajo 2, 3.

16 Fernández Latour, *Cantares,* 240. Two versions of this song were collected, one in San Luis (informant: Luis Quiroga, forty-five years old in 1921), and another in Colonia Rusa, Mendoza (informant: Ramona B. de Lucero, sixty-four years old in 1921).

17 Ignacio Rivas to Wenceslao Paunero, Los Llanos, 4 May 1862, AP, 7–6–16–1254.

18 José Iseas to Wenceslao Paunero, Dolores, 3 June 1863, AP, 7–3–7–658.

19 "Contra Segundo Bazán por abigeato," 1870, AJP (LR), criminal, B–#10, 2, 3, 7.

20 See "Contra Ramón Manrique por robo de dinero," 1873, AJP (LR), criminal, M–#22, 5–6; and "Contra Bernabé, José Angel, Mateo y Facundo Quintero por delito de cuatropea," 1870, AJP (LR), criminal, Q–#4, 1.

21 Fernández Latour, *Cantares,* 264–65. Collected in Huaco, Belén, Catamarca, informant: Segundo Acosta, seventy-five years old in 1921. The compiler found three other, fragmentary versions of the same song in Lorohuasi (informant: Julián Faciano, seventy years old in 1921), Plaza San Pedro (second dispatch), and Huaco (first dispatch), all in Catamarca.

22 Diary entry, 10 July 1867, AFL–PCHL.

23 Fernández Latour, *Cantares,* 263. Collected in Mercedes, San Luis, informant: Eusebia de González, eighty-four years old in 1921.

24 Even in times of peace, like 1855, when the Confederation tried to activate National Guard units to send to the capital city of Paraná as part of a new national army, the gauchos resisted by hiding out; see Joaquín González to Tristán Dávila, Nonogasta, 13 November 1855, AFZ–CTD.

25 Reyes, *Bosquejo Histórico,* 226. According to the First National Census of 1869, there were an estimated 8,849 men (between sixteen and fifty years old) eligible for the draft out of a total population that numbered 48,746.

26 See the testimony of Manuel Ibarra, seventy years old in 1921, in Fernández Latour, *Cantares,* 253; and Exequías Bringas to Nicolás Barros, 1 July 1865, AHLR–CNB, carpeta 12, 8–9.

27   Ibid.

28   Restituta Izaguirre de Dávila to Tristán Dávila, Campanas, 5 November 1865, AFZ–CTD.

29   Wenceslao Paunero to Bartolomé Mitre, San Juan, 27 July 1867, AIM, 7300.

30   Reyes, *Bosquejo Histórico,* 232.

31   Dálmiro Hernández to Wenceslao Paunero, San Luis, 17 July 1867, AIM, 7300.

32   José M. de la Fuente to Bartolomé Mitre, Córdoba, 2 November 1866, AIM, 6173; emphasis in original.

33   Julio Campos to Bartolomé Mitre, Rioja, 1 September 1865, AIM, 6584; emphasis in original.

34   Julio Campos to Tristán Dávila, Rioja, 16 July 1865, in De Paoli and Mercado, *Proceso a los Montoneros,* 64–65.

35   Wenceslao Paunero to Bartolomé Mitre, San Juan, 27 July 1867, AIM, 7300.

36   Fernández Latour, *Cantares,* 80. Collected in Corral de Isaac, La Rioja, informant: Juan Ibañez, seventy-four years old in 1921.

37   CFED, Provincia de La Rioja, dossier 81, Punta de Los Llanos, "Las Montoneras," informant: Manuel Antonio Díaz, seventy years old in 1921.

38   Cited in De Paoli and Mercado, *Proceso a los Montoneros,* 80.

39   Ramón Gil Navarro Ocampo to Justo José Urquiza, Córdoba, 11 February 1876, in AFSB–CRGNO; and Ramón Gil Navarro Ocampo to Justo José Urquiza, Córdoba, 14 February 1867, in AFSB–CRGNO.

40   Reyes, *Bosquejo Histórico,* 226.

41   "Causa criminal seguida de oficio contra los Reos presentes Don Manuel Vicente Bustos (et al.)," 1865, AJF (LR), penal, legajo 1, 96.

42   Cited in De Paoli and Mercado, *Proceso a los Montoneros,* 68–69.

43   Juan Francisco Orihuela to Ricardo Vera, Jachal, 14 September 1862, AGM, 12: 257–58. Other testimony indicates that the gauchos spoke of the possibility that Urquiza might cross the Paraná River and march against Buenos Aires; Domingo F. Sarmiento to Bartolomé Mitre, San Juan, 12 March 1862, AGM, 12: 101. Some knew Mitre as the supreme commander of the national troops, and his figure could be included by some gauchos in political speculations of national dimensions. Thus, after the first rebellion of Chacho, a gaucho said that "the war is over [because] General [Peñaloza] has given guarantees [a pardon] to 'ñor Mitre'" (see "Causa contra Francisco Argañaraz, Angel Mariano Riveros, Javier Gómez y José Ocampo por suponerselos reos de falsedad en la causa criminal seguida a Crisólogo Andrade," 1871, AJF [LR], penal, legajo 5, 23–24; and Navarro Ocampo, *Actor,* 309).

44   In Tucumán, some country people thought of him and "the Queen Victoria of Portugal" as the eventual "godparents of their children," but "because Urquiza was assassinated," this did not come to pass (CFED, Provincia de Catamarca, Recreo, dossier 104 [second dispatch], informant: Natividad de Barrionuevo, eighty years old in 1921).

45   "Causa criminal seguida de oficio contra los Reos presentes Don Manuel Vicente Bustos (et al.)," 1865, AJF (LR), penal, legajo 1, 113–14.

46 Reyes, *Bosquejo Histórico*, 227–28.

47 "Causa criminal contra Agustín Molina, por rebelión," 1872, AJF (LR), penal, legajo 5, 7, 8.

48 Ibid., 6.

49 Ibid., 6, 18–20.

50 See Filemón Posse to José Posse, Catamarca, 4 May 1865, AGM, 26: 132.

51 "Correspondencia para la Regeneración," *La Regeneración* (La Rioja), 18 February 1865.

52 Wenceslao Paunero to Bartolomé Mitre, Córdoba, 31 December 1861, AGM, 10: 259.

53 Copy of the proclamation by Felipe Varela in AP, 7–3–8–682. According to the testimony of the Chilean miner Toribio Urrutia, "peace and friendship with Paraguay" was one of the goals of the rebellion (see "Causa criminal contra Toribio Urrutia (Chileno) por participación con los Rebeldes encabezados por Felipe Varela," 1867, AJF (LR), penal, legajo 2.

54 "Causa criminal contra Fermín Bazán por sedición en los Llanos," 1865, AJP (LR), B–#595, 1; emphasis in original.

55 Ibid., 3.

56 "Sumario instruido por el juez de paz de Belgrano y por orden del Señor Gobernador en campaña sobre los sucesos que se desarrollan desde el 29 de enero pasado, perturbando con la sedición y las montoneras el orden público de la provincia," 1874, *Revista*, 100–101.

57 "Datos Estadísticos de la Provincia de La Rioja, y su Capital," *El Nacional Argentino* (Paraná), 23 August 1856.

58 "Abuso de un Comandante de la Costa Baja," *La Regeneración* (La Rioja), 27 November 1866.

59 "El Fuego de la Rebelión Arde Entre Nosotros Ya," *La Regeneración*, (La Rioja), 27 November 1866; and "Barbaros!" *La Regeneración* (La Rioja), 21 December 1866.

60 "De Donde Surgió el Asesinato del Comandante Herrera?" *La Regeneración* (La Rioja), 30 December 1866.

61 See "Las Víctimas de la Montonera del 67," *La Regeneración*, (La Rioja), 18 August 1867; and Reyes, *Bosquejo Histórico*, 254.

62 Reyes, *Bosquejo Histórico*, 197; and "Abuso de un Comandante de la Costa Baja," *La Regeneración* (La Rioja), 27 November 1866.

63 "Causa criminal sin carátula," 1865, AJP (LR), B–without number, 6, 7, 8.

64 "El Fuego de la Rebelión Arde Entre Nosotros Ya," *La Regeneración* (La Rioja), 16 December 1866.

65 "Causa criminal contra Indalecio Nieto," 1872, AJP (LR), N–without number, 2–5.

66 "Causa criminal contra Eugenio Sosa y Rosa Quintero," 1872, AJP (LR), Q–#5, 7–8.

67 "Las Víctimas de la Montonera del 67," *La Regeneración* (La Rioja), 18 July 1867. Marcelino Reyes, a former Unitarian, also considered Herrera a Unitarian victim of the Federalists; see his *Bosquejo Histórico*, 262.

68 Carrizo, *Cancionero Popular de La Rioja*, 1: 176–77.

1   "Contra los autores y complices del conato de revolución contra las autoridades legales de la provincia," 1869, AJP (LR), criminal, B–#34, 5, 6, 14, 22.

2   Nicolás Barros to Octaviano Navarro, Rioja, 26 January 1869, AHLR–CON, carpeta 11, 168.

3   Samuel Molina to Marcos Paz, Catamarca, 28 December 1861, AFC–CSM.

4   Samuel Molina to Francisco Leguizamón, Catamarca, 2 February 1862, AFC–CSM.

5   Marcos Paz to Bartolomé Mitre, Quilino, 7 February 1862, AGM, 10: 207.

6   José M. de la Fuente to Bartolomé Mitre, Catamarca, 4 May 1868, AIM, 6921; Antonino Taboada to Bartolomé Mitre, Mesillas, 17 July 1867, AIM, 6289; and Antonio Taboada to Bartolomé Mitre, Mesillas, 2 August 1867, AIM, 6291.

7   Bazán et al., *Felipe Varela,* 129.

8   Octaviano Navarro to Antonino Taboada, Catamarca, 30 November 1871, AHLR–CON, carpeta 11, 243–44. In these matters, silence is also telling. As late as 1957, Ramón Rosa Olmos, the dean of Catamarca historians, felt it appropriate not to mention the episode in his *Historia de Catamarca.* In 1992, when I met one of the direct descendants of the Molinas, an old lady born in the early twentieth century, my casual mention of Octaviano prompted this bitter comment: "That traitor!"

9   *Manifiesto del Jeneral Felipe Varela,* 109, 110, 112; and A. Taboada, "La Guerra y la Política en el Interior (Contestación a las Calumnias del General Arrendondo)," in *Los Taboada,* ed. G. Taboada, 1: 613–69.

10   See Luna, *De Comicios,* 152–54; and Letter (without name) to Octaviano Navarro, 12 March 1869, AHLR–CON, carpeta 11, 174.

11   Domingo Villafañe, governor of La Rioja in 1861, shared this assessment of Navarro. A few days before Pavón, Villafañe said to Chacho that he believed that the fate of the whole nation depended on the already inevitable battle between Urquiza and Mitre, and that "the revolutionary movements in some provinces are insignificant." His suggestion was to live with the results of Pavón, which he finally did four months later, when the national troops arrived in La Rioja. Some of his former allies called Villafañe a "brand-new liberal," while others, also outraged, tried to assassinate him. If Villafañe switched so quickly, it must have had to do with the fact that he was not a caudillo with his own power base. Instead, he was a merchant and local administrator. See Domingo Villafañe to Peñaloza, Rioja, 16 September 1861, AHLR–CDV, carpeta 7, 53; Domingo Villafañe to General Rivas, Rioja, 1 May 1862, AGN, X–2–2–2, Archivo General Rivas; and Navarro Ocampo, *Actor,* 175, 197–98.

12   Ramón Gil Navarro Ocampo to Justo José Urquiza, Córdoba, 25 September 1867, AFSB–CRGNO; and Ramón Gil Navarro Ocampo to Justo José Urquiza, Córdoba, 20 September 1867, AFSB–CRGNO.

13   "Contra los autores y cómplices del conato de sublevación y sustracción de presos en el cuartel y cárcel pública de esta ciudad," 1872, AJF (LR), penal, legajo 5, 7. On the organization of the federal courts, see Zimmermann, "Poder Judicial."

14   La Rioja expected to receive 32,500 pesos from the national government in 1870, while only 18,900 pesos in provincial revenues was anticipated. That year's budget

estimated 64,108 pesos in expenses. See Actas de la Legislatura de La Rioja, AGN, VII–21–5–3, 2–12.

15 See Oszlak, *La Formación del Estado Argentino,* 124.

16 Of a total of eighty-four officers and soldiers, thirty-seven were from other provinces (see *Censo Nacional,* 1869, vol. 299, AGN).

17 See "Mensaje del Gobernador Jose Benjamín de la Vega," 25 August 1869, Actas de la Legislatura de La Rioja, AGN, VII–21–5–2, 395–402.

18 Ibid.

19 "Circular del Gobierno de la provincia a los Jueces departamentales de Costa Alta, San Martín, Belgrano e Independencia," 26 June 1869, AHLR, Copiador notas al Interior de la provincia, 1: 39–40.

20 "Mensaje del Gobernador Jose Benjamín de la Vega," 395–402.

21 Some of the last names of the 189 teachers that gathered the information include Dávila, Peñaloza, Bazán, Zalazar, Carrizo, Brizuela, Tello, Romero, Nieto, Millicay, and Miranday.

22 CFED, Provincia de San Juan, Valle Fertil, dossier 50, "Tradiciones Populares."

23 CFED, Provincia de La Rioja, Plaza Vieja, dossier 25, "Relatos Históricos," 8. Likewise, for a story that portrayed Facundo as an agrarian hero, see CFED, Catamarca, Coneta, dossier 6, "Anécdota," informant: no name, forty-eight years old in 1921.

24 Review of the first edition of *La Vuelta de Martín Fierro* in *Anvario Bibliográfico Argentina* (Buenos Aires) 1 (1879): 270–73. This is the quotation that opens the book on p. vii.

Conclusions

1 See Oszlak, *La Formación del Estado Argentino.*

2 Ibid.

3 See Lynch, *Argentine Dictator;* and, "From Independence to National Organization," 1–46.

4 On "barbarian democracy," see Sarmiento, *Facundo.* On "inorganic democracy," see Burns, *The Poverty of Progress.*

5 See Ortega Peña and Duhalde, *Felipe Varela Contra el Imperio Británico.*

6 See Lynch, *Argentine Dictator;* and Graham, *Patronage and Politics in Nineteenth-Century Brazil.*

7 For a similar argument, see Chasteen, *Heroes on Horseback.*

8 On the concept of factional politics, see Halperín Donghi, *Proyecto y Construcción.* For a similar argument in the Brazilian case, see Graham, *Patronage and Politics in Nineteenth-Century Brazil.*

9 For the print capitalism argument, see Anderson, *Imagined Communities.*

10 Joseph and Nugent, *Everyday Forms of State Formation,* 12. See also Mallon, *Peasant and Nation;* and Wells and Joseph, *Summer of Discontent, Seasons of Upheavals.*

11 See Mallon, *Peasant and Nation.*

12 See Mallon, *Peasant and Nation;* Walker, *Smoldering Ashes;* and Guardino, *Peasants, Politics, and the Formation of Mexico's National State.*

13 See Walker, *Smoldering Ashes;* and Guardino, *Peasants, Politics, and the Formation of Mexico's National State.*

14 See Van Young, "To See Someone Not Seeing," and "The New Cultural History"; Joseph and Nugent, *Everyday Forms of State Formation;* and Knight, "Weapon and Arches in the Mexican Revolutionary Landscape," and "Rethinking the Tómochic Rebellion."

15 Wells and Joseph, *Summer of Discontent, Seasons of Upheavals,* 11.

16 Van Young, "The New Cultural History," 228.

17 See Walker, *Smoldering Ashes;* and Vaughan, "Cultural Approaches."

BIBLIOGRAPHY

Archives and Abbreviations

LA RIOJA

AFL: Archivo Familia Lagos
   PCHL: Papeles Coronel Hilario Lagos (hijo)
AFZ: Archivo de la Familia Zamora
   CTD: Correspondencia Tristán Dávila
   PFI: Papeles Familia Izaguirre
AHLR: Archivo Histórico de La Rioja
   CDV: Correspondencia Domingo Villafañe
   CNB: Correspondencia Nicolás Barros
   CON: Correspondencia Octaviano Navarro
AJF (LR): Archivo de la Justicia Federal (La Rioja)
AJP (LR): Archivo de la Justicia Provincial (La Rioja)
Archivo de Miguel Bravo Tedín

CÓRDOBA

AFSB: Archivo de María del Carmen Ferreira de Sánchez Bretón
   CRGNO: Correspondencia Ramón Gil Navarro Ocampo
Archivo del Arzobispado de Córdoba

BUENOS AIRES

AFC: Archivo de la Familia Castro
   CSM: Correspondencia Samuel Molina
AGN: Archivo General de la Nación
AIM: Archivo Inedito del General Mitre (Museo Mitre)
AP: Archivo del General Wenceslao Paunero (Museo Mitre)
AS: Archivo de Domingo F. Sarmiento (Museo Histórico Sarmiento)
CFED: Coleción de Folklore de la Encuesta Docente in Instituto Nacional de Antropología y Pensamiento Latinoamericano

LA PLATA (PROVINCE OF BUENOS AIRES)
Newspapers in the Hemeroteca of the main library of the University of La Plata
El Famatina Reformado (La Rioja), 1862–1863
El Famatina (La Rioja), 1863
El Riojano (La Rioja), 1863
La Regeneración (La Rioja), 1866–1868
El Eco de Córdoba, 1862–1863
El Imparcial (Córdoba), 1863
El Progreso (Córdoba), 1868–1869
El Nacional Argentino (Paraná), 1856–1859

BERKELEY
Private Diary of Ramón Gil Navarro Ocampo, Bancroft Library, University of California,
Berkeley

ABBREVIATIONS OF PUBLISHED CORRESPONDENCE
AGM: Archivo del General Bartolomé Mitre
AMP: Archivo de Marcos Paz
AQ: Archivo de Facundo Quiroga

Published Documents, Books, and Articles

Adelman, Jeremy. *Republic of Capital: Buenos Aires and the Legal Transformation of the
Atlantic World.* Stanford, Calif.: Stanford University Press, 1999.
Agulhon, Maurice. *La Republique Au Village: Les Populations du Var de La Révolution a la II
République.* Paris: Editions du Seuil, 1979.
Aldao, Carlos. "Prólogo del Traductor." In Francis Bond Head, *Las Pampas y Los Andes.*
Buenos Aires: Vaccaro, 1920.
Anderson, Benedict. *Imagined Communities: Reflections on the Origin and the Spread of
Nationalism.* London: Verso, 1983.
Archivo del Brigadier General Juan Facundo Quiroga (AQ). 4 vols. Buenos Aires: Universi-
dad de Buenos Aires, 1957–1988.
Archivo del General Bartolomé Mitre: Documentos y Correspondencia (AGM). 28 vols. Buenos
Aires, 1911–1914.
Barrán, José Pedro. *Historia de la Sensibilidad en el Uruguay.* (2 vols.) (*La Cultura Bárbara.*
vol. 1.) Montevideo, Uruguay: Facultad de Humanidades y Ciencias, 1990.
Bazán, Abel. *Vida de San Nicolás de Bari y Apuntes Históricos Sobre su Milagrosa Imágen que
se Venera en La Rioja (República Argentina).* Córdoba, Argentina: La Industrial, 1907.
Bazán, Armando Raúl. "Las Bases Sociales de la Montonera." In *Angel Vicente Peñaloza.*
Buenos Aires: Hachette, 1969.
———. *Historia de La Rioja.* Buenos Aires: Plus Ultra, 1979.
Bazán, Armando Raúl, Garpa H. Guzmán, Gerardo Pérez Fuentes and Ramón R. Olmos.
Felipe Varela. Su historia. Buenos Aires: Plus Ultra, 1975.

Benarós, León. "Estudio preliminar," in Gutierrez, Eduardo. *Los Montoneros*. Buenos Aires: Hachette, 1961.

Bialet y Masse, Juan. *Provincia de La Rioja, 1877: Memoria del Ex-Medico Titular y Movimiento Estadístico de la Población desde 1853 hasta 1877 Inclusive, por el Dr. Juan Bialet y Masse*. Buenos Aires: Imprenta Europea, 1878.

Blassingame, John, ed. *Slave Testimony*. Baton Rouge: Louisiana State University Press, 1977.

Boman, Eric. "Pueblos de Indios del Antiguo Curato de San Blas de los Sauces (Provincias de La Rioja y Catamarca)." In *Anales del Museo Nacional de Historia Natural Bernardino Rivadavia*. Vol. 35. Buenos Aires, 1927–1932.

Borges, Jorge Luis. *Obras Completas*. 5 vols. Buenos Aires: Emece, 1974–1996.

———. *Textos Recobrados, 1919–1929*. Buenos Aires: Emece, 1997.

Bosch, Beatriz. "Urquiza y el Ultimo Levantamiento del Chacho." In *Angel Vicente Peñaloza*. Buenos Aires: Hachette, 1969.

Botana, Natalio. *El Orden Conservador*. Buenos Aires: Sudamericana, 1977.

———. *La Tradición Republicana*. Buenos Aires: Sudamericana, 1983.

Bunkley, Allison. *Vida de Sarmiento*. Buenos Aires: Eudeba, 1966.

Burgin, Miron. *Aspectos Económicos del Federalismo Argentino*. Buenos Aires: Hachette, 1960.

Burke, Peter. *Popular Culture in Early Modern Europe*. New York: Harper and Row, 1978.

Burns, E. Bradford. *The Poverty of Progress: Latin America in the Nineteenth Century*. Berkeley: University of California Press, 1980.

Carmagnani, Marcello, ed. *Federalismos Latinoamericanos: Mexico, Brasil, Argentina*. Mexico: Fondo de Cultura Económica and Fideicomiso Historia de las Americas, 1993.

Carranza, Adolfo P. *El Clero Argentino de 1810 a 1830*. 2 vols. Buenos Aires: M. A. Rosas, 1907.

Carrizo, Juan Alfonso. *Antiguos Cantos Populares Argentinos*. Buenos Aires: Silla, 1926.

———. *Cancionero Popular de Jujuy*. Buenos Aires, 1935.

———. *Cancionero Popular de La Rioja*. 3 vols. Buenos Aires: Baiocco, 1942.

———. *Cancionero Popular de Salta*. Buenos Aires: Baiocco, 1933.

———. *Cancionero Popular de Tucumán*. 2 vols. Buenos Aires: Baiocco, 1937.

———. *Selección del Cancionero Popular de La Rioja*. Buenos Aires: Dictio, 1987.

Castro, Antonio P., ed. *Epistolario entre Sarmiento y Posse, 1845–1888*. Buenos Aires: Museo Histórico Sarmiento, 1946–1947.

Chasteen, John Charles. *Heroes on Horseback: A Life and Times of the Last Gaucho Caudillos*. Albuquerque: University of New Mexico Press, 1995.

Chávez, Fermín. *Vida del Chacho*. 2d ed. Buenos Aires: Theoria, 1967.

———. *El Revisionismo y Las Montoneras*. Buenos Aires: Theoria, 1984.

Chiaramonte, José Carlos. *Ciudades, Provincias, Estados: Los Orígenes de la Nación Argentina, 1800–1846*. Buenos Aires: Ariel, 1997.

———. "Finanzas Públicas de las Provincias del Litoral, 1821–1841." *Anuario del Instituto de Estudios Históricos y Sociales* 1 (1986): 159–98.

———. "Legalidad Constitucional o Caudillismo: El Problema del Orden Social en el Surgimiento de los Estados Autónomos del Litoral Argentino en la Primera Mitad del Siglo XIX." *Desarrollo Económico* 26, no. 102 (July–September 1986): 175–96.

———. *Mercaderes del Litoral.* Buenos Aires: Fondo de Cultura Económica, 1991.

Chiaramonte, José Carlos, Guillermo Ernesto Cussiánovich, and Sonia Tedeschi. "Finanzas Públicas y Política Interprovincial: Santa Fe y su Dependencia de Buenos Aires en la Epoca de Estanislao López." *Boletín del Instituto de Historia Argentina y Americana Doctor Emilio Ravignani* 8, 2nd semester (1993), 77–116.

Darnton, Robert. *The Great Cat Massacre and Other Episodes in French Cultural History.* New York: Vintage, 1984.

Dávila, Domingo B. "Orígenes Nacionales: Narraciones Riojanas." In *Revista de Derecho, Historia y Letras.* Vols. 3–5. Buenos Aires, 1899.

Dávila, Guillermo. "El Mineral de Famatina." In *La Revista de Buenos Aires.* Vol. 23. Buenos Aires, 1870.

De la Colina, Salvador. *Crónicas Riojanas y Catamarqueñas.* Buenos Aires: Revista Argentina de Ciencias Políticas, 1912.

De la Vega Díaz, Dardo. *Cuestiones de Historia Menuda.* La Rioja: , 1938.

———. *Mitre y el Chacho: La Rioja en la Reorganización del País.* La Rioja: Testori, 1939.

de Moussy, Víctor Martín. *Description Geographique et Statistique de la Confederation Argentine.* 3 vols. Paris, 1860–1864.

Denis, Pierre. *La Valorización del País: La República Argentina.* 1920. Reprint, Buenos Aires: Hachette, 1987.

De Paoli, Pedro. *Facundo: Vida del Brigadier General Don Juan Facundo Quiroga, Víctima Suprema de la Impostura.* Buenos Aires, 1960.

De Paoli, Pedro, and Manuel Mercado. *Proceso a los Montoneros y Guerra del Paraguay.* Buenos Aires: Eudeba, 1974.

Di Lullo, Orestes. *Cancionero Popular de Santiago del Estero.* Buenos Aires: Baiocco, 1937.

Fernández, Francisco F. *Solané.* Buenos Aires: Universidad de Buenos Aires, 1926.

Fernández Latour, Olga. *Cantares Históricos de la Tradición Argentina.* Buenos Aires: Instituto Nacional de Investigaciones Folklóricas, 1960.

Fitte, Ernesto J. *Bienes Sucesorios del Brigadier General Don Juan Facundo Quiroga.* Buenos Aires: Academia Nacional de la Historia, 1971.

French, J. O. "On the Province of La Rioja in South America to Accompany a Map." *Journal of the Royal Geographic Society of London* 9 (1839): 381–406.

Garavaglia, Juan C., and Jorge D. Gelman. "Rural History of the Rio de la Plata, 1600–1850: Results of a Historiographical Renaissance." *Latin American Research Review,* 30, no. 3 (1995): 75–105.

Geertz, Clifford. *Local Knowledge: Further Essays in Interpretive Anthropology.* New York: Basic Books, 1983.

Genovese, Eugene. *Roll, Jordan, Roll.* New York: Vintage Books, 1976.

Goldman, Noemí. "El Levantamiento de Montoneras contra Gringos y Masones en Tucumán, 1887: Tradición Oral y Cultura Popular." *Boletín del Instituto de Historia Argentina y Americana Dr. Emilio Ravignani* 2, 1st semester, 47–73.

Goldman, Noemí, and Ricardo Salvatore, eds. *Caudillismos Rioplatenses: Nuevas Miradas a un Viejo Problema.* Buenos Aires: Eudeba, 1998.

González, Joaquín Víctor. *Mis Montañas*. 1893. Reprint, Buenos Aires: Estrada, 1944.

Gootenberg, Paul. *Between Silver and Guano*. Princeton, N.J.: Princeton University Press, 1989.

Graham, Richard. *Patronage and Politics in Nineteenth-Century Brazil*. Stanford, Calif.: Stanford University Press, 1991.

Guardino, Peter F. *Peasants, Politics, and the Formation of Mexico's National State: Guerrero, 1800–1857*. Stanford, Calif.: Stanford University Press, 1996.

Guiraldes, Ricardo. *Cuentos de Muerte y de Sangre*. 1915. Reprint, Madrid: Espasa-Calpe, 1933.

Gutiérrez, Eduardo. *El Chacho*. 1886. Reprint, Buenos Aires: Hachette, 1960.

———. *Los Montoneros*. 1886. Reprint, Buenos Aires: Hachette, 1961.

———. *La Muerte de un Heroe*. Buenos Aires: Tommasi, n.d.

Guzmán, María Florencia. "Los mulatos-mestizos en la Jurisdicción Riojana a fines del siglo XVIII: El caso de los Llanos." *Temas de Asia y Africa* 2 (1993): 71–107.

Halperín Donghi, Tulio. *The Contemporary History of Latin America*. Durham, N.C.: Duke University Press, 1993.

———. *Hispanoamérica Después de la Independencia*. Buenos Aires: Paidós, 1972.

———. *José Hernández y Sus Mundos*. Buenos Aires: Sudamericana, 1985.

———. *Proyecto y Construcción de una Nación: Argentina (1846–1880)*. Buenos Aires: Ariel, 1995.

———. *De la Revolución de la Independencia a la Confederación Rosista*. Buenos Aires: Paidós, 1985.

———. *Revolución y Guerra: La Formación de una Elite Dirigente en la Argentina Criolla*. Buenos Aires: Siglo XXI, 1972.

Heras, Carlos, ed. *Archivo del Coronel Doctor Marcos Paz* (AMP). *Paz* 5 vols. La Plata, Argentina: Universidad Nacional de la Plata, 1961.

Hernández, Jose. *Vida del Chacho*. In *Vidas del Chacho,* edited by Pedro Orgambide. Buenos Aires: Rodolfo Alonso, 1973.

Hudson, William Henry. *Far Away and Long Ago*. 1918. Reprint, New York: Lyons and Burford, 1997.

———. *The Purple Land That England Lost: Travels and Adventures in the Banda Oriental, South America*. 1885. Reprint, New York: AMS Press, 1968.

"Interrogatorio de Melitón Córdoba a José Mercedes Chumbita (preso), Machigasta, 12/6/63." *Revista de la Junta de Historia y Letras de La Rioja* 2, no. 4 (1943): 51.

Joseph, Gilbert M., and Daniel Nugent, eds. *Everyday Forms of State Formation: Revolution and the Negotiation of Rule in Modern Mexico*. Durham, N.C.: Duke University Press, 1994.

Knight, Alan. "The Mexican Revolution: Bourgeois? Nationalist? Or Just a Great Rebellion?" *Bulletin of Latin American Research* 4, no. 2 (1985): 1–37.

———. "Peasant and Caudillo in Revolutionary Mexico, 1910–1917." In *Caudillo and Peasant in the Mexican Revolution,* edited by David Brading. Cambridge, U.K.: Cambridge University Press, 1980.

———. "Rethinking the Tomóchic Rebellion." Paper presented at the American Historical Association Annual Meeting, Washington, D.C., January 1999.

———. "Weapons and Arches in the Mexican Revolutionary Landscape." In *Everyday Forms of State Formation: Revolution and the Negotiation of Rule in Modern Mexico*, edited by Gilbert M. Joseph and Daniel Nugent (Durham, N.C.: Duke University Press, 1994).

Langer, Eric. "Espacios Coloniales y Economías Nacionales: Bolivia y el Norte Argentino (1810–1930)." *Siglo XIX* 2, no. 4 (1987): 135–60.

Latzina, Francisco. *L'Agriculture et L'Elevage Dans la République Argentine*. Paris: Mouillot, 1889.

Levine, Lawrence. *Black Culture and Black Consciousness*. Oxford: Oxford University Press, 1977.

Levine, Robert M. *Vale of Tears: Revisiting the Canudos Massacre in Northeastern Brazil, 1891–1897*. Berkeley: University of California Press, 1992.

Lewin, Boleslao. *La Insurreción de Tupac Amaru*. Buenos Aires: Eudeba, 1987.

Luna, Félix. *Los Caudillos*. Buenos Aires: Planeta, 1988.

———. "El Chacho en la Literatura Nacional." In *Angel Vicente Peñaloza*. Buenos Aires: Hachette, 1969.

———. *De Comicios y Entreveros*. Buenos Aires: Schapire Editor, 1976.

Lynch, John. *Argentine Dictator: Juan Manuel de Rosas, 1829–1852*. Oxford: Clarendon Press, 1981.

———. *Caudillos in Spanish America, 1800–1850*. Oxford: Clarendon Press, 1992.

———. "From Independence to National Organization." In *Argentina since Independence*, edited by Leslie Bethell. Cambridge: Cambridge University Press, 1993.

———. *Massacre in the Pampas, 1872: Britain and Argentina in the Age of Migration*. Norman: University of Oklahoma Press, 1998.

Maeder, Ernesto J. *Evolución Demográfica Argentina de 1810 a 1869*. Buenos Aires: Eudeba, 1969.

Mallon, Florencia E. *Peasant and Nation: The Making of Postcolonial Mexico and Peru*. Berkeley: University of California Press, 1995.

Manifiesto del Jeneral Felipe Varela a los Pueblos Americanos Sobre los Acontecimientos Políticos de la República Argentina en los Años 1866 y 1867. Notes and introduction by Rodolfo Ortega Peña and Eduardo Luis Duhalde. 1868. Reprint, Buenos Aires: Sudestada, 1968.

Mansilla, Lucio V. *Entre-Nos: Causeries de los jueves*. 1889–1890. Reprint, Buenos Aires: Hachette, 1963.

———. *Una excursión a los indios ranqueles*. 2 vols. 1870. Reprint, Buenos Aires: Kapelusz, 1966.

Martínez Estrada, Ezequiel. *Muerte y Transfiguración de Martín Fierro*. 2d ed. 2 vols. Buenos Aires: Fondo de Cultura Económica, 1958.

Memoria del Ministerio del Interior. Buenos Aires, 1864.

Mercado, Manuel G. *La Degollación del Chacho*. Buenos Aires: Theoria, 1966.

———. *Las Quince Muertes del Chacho*. La Rioja, 1974.

Mitre-Sarmiento: Correspondencia, 1846–1868. Buenos Aires, 1911.

Myers, Jorge. *Orden y Virtud: El discurso Republicano en el Régimen Rosista*. Buenos Aires: Universidad Nacional de Quilmes, 1995.

Nario, Hugo. *Los Crímenes del Tandil, 1872.* Buenos Aires: Centro Editor de America Latina, 1983.

———. *Tata Dios: El Mesías de la Ultima Montonera.* Buenos Aires: Plus Ultra, 1976.

Navarro Ocampo, Ramón Gil. *Actor, Testigo y Mártir.* 1862. Written in 1862, First published in 1984, Córdoba, Argentina: Lerner, 1984.

Olivera, Gabriela. *Transformaciones de la Economía Familiar: Las Familias Campesinas y las Migraciones en Tres Areas de Los Llanos Riojanos.* 1989. Mimeographed paper.

Olmos, Ramón R. *Historia de Catamarca.* Catamarca, Argentina: La Unión, 1957.

Ortega Peña, Rodolfo, and Eduardo Luis Duhalde. *Felipe Varela Contra el Imperio Británico (Las Masas de la Unión Americana Enfrentan a las Potencias Europeas).* Buenos Aires: Sudestada, 1966.

Oszlak, Oscar. *La Formación del Estado Argentino.* Buenos Aires: Editorial de Belgrano, 1985.

Paz, José María. *Memorias Postumas.* 4 vols. Buenos Aires: Schapire, 1968.

Perdue, Charles. Introduction to *Weevils in the Wheat: Interviews with Virginia Ex-Slaves.* Edited by Charles L. Perdue Jr., Thomas E. Barden, and Robert K. Phillips. Charlottesville: University Press of Virginia, 1976.

Pérez Fuentes, Gerardo. "El Chacho y el Pronunciamiento del 2 de Marzo de 1848 en La Rioja." In *Angel Vicente Peñaloza.* Buenos Aires: Hachette, 1969.

Pomer, León. *Cinco Años de Guerra Civil (1865-1870).* Buenos Aires: Amorrortu, 1985.

Portelli, Alessandro. *The Death of Luigi Trastulli and Other Stories: Form and Meaning in Oral History.* Albany: State University of New York Press, 1991.

Primer Censo Nacional. Buenos Aires, 1869.

Registro Oficial de la Provincia de La Rioja. 3 vols. Buenos Aires: Coni, 1890.

Reis, João José. *Slave Rebellion in Brazil: The Muslim Uprising of 1835 in Bahia.* Translated by Arthur Brakel. Baltimore, Md.: Johns Hopkins University Press, 1993.

Reyes, Marcelino. *Bosquejo Histórico de la Provincia de La Rioja, 1543-1867.* Buenos Aires: H. Cattáneo, 1913.

Rickard, Ignacio F. *The Mineral and Other Resources of the Argentine Republic (La Plata).* London, 1870.

Rodríguez, Julio Cesar. *Historia Judicial de Catamarca.* Catamarca: El Ambato, 1953.

Roldán, D., and F. Coppari. "La Personalidad del Chacho en los Llanos de La Rioja." In *Revista de la Junta de Historia y Letras de La Rioja.* Vol. 4. La Rioja, 1945.

Romano, Silvia. "Finanzas Públicas de la Provincia de Córdoba, 1830-1855." *Boletín del Instituto de Historia Argentina y Americana Doctor Emilio Ravignani* 6 (1992): 99-147.

Rosal, Miguel. "El Interior frente a Buenos Aires: Flujos Comerciales e Integración Económica, 1831-1850." *Secuencia* 31 (1995).

Sábato, Hilda. *Agrarian Capitalism and the World Market: Buenos Aires in the Pastoral Age, 1840-1890.* Albuquerque: University of New Mexico Press, 1990.

———. *La Política en las Calles: Entre el Voto y la Movilización, Buenos Aires, 1862-1880.* Buenos Aires: Sudamericana, 1998.

Salomón, Noe. *Realidad, Ideología y Literatura en el "Facundo" de D. F. Sarmiento.* Amsterdam: Rodopi, 1984.

Salvatore, Ricardo. "Fiestas Federales: Representaciones de la República en el Buenos Aires Rosista." *Entrepasados* 4, no. 11 (1996): 45–68.

Sarmiento, Domingo F. *El Chacho: último caudillo de la montonera de los Llanos.* In *Vidas del Chacho,* edited by Pedro Orgambide. Buenos Aires: Rodolfo Alonso, 1973.

———. *Facundo.* Caracas: Biblioteca Ayacucho, 1977.

———. *Recuerdos de Provincia.* 1850. Reprint, Buenos Aires: Losada, 1995.

Schmit, Roberto, and Miguel Rosal. "Las Exportaciones del Litoral Argentino al Puerto de Buenos Aires entre 1783 y 1850." In *Revista de Historia Económica.* Vol. 13. Madrid, 1995.

Scott, James C. *Domination and the Arts of Resistance: Hidden Transcripts.* New Haven, Conn.: Yale University Press, 1990.

———. "Patron-Client Politics and Political Change in Southeast Asia." In *Friends, Followers, and Factions: A Reader in Political Clientelism,* edited by Steffen W. Schmidt et al. Berkeley: University of California Press, 1977.

———. *Weapons of the Weak: Everyday Forms of Peasant Resistance.* New Haven, Conn.: Yale University Press, 1985.

Shumway, Nicolas. *The Invention of Argentina.* Berkeley: University of California Press, 1991.

Slatta, Richard. *Los Gauchos y el Ocaso de la Frontera.* Buenos Aires: Sudamericana, 1985.

Stern, Steve J., ed. *Resistance, Rebellion, and Consciousness in the Andean Peasant World, Eighteenth to Twentieth Centuries.* Madison: University of Wisconsin Press, 1987.

Stevens, Donald F. *Origins of Political Instability in Early Republican Mexico.* Durham, N.C.: Duke University Press, 1991.

"Sumario instruído por el juez de paz de Belgrano y por orden del Sr. Gobernardor en campaña sobre los sucesos que se desarrollan desde el 29 de enero pasado, perturbando con la sedición y las montoneras el orden público de esta provincia, 1874." *Revista de la Junta de historia y Letras de la Provincia de La Rioja* 2, no. 3 (1943): 80–107.

Taboada, Antonino. "La Guerra y la Política en el Interior (Contestación a las Calumnias del General Arredondo)." In *Los Taboada,* edited by Gaspar Taboada. Vol. 1 Buenos Aires: Imprenta López, 1929–1942.

Taboada, Gaspar, ed. *Los Taboada.* 5 vols. Buenos Aires: Imprenta López, 1929–1942.

Terán, Oscar. *Alberdi Póstumo.* Buenos Aires: Puntosur, 1988.

Thompson, Stith. *The Folktale.* New York: Dryden Press, 1946.

Thurner, Mark. *From Two Republics to One Divided: Contradictions of Postcolonial Nationmaking in Andean Peru.* Durham, N.C.: Duke University Press, 1997.

Van Young, Eric. "The New Cultural History Comes to Old Mexico." *Hispanic American Historical Review* 79, no. 2 (1999): 211–47.

———. "The Raw and the Cooked: Elite and Popular Ideology in Mexico, 1808–1821." In *The Middle Period in Latin America: Values and Attitudes in the Seventeenth to Nineteenth Centuries,* edited by Mark D. Szuchman. Boulder, Colo.: Lynne Rienner Publishers, 1989.

———. "To See Someone Not Seeing: Historical Studies of Peasants and Politics in Mexico." *Mexican Studies/Estudios Mexicanos* 6, no. 1 (1990): 133–59.

Vaughan, Mary Kay. "Cultural Approaches to Peasant Politics in the Mexican Revolution." *Hispanic American Historical Review* 79, no. 2 (1999): 269–305.

Villafañe, Benjamín. *Reminiscencias Históricas de un Patriota.* Tucumán, Fundación Banco Comercial del Norte, 1972.

Vovelle, Michel. "La Representation Populaire de la Monarchie." In *The French Revolution and the Creation of Modern Political Culture,* edited by Keith Baker. Vol. 1. New York: Pergamon Press, 1987–1994.

Walker, Charles F. *Smoldering Ashes: Cuzco and the Creation of Republican Peru, 1780–1840.* Durham, N.C.: Duke University Press, 1999.

Wells, Allen, and Gilbert M. Joseph. *Summer of Discontent, Seasons of Upheaval: Elite Politics and Rural Insurgency in Yucatán, 1876–1915.* Stanford, Calif.: Stanford University Press, 1996.

Wolf, Eric, and Edward Hansen. "Caudillo Politics: A Structural Analysis." *Comparative Studies in Society and History* 9 (January 1967): 168–79.

Woodward, Comer Vann. "History from Slave Sources: A Review Article." *American Historical Review* 79, no. 2 (1974): 470–81.

Zalazar, Ernesto S. *Montonereando.* La Rioja, 1967.

Zimmermann, Eduardo A. "El Poder Judicial la construcción del Estado y el federalismo: Argentina, 1860–1880." In *In Search of a New Order: Essays on the Politics and Society of Nineteenth-Century Latin America,* edited by Eduardo Posada-Carbó. London: University of London, Institute of Latin American Studies, 1998.

INDEX

Agregados, 64, 208n. 16
Alberdi, Juan Bautista, 2, 155
Angel, Carlos, 22, 47, 84, 97
Arauco, 55–58, 149
Argentine Confederation, 2, 121, 161
Arredondo, José Miguel, 12, 22, 158
Avellaneda, Nicolás, 8
Aymogasta, 55, 56, 57, 158, 206n. 88

Banderita, 11
Barranca Yaco, 131, 133
Blacks, 70–71, 143–44, 145–47
Borges, Jorge Luis, vii, 2
Brizuela, Tomás, 30, 104
Buenos Aires-centered historiography, 5–6

Cabrera, Esteban, 47
Campos, Julio, 170, 171, 172, 174
Carrizo, Berna, 13, 69, 71, 79, 80
Carrizo, José Manuel, 47, 54
Caseros, 8, 91
Castro Barros, Pedro Inacio de, 156
Caucete, 13, 99
Caudillismo, 3–4
Caudillo: as authority, 125–27; and con-
    fession, 229n. 58; as father, 126–27;
    as hero, 130–36; similarity with kings,
    125–26; and the supernatural, 136–38

Charisma, 113–15, 190
Chumbita, Mercedes, 56, 57, 58, 206n. 96
Chumbita, Severo, 56, 57, 80, 83, 109,
    110, 111, 158, 206nn. 87, 94, and 96,
    218n. 70
Coalition of the North, 10, 54
Comuneros, 32, 48, 202n. 19; of a *merced,*
    66, 67
Costas of the Llanos, 61
Criador, 10, 68, 70–74

Dávila family, 31, 58, 111, 203n. 32;
    Cesario, 110; Exipión, 107–10; Miguel,
    34, 54, 59; Nicolás, 34; Tristán, 54–55,
    91, 92, 205n. 79
Del Moral family, 55–58, 205–6n. 83

Elizondo, Sebastián, 15, 181, 182
Encounter, 150
Ethnicity and politics, 143–52

Federalism, 1, 5, 17, 19; and Catholicism,
    152–63; as community, 173; as Con-
    stitutional Party, 22; and defense of
    political autonomy, 153, 159; in Fama-
    tina, 47–49; and oral culture, 117; and
    Quiroga, 190–91; and subsistence, 60,
    68, 207n. 106

Federalists: as bandits, 166, 169, 227n. 12; as *chachinos* or *chachistas,* 106, 108, 109, 129, 130, 190
Folklore: Colección de Folklore de la Encuesta Docente, 115, 186, 219n. 11.; and methodology, 122–25; and popular politics, 59, 193

Gaucho, 75–77, 104, 105, 158–59, 171, 195n. 2
Gauchos motivations, 4, 94–100, 189, 193
Guaja, 61
Guanacache, 58
Guayama, Santos, 77, 181
Gutiérrez, Eduardo, vii, 2

Halperín Donghi, Tulio, 3, 5
Heretics, 143, 153, 158, 159. *See also* Masons; Protestants
Hernández, José, vii, 2
Herrera, Andrés Galo, 13, 177–80

Inca, 150, 151, 227–28n. 27
Indians, 143, 144, 145, 149
Irrazábal, Pablo, 13, 27, 96, 133, 134, 135, 224n. 81
Iseas, José, 167

Labrador, 27, 37–38, 63–65, 202n. 19
Lagos, Hilario, 168
Lamadrid, Gregorio Aráoz de, 54
Linares, José María, 45, 54, 166, 170, 175
Llanos, Lucas, 21, 79, 80, 83

Machigasta, 56, 57, 149, 206n. 88
Martín Fierro, vii, 187
Masons, 159, 160, 161. *See also* Heretics
Merced, 66–68
Mitre, Bartolomé, 8, 174, 232n. 43
Moctezuma, 118, 119
Molina family, 182–83
Montonera, 2, 78, 86–89
Montonero, 77–78, and Peronism, 3

National Organization, 8
Navarro Ocampo, Ramón Gil, 25, 226n. 111
Navarro Octaviano, 11, 96, 182–83, 234n. 11; as father, 127
Nieto, Indalecio, 80, 83
Norte Chico (Chile), 40, 121, 204n. 49

Ocampo family, 31, 58, 118, 203n. 32
Olta, 13, 103, 129
Oral culture, 113, 115–25

Paraguay, war with, 13, 169, 171, 176
Patria, 91, 92, 99, 159, 168, 175, 216n. 25
Patron-client relations: and emotional attachment, 103, 105; and justice, 27; oral representations of, 128–30; and sociability, 103–5
Paunero, Wenceslao, 25, 165
Pavón, 8, 11
Paz, José María, 25, 116, 137, 156, 220n. 19
Peñaloza, Angel Vicente(El Chacho), 1, 2, 10, 11, 25, 26, 27, 58, 69, 71, 72, 94, 96, 99, 100, 102, 103, 104, 116, 133, 181, 184, 217n. 46
Pérez, Santos, 87, 130–33
Pilquineros, 43, 50–51
Playas, 12
Protestants, 159. *See also* Heretics; Masons
Pueblas, Juan Gabriel, 96
Pueblos, 36
Puesto, 34

Quechua, 149, 150
Quiroga, Facundo, 2, 25, 54, 58, 59, 69, 71, 72, 96, 100, 104, 116, 119, 120, 138–40, 186, 210n. 55, 211n. 64, 219n. 10, 220n. 19; and Catholicism, 153–57, 159; and Chacho, 140–42; and ethnicity and blacks, 146–48; as father, 148, 222n. 53; as Tiger, 225n. 103

Rivadavia, Bernardino, 8, 152, 153, 155, 160, 186

Rivas, Ignacio, 94, 165
Romero, Victoria, 89, 90, 214n. 50
Rosas, Juan Manuel, 8, 73, 74, 118, 121, 157

Saá, Juan, 14, 86, 169, 171
San Antonio, 61, 128
San Nicolás de Bari, 149
Sandes, Ambrosio, 164, 165, 166
Sañogasta, 39, 203n. 32
Sarmiento, Domingo F., 1, 2, 3, 8, 26, 51, 74, 113, 148, 151, 152
Savages, 1, 25, 91, 99, 129, 151, 159, 160, 184, 185, 191, 192
Scott, James C., 114
"Sons" of caudillos, 1, 99, 222nn. 53, 54

Taboada family, 183–84
Tello, Hipólito, 30
Tierras comunales, 39
Trickster tale, 59, 207n. 101
Tupac Amaru, 151

Unitarianism, 1, 5, 17; continuity of, 25; in Famatina, 45–46; and fiscal poverty, 19–20; and hunger, 60; in the interior, 21, 23; and justice, 28–29; in La Rioja, 21, 22, 30–31; and mobilizations, 106–12; and Oral culture, 117
Unitarians: as doctors, 30; as liberals, 24, 25, 199n. 30; Pure, 24. *See also* Savages
Urquiza, Justo J., 8, 11, 12, 14, 73, 163, 173, 174, 183, 232n. 43

Varela, Felipe, 2, 14, 22, 152, 181, 182, 183; and Chilean government, 197n. 26
Vera family: Gregorio, 27; José María, 26; Ricardo, 27, 69, 71, 133, 134, 135, 170, 172, 173, 224n. 81
Videla, Juan de Dios, 14
Villafañe, Domingo, 22, 234n. 11
Villains, 130–36
Vuelta de Martín Fierro, vii, 187

Water and irrigation, 42, 55 58
Whites, 143–44, 145–47, 152
Workers, 65–66

Zalazar, Aurelio, 13, 79, 80, 83, 84, 171–75, 218n. 70

Ariel de la Fuente is Assistant Professor in the Department of History
at Purdue University.

Library of Congress Cataloging-in-Publication Data

De la Fuente, Ariel.

Children of Facundo : caudillo and gaucho insurgency during the Argentine
state-formation process (La Rioja, 1853–1870) / Ariel de la Fuente.

Originally presented as author's thesis (Ph.D.)

State University of New York at Stony Brook.

Includes bibliographical references (p.) and index.

ISBN 0-8223-2582-9 (alk. paper) — ISBN 0-8223-2596-9 (pbk. : alk. paper)

1. La Rioja (Argentina : Province)—History—19th century. 2. Government,
Resistance to—Argentina—La Rioja (Province)—History. 3. Caudillos—
Argentina—La Rioja (Province)—History—19th century. 4. Gauchos—
Argentina—La Rioja (Province)—History—19th century. 5. Federal
government—Argentina—History—19th century. I. Title.

F2956 .D45   2000   982'.4605—dc21   00-010751